PLATE II   *Frank H. Schell*   MARCH OF THE FEDERAL 19TH CORPS TO PORT HUDSON

The
AMERICAN HERITAGE

Century Collection of

CIVIL WAR ART

EDITOR

STEPHEN W. SEARS

FOREWORD

BRUCE CATTON

Published by AMERICAN HERITAGE PUBLISHING CO., INC., NEW YORK

Book Trade Distribution by McGRAW-HILL BOOK COMPANY

The AMERICAN HERITAGE
Century Collection of
CIVIL WAR ART

EDITOR
Stephen W. Sears

ART DIRECTOR
Murray Belsky

RESEARCHER
Laura Lane Masters

COPY EDITOR
Kaari Ward

———

AMERICAN HERITAGE
PUBLISHING CO., INC.

PRESIDENT AND PUBLISHER
Paul Gottlieb

GENERAL MANAGER, BOOK DIVISION
Kenneth W. Leish

EDITORIAL ART DIRECTOR
Murray Belsky

———

Copyright © 1974 by American Heritage Publishing
Co., Inc., a subsidiary of McGraw-Hill, Inc.,
1221 Avenue of the Americas, New York, N.Y. 10020.
All rights reserved. Printed in the United States of
America. No part of this publication may be reproduced, stored in a retrieval system, or transmitted,
in any form or by any means, electronic, mechanical,
photocopying, recording, or otherwise, without the
prior written permission of the publisher.

Library of Congress Cataloging in Publication Data:
page 400

ISBN 07-010267-8

PLATE III   *Walton Taber*   NATIONAL CEMETERY, CORINTH, MISSISSIPPI

The illustration on page 1 (Plate I) is titled *Confederate Canteen*
and was drawn by Walton Taber; the canteen, made of wood, was found
on the Antietam battlefield. Plate II, facing the title page, derives from
a sketch done by Schell on March 14, 1863, when he was covering
the Port Hudson campaign for *Leslie's Illustrated Weekly*.
Plate III (above) was based on a photograph taken in 1884.

Table of Contents

Foreword

BRUCE CATTON

Nineteen years had passed since the two generals sat down together at Appomattox Court House. In the next presidential election votes would be cast by men who had been born since the war ended. No one under 30 had more than a dim childhood memory of the war, as of something vast and fabulous and exciting that had somehow happened beyond the horizon, out of sight and out of hearing. Those who had actually been in the war, carrying the reality of its bitter taste and smell, its murky shadows and darker terror forever with them like old Pilgrim's bundle, were now in their forties, or beyond them. At the veterans' annual reunions it began to be noticed that each year a few more of the old comrades were gone. Time no longer moved slowly; the longer you lived, the faster time went, and it was possible now to realize that some day no one in all the world would really remember the American Civil War.

That war had been the biggest thing that ever happened on this side of the globe. No one was quite certain just what it meant—or, perhaps more accurately, a good many men thought they were certain but they could not agree with each other—but it was clear to everyone that it meant something prodigious. In one way or another it had been a time of greatness, even if one had to confess, in the end, that the greatness simply measured unrelieved tragedy and loss. Whether it was something to live down or to live up to, Americans would carry it in their bones and sinews as long as the name of their country meant anything. And now, before the light departed from that haunted landscape with its terrible names and memories, it was time to put the business in some sort of focus. What had it all been like? What had it meant, how had it been for the men who lived through it? Above all—for memory is sharpest and most understanding when it takes visual shape—what had it looked like?

Thinking along these lines, the editors of *Century* magazine proceeded to do a great thing.

They collected accounts of all the major campaigns and battles of the war written by men who had been in them; by major generals and by private soldiers and by all ranks and conditions in between, by men who had served on both sides, each man required only to tell it the way it was—the way, that is to say, it was *to him*, his account of it usually balanced or amplified by the accounts of other men who saw it through different eyes and who, when they came to write, drew upon a different set of memories.

Out of all of this came a composite history such as no war had ever had before. The accounts ran in the magazine, issue after issue for three years, and finally they were published in massive hard-cover form—the legendary *Battles and Leaders of the Civil War*, in four bulky volumes, the broad and solid foundation, ever since, for students of that war.

Furthermore, having collected writers to describe the war, the *Century* editors had gone looking for artists, for the *Battles and Leaders* series was fully illustrated. This proved to be a most important decision.

6

We take illustrations for granted nowadays, the era of the picture book having dawned some time ago. But nothing of the kind was taken for granted in the 1880's simply because the process of turning a drawing or a photograph into something that would adorn the printed page had always been most roundabout and unsatisfactory. Photographs could not be faithfully reproduced at all. The pencil or pen-and-ink artist, doing on-the-spot reporting, was at the mercy of the wood engraver back in the office; what the artist drew was not so much reproduced as copied by the engraver, who was working in a hurry. The results usually were unfortunate.

As a consequence, contemporary accounts of the Civil War had been most imperfectly illustrated, even though such papers as *Harper's Weekly* and *Frank Leslie's* and the *New York Illustrated News* spent a good deal of money hiring combat artists. Some of these artists were surprisingly good, but the odds were against them; the game, so to speak, was rigged so that they could not win, even though they accompanied the armies, witnessed the battles, and did their best to send in good work. For the artist was entrusting his work to distant technicians who had to obey the rigid demands of the imperfect medium they worked in rather than the requirements of artistic and reportorial integrity. This was so much the case that the artist who was in a hurry to get his material back to the office sent off unfinished sketches, with figures in the foreground blocked in roughly and the rest of the space taken up with quick outlines and with written directions to the wood engraver—"trees here," "artillery in park," and so on.

By the time *Battles and Leaders* went to press, things were somewhat different. Photographs still were all but unreproducible; many photographs of individuals were indeed utilized in the series, but they were not turned into halftones because the halftone process had not yet been perfected; instead, skilled craftsmen used these portraits as models for engravings, with very good results. And for the sketch artists whose work had been so woefully butchered during the war, a new day had dawned. For one thing, nobody any longer was rushed for time; for another, the technique of turning a drawing into a wood engraving had been vastly improved. What the artist drew could be seen now, on the printed page, looking much more as he had actually drawn it. (On the following pages, of course, it is at last possible to see what the artists actually did draw, reproduced directly from their originals with the painstaking fidelity of modern-day printing.)

The *Century* editors discovered that a great deal of material was available. By and large this material came from three groups. First, and most important, were the combat artists themselves—the men who had gone with the armies and who, for the most part, had had to be satisfied with sending off incomplete sketches. Some of these men, later on, had worked up finished drawings from their sketches; others did so now, delighted by the prospect that their work would at last gain publication in more proper form. Next, there was a group of men who had served in the war as soldiers and who made a living as artists later; these men simply drew what they remembered. Finally, there were a number of professional illustrators of the day, who worked from whatever they could lay their hands on— Brady and Gardner photographs, wartime lithographs and sketchbooks, or photographs made since the war to show how the land lay on this or that battlefield. In many cases, also, this third group worked entirely from the imagination, supplemented by conversations with veterans who had been present at the scene.

All in all, the *Century* editors used the work of some 70 artists, from whom they got a total of about a thousand pictures. (The aforementioned portraits brought the grand total of illustrations to over 1,700.) It should be noted that just as the editors had taken extreme pains to get accuracy in the written material, so also equal pains were taken with the art work. Everything that could be done to provide a faithful pictorial representation of the war was done, and if in the end it remains true that no artist but one of Goya's genius could really convey the ultimate reality of war, these men did well enough.

In some ways the pictures in *Battles and Leaders* may actually have been more important than the narratives. For the first time a nation that had fought a great war was enabled to visualize the experience. It could *see* what it had done. The vision no doubt was incomplete and imperfect, but it was much more complete and faithful than anything that had ever been done before. The age of the "court painter," who covered palace walls with scenes of immaculate armies in beautiful uniforms, maneuvering bloodlessly before guns that did nothing worse than emit graceful puff-balls of white smoke, had never produced anything like this. The American was able to see his soldiers as flesh-and-blood human beings operating on homely, recognizable American fields, with familiar cabins, houses, and rickety culverts in the background.

I think some of the people who rejoiced in this most were the veterans themselves.

In the small town where I lived as a boy, in backwoods Michigan, it happened that my father got the first set of *Battles and Leaders* that had appeared in this area. He must have picked up a latter-day printing because this was around 1910 or 1912, but it does not matter. It was the first set in town, word of it got about, and during the next few months I believe almost every Civil War veteran in the neighborhood came in to borrow one of the volumes, or at least to ask the privilege of sitting down and looking at one on the front porch. As I remember it, what engaged the interest of these old gentlemen the most were the pictures. To read about the old battles was well enough, but actually to see the pictures apparently was much better. Those books of ours got intensive usage.

Many years after this I found it necessary to examine several hundred regimental histories of the war. Almost without exception these were artless, informal little books, written by one or more survivors of the regiment (or by a committee chosen more or less at random) and printed, usually, by a local job printing house. Practically none got into regular trade distribution; they were designed for use by the regimental survivors and their families, and I don't imagine more than a few hundred copies of any of them ever got printed. But the point is that most of these little histories reproduced one or more of the *Battles and Leaders* pictures. I suppose some of them were just plain pirated, but I also suppose that any regimental association that asked permission to use the material got it instantly. Those books were not in competition with anybody—and the eagerness with which they used the reproductions when they got them shows how the old soldiers regarded the work the artists had done.

The *Battles and Leaders* collection saw the light at a psychological moment. The men who had been in the war were beginning to enter full-blown middle age, and once fairly into that, the rocker in the chimney corner is not really very far away; and as the wartime generation grew older a new generation that knew the war only at second-hand came along. Very likely the veterans and their tales had begun to get just a little tiresome, and the new generation had other things on its mind, and who wanted to hear all the time about the great things Dad did when he was young, anyway? And just then these four big volumes came along. . . .

This set the tone for what happened thereafter. Not only did it focus fresh attention on the Civil War just when the innumerable concerns of a very busy country were about to crowd it out of sight, but it conditioned a whole generation, some of whose members were going to write about the war as historians. The orchestra was going to be tuned, in a sense, to the note sounded on this gong.

For one thing, this meant that to a considerable extent the war would be discussed, then and thenceforward, as a common national possession. Different viewpoints, of course, remain, and there are plenty of people in the North and the South alike who cherish these viewpoints strongly and can grow quite warm arguing about them. But the many who have written about the war during the last eight or nine decades have not been devoting themselves to two different wars, one for the North and one for the South. They have tried to show what the affair was really like, how things happened and why, what deep currents and forces in the national character (the character of one nation, that is, not of two) brought the conflict on and made it go as it did, and what the present and future effects on the nation are likely to be.

For another thing, there are the pictures. When we consider them we are obliged to consider the profound differences between the photograph and the drawing, in line or in water color. *Battles and Leaders*, to repeat, came out before there was a practical process for reproducing photographs accurately in halftone, so it relied on the artist and the illustrator. This made an enormous difference.

The photograph in that era was very literal-minded. It captured nothing that the eye of a totally unimaginative human being could not see. It had no overtones; it presented the landscape as it found it. The whole was never greater than the sum of its parts.

But when the pen of the artist gets to work, there is a subtle change. For example, it often happened in the *Battles and Leaders* series that the editors wanted to show what all or part of a certain battlefield had looked like, and so they procured a photograph of it—and then, because there was no other way to prepare it for the printed page, had a pen-and-ink artist make a copy of it. The artist might do his best to make an accurate, unemotional reproduction—and yet, somehow, the finished product, the picture that finally appeared in the book, would be subtly but unmistakably different. The picture drawn by the artist would say something, or at least hint at something, that was not in the photograph.

This is bound to be true, of course, when an action picture is to be presented. Here the artist prevailed, because with the cumbersome wet-plate cameras of the 1860's it was virtually impossible to take an action picture. Many of the battle scenes in this book are the work of men who were there, either representing the illustrated papers or serving in the ranks. Others are the work of an illustrator, who could visit the scene where the action took place, study photographs, talk to eyewitnesses, and then try to be wholly objective in what he drew; nevertheless something peculiar to himself would put its own flavor in the result. Inevitably, whether eyewitness artist or illustrator, he would show the world as he saw it rather than the world as it really was.

This happens, to a greater or lesser degree, all along the line. A different sort of light falls on the landscape when the drawing is made. It is the light that never was, and the picture in spite of everything becomes picturesque.

The editors and the artists, in other words, may have wished to be the most ruthless realists on earth, but they became romanticists against their will. They put a strange pastoral tint on the grimmest battlefield. They portrayed desperate action—which, as likely as not, the artist witnessed—as something the viewer would rather like to have been in, so that in the end even the veterans themselves became bemused . . . as witness the old gentlemen who came to our house to look at these pictures, translating the reality that they knew all too well into the fiction in which imagination led old men's memories down shady lanes.

These drawings, to be sure, were an enormous improvement on the gaudy colors and dramatic posturings of the court painters, whose battles from Fontenoy to Waterloo all looked alike. The European painters concentrated on kings, dukes, marshals, and others of high position; the American artists came down to the rank and file and depicted a war in which the ordinary man was the important figure. Yet there is a fundamental similarity. People who die in these pictures almost always do so without the hideous grotesqueries violent death strews across the field. Even the drawings of the dead at, say, Antietam do not have the bloated, pitiful look of the photographs on which they were based; they are, somehow, the honored dead.

The pictures presented in this book, then—a carefully winnowed collection of the art the *Century* editors commissioned—lack the hard, matter-of-fact realism of the camera. That is by no means a fatal defect; indeed, it is necessary to point out that while the camera shows what it sees with pitiless accuracy, the man who holds the camera, or the people who send him forth, may have very definite ideas about the shorn lambs to whom the winds of war have to be tempered. However that may be, these pictures played an important part in helping to flavor the national response to an unforgettable war. All in all, they probably did America a great deal of good.

For this reason: the Civil War (and this can never be said too often) was brutally hard, cruel, painful, and deeply tragic. It was as divisive an experience as the country could have had. Fought with intense passion, it led the men of the two sections to do things to each other that would seem to have been wholly unforgivable. North and South together, it took more than 600,000 lives; and if it lacked the cynical, coldly contrived cruelty of totalitarian wars as a later generation would know them, it was in all conscience bad enough . . . as bad, undoubtedly, as people of the mid-nineteenth century could imagine.

In the 1880's this had receded from the forefront of the American consciousness, but it was not really so very far away. The whole of it, one would suppose, should have remained as an utterly indigestible lump in the American memory—something that would poison national life for generations to come.

But it did not happen that way. Instead, in the strangest and seemingly most illogical manner, the whole experience became a legend. Instead of being something recalled with dread and bitterness, it passed into romance. People began to murmur softly about the Boys in Blue and the Boys in Gray; they built a whole host of novels, songs, and plays (most of them, sad to say, trashy enough and to spare) about what, in euphemistic triumph, they came to call "the late unpleasantness"; and the terrible war slowly but surely became a common possession, to be remembered fondly and without bitterness . . . or at least without more bitterness than could be handled.

This, to be sure, did not happen immediately. There was much ill feeling, north and south of the Mason-Dixon line, during the hard years of the Ku Klux Klan and the "bloody shirt," the carpetbagger and the occupation troops. If a thoughtful American in those days might have feared that the nation would never be truly at peace with itself, nobody could have blamed him.

But it worked out, at last, over the long pull; and surely one important factor in the matter of healing was the noble *Battles and Leaders* collection of pictures and accounts, which resolutely and without making a fuss about it treated the great tragedy as a matter of pride and loss for people of both sides. There was no attempt to draw a moral, to preach, or to urge mutual forgiveness; there was simply the unspoken assumption behind every paragraph and every picture that somewhere beyond guilt and beyond blame the people of America had fought to extricate themselves from an unendurable situation and, doing so, had established a better base for all future years.

These pictures helped to filter out the evil and the ugliness. If they unintentionally lent a tinge of romance to what was underneath everything a matter of unrelieved tragedy, it was a romance the country desperately needed. Unvarnished realism was the last thing America wanted in that postwar generation. It had lived with that realism for four dreadful years, and if it ever forgot about it there were gravestones enough, from Minnesota to Florida, to bring it back to mind. The country needed to see the passions that brought on the war and the strengths that had endured it, so that out of what men had been and done they could find the heart to take them into the future.

For that, cold realism would not be enough. The moment of shock, when realism is desperately needed, passes; after that, people who have been profoundly disillusioned need something to take them out of despair. They need to remember not merely what they did but what they meant while they were doing it; if hard events had shattered faith, it was necessary at least to regain the emotional attitude that made faith possible.

Furthermore, the strange light that rested on man and earth in the artists' pictures had really been there. America would never again look quite the same as it had looked in the 1860's—partly because the war had been fought, even more because the earth had spun on into a different part of the sky, a different part of time—but one of the realities on which the future had to be built was the cherished memory of how it had looked when the old daylight still touched the hills.

So the achievement of assembling and publishing the great volumes of *Battles and Leaders* was of massive importance. We are still living our way out of the era that was broken up by the Civil War. The pain and loss which that war caused, like the follies and stupidities that brought on the war in the first place, are gone forever. But the responsibilities that arise when one era ends and another begins are still with us, and they will never be discharged by cynics. To share, even at long remove, in the sentiment, in the hopes and the strange dreams that turned the nation's greatest time of trial into legend and romance, is after all to share in great strength and determination. The people who idealized that war were people who had gone through the fire. If they had a certain tendency to see things through an October haze, they had earned the right to look at them any way they chose. It was young Captain Oliver Wendell Holmes, thrice-wounded and of proven valor, who left the army in 1864 utterly disillusioned, privately confessing that the war for reunion could not and possibly should not be won—and who, twenty years later, wrote that through great good fortune he and the men of his generation who served in the war had lived through a time when "our lips were touched with fire."

. . . In any case, here are the pictures, a fine wealth of them. They are worth looking at.

Introduction

In the Foreword and in the commentaries on the Century Collection pictures that follow, there is frequent reference to the *Century* editors. They should be introduced. In the editor's chair throughout the magazine's era of greatest influence was Richard Watson Gilder, who held the position for 28 years (1881-1909). His associates Robert Underwood Johnson and Clarence Clough Buel conceived the *Battles and Leaders* series and were put in command of it. Alexander W. Drake and W. Lewis Fraser of the art department managed the illustration program. The *Century*'s printer, the celebrated Theodore Low De Vinne, ensured a well crafted final product.

The *Battles and Leaders* project was the biggest and most ambitious undertaking in the magazine's history. "This war-series is a flank movement on all our rivals," Gilder explained to the Century Company's president four months before the first "war paper" was published. "It is a great scheme in itself—something that would not have been done save for the Century—and even if done, not so well done. The 'young men' at the office [Buel and Johnson] have managed & are managing it with the greatest skill & wisdom." In a note to Johnson a few days later, he was even more expansive: "This war series is the most important thing, historically, I ever expect to live to see in this century."

Gilder's optimism was rewarded. The project was more than historically significant; it was also a ringing popular and commercial success. Between 1884 and 1887, the life span of the series, the magazine's circulation doubled, to a quarter-million, and when the war papers were collected, rearranged, fleshed out with additional articles and illustrations, and published between hard covers as *Battles and Leaders of the Civil War* (1888), over 75,000 four-volume sets were sold—a very respectable showing for that day. It is estimated that the Century Company earned a million dollars from the *Battles and Leaders* project.

After the art work for the series had been engraved, it was filed away in the Century Company art department. How long it remained there cannot be stated precisely, but the most likely period of its disposal would seem to be between about 1925, when *Century* ceased being an illustrated magazine, and 1930, when it ceased entirely. In any event, a large share of the *Battles and Leaders* pictures, plus additional art that had illustrated other Civil War articles in *Century* or in *St. Nicholas*, the company's young people's magazine, was acquired by a Civil War buff named General William Cannon Rivers.

Rivers was a West Pointer (class of 1887) whose military career went all the way back to the Northern Cheyenne and Sioux uprisings in the early 1890's. His service record included the Spanish-American War, more than a decade of duty in the Philippines, and a combat command with the field artillery in World War I. From 1923 to 1927 he was stationed in the inspector general's office at Governor's Island in New York (at which time, family tradition has it, he acquired the Century Collection), and when he retired in 1930 he was the army's inspector general.

Rivers continued living in New York until 1942, when he moved to Warrenton, North Carolina; there, a year later, he died at the age of 77.

When the general's widow incurred a protracted illness, the Civil War art, packed into three old trunks that dated from Rivers' service in the Philippines, was deposited in a storage warehouse in nearby Raleigh. In 1964, upon Mrs. Rivers' death, the collection was inherited by her son, James Battle Rivers. A West Pointer like his father, the younger Rivers had resigned from the army in 1924 in favor of a business career. The pictures, still in the Philippine trunks, were stored in the attic of the Rivers home near the Vieux Carré in New Orleans. After the death of James Battle Rivers in 1972, the collection was acquired by Robert B. Mayo, a Civil War collector and the director of the Valentine Museum in Richmond. American Heritage purchased the collection from Mr. Mayo in 1973. His assistance in developing the provenance of the art and his permission to utilize 16 *Century* drawings from his private collection are gratefully acknowledged.

The plates that follow—reproduced for the first time as the artists drew them—are arranged either chronologically by campaign or in specialized topical chapters. Small reproductions of the rest of the collection appear in the Catalogue that begins on page 354. Although the chapter-opening narratives and the picture commentaries attempt to establish historical contexts, this book does not pretend to be a history of the Civil War. Its pace and coverage are dictated entirely by the contents of the collection. For example, the early naval actions on the Mississippi get more space than the Battle of Gettysburg simply because the naval pictures are of high quality and because sometime in the last 90 years most of the *Battles and Leaders* Gettysburg pictures were skimmed off.

Each of the plates is reproduced in two or three colors directly from the art itself. Sheets are sometimes cropped in the interest of clear reproduction, but in no instance has the picture area of any piece of art been cropped. The process by which one of these drawings became a woodcut in the 1880's—it was photographed to size directly on the block (a technique developed by Alexander Drake), after which the engraver cut the block, using the original only for reference—meant that it was treated with less than sacrosanct care. *Century* art directors scrawled dimensions and instructions across the sheets, to which were added "date wanted" stamps in purple ink and engraver's file numbers; not infrequently these graffiti intruded on the picture area. In the plates such intrusions have been removed or minimized where practical, the goal being to reproduce every picture as closely as possible to the way the artist drew it—with allowances, of course, for nine decades of wear and tear. Any writing that appears in the reproduction is, in the great majority of cases, the artist's. Since few originals were titled, descriptive titles have been supplied.

The American Heritage Century Collection includes approximately half of the original art commissioned for the *Battles and Leaders* project (exclusive of portraits and maps). The dozen drawings by Winslow Homer, the best known of the project's artists, were long since removed, to surface later in various collections across the country. The same is true of the Joseph Pennell drawings. At some point Franklin D. Roosevelt acquired ten *Battles and Leaders* naval subjects for his collection, and various other drawings have been traced to museums or private collections. The Rivers family gave a number of pieces away. Considering the tattered condition of some of the surviving pictures, no doubt a fair proportion of the drawings fell victim to damage or disintegration over the years. Where are the rest of the pictures? Perhaps even now they are gathering dust in a trunk in the corner of an attic somewhere.

—Stephen W. Sears

I Shots Fired in Anger

THIS FIRST SEGMENT of the Century Collection offers a glimpse of the opening phase of the Civil War—lasting roughly a year—in which the political maneuvering was more significant than the fighting. Battles were few and casualties low; not until the major campaigns began, in the spring of 1862, would Americans confront endless casualty lists and begin to see war's true face. Rather, the great question in these early months was which way the border states of Maryland, Kentucky, and Missouri would go—whether the dividing line between North and South would be, as Jefferson Davis fervently hoped, the Ohio River. In the end all three states remained in the Union, but the complex way in which this happened was hardly anything that a newspaper's special artist could sketch or that the Century Company's illustrators wanted to tackle. So the pictorial coverage of the contest for the border states focused on whatever shooting took place there.

The *Century* editors often used what they called "initial" pictures to lead off their *Battles and Leaders* essays. These would "stage-set" or typify the subject matter to follow. The device is repeated here. Taber's Plate 1, based on a gag photograph, is entirely appropriate to the prevailing attitude in those first months of war. After their victory at Bull Run, the Confederates entrenched themselves for more than seven months around Manassas Junction and Centreville. When they pulled out the next spring, the Federals discovered those fortifications to be far less formidable than they had seemed, for the artillery-poor Rebels had painted and shaped a good number of logs into "Quaker guns." Yankee soldiers got a good laugh out of this and had their pictures taken with the harmless artifacts, and the whole thing seemed proof that war was an adventure. Shots had been fired in anger, but much innocence remained.

Walton Taber, the most prolific of the *Battles and Leaders* artist corps, is responsible for the largest single share of pictures in the Century Collection. Very little is known about Taber, except that the bulk of his illustration work was for the Century Company; it is probable that he was a staff artist. As will be seen in this

PLATE 1 *Walton Taber* CONFEDERATE QUAKER GUN

chapter, in most instances he worked from photographs, lithographs, or other wartime sources, but he also produced a considerable body of original illustration. As Plates 22 and 23 testify, his skill in draftsmanship and composition was considerable.

This chapter also introduces another artist who is a mainstay of the collection: Theodore R. Davis. Davis was a *Harper's Weekly* "special" throughout the war (and, in fact, for two decades after the war), and no other combat artist covered more theaters of action. Over 250 of his drawings appeared as woodcuts in *Harper's* during the war years. The eight Davis drawings and water colors reproduced here had their origins in a tour of the South he made in the spring of 1861 in company with William Howard Russell of the London *Times*. Traveling with the celebrated English journalist and claiming to be in the employ of the *Illustrated London News* opened Southern doors for Davis that would have been slammed in his face had he shown the credentials of the hated *Harper's Weekly*. This subterfuge apparently raised Russell's hackles, and he complained to *Harper's* that he had been taken in by its 21-year-old artist. In any event, Davis gained much from the association. His drawings of Montgomery (Plate 3) and Pensacola Harbor (Plate 5) derive from direct observation; the others are combinations of observation and illustration. His Fort Sumter series (Plates 6-9), for example, does not represent eyewitness pictorial reporting, for he and Russell did not reach Charleston until two days after Sumter's surrender, yet Davis did tour the fort and harbor, and had ample opportunity to fill his sketchbook with such features as Sumter's barbette battery (Plate 9).

Coverage of these early months of the war opens with Fort Sumter, continues with the immediate aftermath and the fight at Bull Run, and concludes with the first clashes in the Western border states of Kentucky and Missouri. These pictures, it will be noted, are singularly bloodless. In Plate 27 a man is indeed shot, but it is dramatically, on a rearing horse, highly appropriate to a romantic vision of warfare. This is generally true of the entire *Battles and Leaders* pictorial coverage of this period. "You are green, it is true," Lincoln had told his General McDowell before Bull Run. "But they are green also. You are all green alike." Like the rookie soldiers, the artists of this war had their illusions, and they, too, would lose them with all speed when the real fighting began.

PLATE 2 *Edwin J. Meeker*
SECESSION HALL, CHARLESTON

A long stride toward war was taken on December 20, 1860, when South Carolina's Ordinance of Secession was adopted in St. Andrews' Hall (center). The building was promptly rechristened Secession Hall, but its new fame was brief; within a year it was gutted by fire.

PLATE 3 *Theodore R. Davis*
VIEW OF MONTGOMERY, ALABAMA

With the inauguration of Jefferson Davis at the capitol
in Montgomery, Alabama, in February, 1861, the house was
truly divided, with two capitals and two Presidents.
In Theodore Davis' water color, the capitol building,
as the artist described it, "is the crowning object of
the landscape." He worked from sketches made in
May, 1861, when he and correspondent William Howard
Russell of the *Times* of London visited Montgomery.
Walton Taber based the drawing below of one of
Washington's landmarks on a Mathew Brady photograph.

PLATE 4 *Walton Taber* THE OLD NAVY DEPARTMENT BUILDING, WASHINGTON

PLATE 5   *Theodore R. Davis*   PENSACOLA HARBOR FROM THE BAR

PLATE 6   *Theodore R. Davis*   EVACUATION OF FORT MOULTRIE

For a time during those high-tension early months of 1861 it seemed
as likely that the spark to ignite civil war would be struck at
Fort Pickens in Pensacola Harbor as at Charleston's Fort Sumter. But
Pickens was easily reinforced and Floridians were less trigger-tempered
than South Carolinians, and so the fort remained firmly in Union
hands. Davis sketched it as it looked when he visited there in May,
with the crisis passed and the cruiser *Powhatan* in attendance.
At Charleston, however, the pressure rose. Plate 6 shows Major
Robert Anderson's garrison rowing out to Fort Sumter, a more
defensible position than Fort Moultrie (right). Two weeks later,
on January 9, 1861, the supply ship *Star of the West* was turned back
by Southern harbor batteries; in Davis' drawing (with the *Star
of the West* as an inset), the Sumter garrison watches helplessly.

PLATE 7   *Theodore R. Davis*   FIRING ON THE "STAR OF THE WEST"

The signal to open fire was a shell from

PLATE 8   *Theodore R. Davis*   THE OPENING OF THE CIVIL WAR

"At half past four the heavy booming of a cannon," wrote the Charleston diarist
Mary Boykin Chesnut. "I sprang out of bed, and on my knees prostrate
I prayed as I never prayed before." The precise moment when war began is the
subject of Davis' water color: a signal shell fired from Fort Johnson
(far left) explodes squarely over Fort Sumter at 4:30 on the morning of April 12,
1861. In the foreground is the Confederate armored battery on Cummings
Point, just three-quarters of a mile from Sumter. Avid secessionist
Edmund Ruffin had the honor of firing its first round, which in legend, if not
in fact, was the Civil War's first shot fired in anger. During the subsequent
bombardment Major Anderson returned fire only from the protected lower
batteries, to minimize his casualties. This policy of restraint became too
much for Sergeant John Carmody; Davis sketched the result (Plate 9). Carmody
dashed up to the exposed barbette battery and fired off every gun that bore on
Fort Moultrie. The Rebels opened a furious cannonade to silence this threat.
"But the contest was merely Carmody against the Confederate States," recounted
one of Sumter's officers, "and Carmody had to back down, not because he
was beaten, but because he was unable, single-handed, to reload his guns."

20

PLATE 9 *Theodore R. Davis* SERGEANT CARMODY MANS THE BARBETTE BATTERY

On April 14, outgunned and with no hope of rescue, Anderson surrendered Fort Sumter. The 4,000 rounds fired had killed no one; the only casualties were two of Anderson's men, dead from an explosion of ready ammunition during the garrison's final salute to the flag. A Charleston photographer promptly arrived to take pictures for General Beauregard's report of the action, and they are the basis for these Taber drawings. Below is the exterior wall of Sumter that faced the Cummings Point battery. Heavy shot damage was inflicted here by a powerful English-made rifled cannon before it ran out of ammunition. Plate 10 shows the interior of the same wall and the fort's splintered flagstaff. Sumter's barbette and double row of casemates are visible in Plate 12. At center is a furnace for heating shot, and at left, three makeshift 8-inch mortars. The Confederate flag is rigged to the fort's gun derrick.

PLATE 10   *Walton Taber*   FORT SUMTER CASEMATES IN RUINS

PLATE 11   *Walton Taber*   SOUTHWEST FACE OF FORT SUMTER

PLATE 12   *Walton Taber*   INTERIOR OF FORT SUMTER AFTER THE SURRENDER

PLATE 13   *Theodore R. Davis*   ARRIVAL OF THE ORIGINAL CONTRABAND AT FORTRESS MONROE

The arrival of the Original Contraband at Fortress Monroe —

After Sumter, one place Washington quickly moved to hold was Fortress Monroe,
at the tip of the Virginia peninsula. In command there was Massachusetts' very
political general, Benjamin Butler, and in late May of 1861, as painted by
Davis, fugitive slaves sought refuge in his fort. Seen "as property liable
to be used in aid of rebellion," Butler declared them contraband of war,
giving new meaning to an old phrase and driving a nail into slavery's coffin.

PLATE 14   *Edwin J. Meeker*   THE WASHINGTON ARSENAL

Lincoln's call for 75,000 militia to suppress "combinations too powerful to be suppressed by the ordinary course of judicial proceedings" was answered enthusiastically enough, but his immediate problem was a shortage of troops to protect Washington. This peaceful tableau of officers and their ladies in the arsenal courtyard, after a photograph by A. J. Russell, was entirely untypical of the period after Fort Sumter; the place was, in fact, a frantic bustle of hurrying officers and clamorous militiamen drawing arms. For more than a week the capital was isolated by Maryland secessionists. Finally, on April 27, the 7th New York arrived and communications with the North were reopened.

New York's Seventh was something of a white-glove regiment,
with elegant uniforms and an elevated social standing,
and it was more than ready for adventure. "Our men were gay
and careless," wrote one of the New Yorkers. "They looked
battle in the face with a smile." After a spectacular
send-off parade down Broadway, the Seventh entrained for
Philadelphia. With the rail line south blocked at Baltimore,
it then had to make a long detour around Cape Charles
and up the Chesapeake to Annapolis aboard the side-wheeler
Boston. Artist Davis, who had recently recorded views
of Annapolis for *Harper's Weekly*, turned to his sketchbook to
make this water color of the *Boston's* arrival at the Naval
School dock. Finally, after a sobering 20-mile march and
another train ride, the regiment reached Washington—much
to the President's relief—and was quartered in the Capitol.

PLATE 15   *Theodore R. Davis*   ARRIVAL OF THE 7TH NEW YORK AT ANNAPOLIS

Two days after Lincoln called for troops, Virginia's state convention voted for secession; the day after that, Virginia troops seized the government armory at Harper's Ferry. The 43-man garrison had put the torch to the arsenal before pulling out, but the Virginians were able to salvage many arms parts and much of the rifle-making machinery. Two months later, when the Confederates in turn had to withdraw, they burned the Baltimore & Ohio's bridge over the Potomac. Plate 16, after James Gardner's 1865 photograph, shows the bridge as it was rebuilt. The Baltimore & Ohio was also involved in a long, tangled struggle in western Virginia between Yankees trying to keep the line open and Rebels trying to shut it down. Robert E. Lee received no acclaim for his part in the campaign, and George B. McClellan received entirely too much. Plate 17—a Confederate gun crew preparing to shell a Federal camp far below—represents a typical skirmish in that rugged terrain. Sheppard based his drawing on a sketch by a Confederate who witnessed the action late in the fall of 1861.

PLATE 16   *Walton Taber*   Harper's Ferry, Looking down the Potomac

PLATE 17   *William L. Sheppard*   FLOYD'S COMMAND, GAULEY BRIDGE, VIRGINIA

PLATE 18   *Walton Taber*   THE McLEAN HOUSE

PLATE 19   *J. D. Woodward*   THE ROBINSON HOUSE

Here are landmarks of Bull Run, the battle of the amateurs, drawn from photographs taken by Alexander Gardner or other Brady assistants in 1862 after the Confederates pulled back toward Richmond. Wilmer McLean's tidy brick house was General Beauregard's headquarters on the eve of battle. A stray Yankee shell, Beauregard recounts, exploded in the McLean fireplace, abruptly depriving the general of his noon meal. When McLean's farm was again overrun in the second battle at Bull Run, he hastened far from the war zone, to the quiet village of Appomattox Court House. It was near the house of James Robinson, a free Negro, that General T. J. Jackson won an immortal nickname when his brigade stood "like a stone wall." Sudley Church overlooked the route of the Federal flank march that initiated the fighting. It was a field hospital in both Bull Run battles. A section of Beauregard's fortifications is depicted in Plate 21; winners of the field, the Confederates dug in here and spent the winter 25 miles from Washington.

PLATE 20   *J. D. Woodward*   SUDLEY CHURCH

PLATE 21   *Harry Fenn*   CONFEDERATE FORTIFICATIONS AT MANASSAS JUNCTION

PLATE 22 *Walton Taber*
SIEGE OF LEXINGTON, MISSOURI

PLATE 23 *Walton Taber* OFF TO THE WAR

The sharp, scattered combats and convoluted political
maneuvers by which the Lincoln administration struggled to
hold on to the border state of Missouri early in the war
attracted only a few photographers and newspaper artists.
To expand the pictorial coverage of this section in
Battles and Leaders, the *Century* editors went to their top
illustrator, Walton Taber. *Off to the War* pointed up
the opportunity for rapid troop movement by rail, especially
in the Western theater; the Civil War would be the first
"railroad war." In Plate 22 Taber portrays an incident
in the Confederate capture of Lexington in September, 1861.
For over a week a force of Yankees, well dug in on a hilltop,
held out stubbornly against the 18,000-man besieging
army of Sterling Price. Then the Rebels hit on the strategem
of advancing behind a mobile breastwork of hemp bales,
soaked in water to make them proof against heated shot.
The badly outnumbered Federals could find no way to counter
this, and on the ninth day of the siege they surrendered.

PLATE 24 *Harry Fenn* THE BATTLE OF BELMONT

Even before 1861 was out, the contest for control of the Mississippi
River was well begun. The Federal staging area was Cairo, Illinois,
where the Ohio River enters the Mississippi. Under U.S. Grant's
command, supply and repair facilities, such as the wharf boat
opposite, were assembled and troop levies drilled. Downriver, on a
high Kentucky bluff, was the Southern stronghold of Columbus.
On November 7 Grant and 3,100 men went ashore at Belmont, Missouri,
across the river from Columbus, looking for trouble. They found it,
more than they could handle, and were lucky to get away at all.
In the water color above, Grant's two wooden gunboats, *Tyler*
and *Lexington*, try fruitlessly to silence the Columbus batteries.
In Plate 26 Grant's battered force is taken back aboard its transports
under the protecting fire of the gunboats. Both pictures derive
from the wartime sketches (all of which have apparently since disappeared)
of Henry Walke, who commanded gunboat *Tyler* in this action.

PLATE 25   *Walter H. Goater*   WHARF BOAT, CAIRO, ILLINOIS

PLATE 26   *Frank H. Schell and Thomas Hogan*
THE BATTLE OF BELMONT: RE-EMBARKATION OF GRANT'S TROOPS

PLATE 27   *Walton Taber*   THE BATTLE OF LOGAN'S CROSSROADS

Logan's Crossroads, fought in south-central Kentucky on January 19, 1862, was a small action (some 800 total casualties) with large strategic consequences, for it deflated Confederate hopes of holding Kentucky. Taber's drawing is a free adaption of a lithographed view by Private Alfred E. Mathews of the 31st Ohio. The figure on the rearing horse (left) is the Confederate commander, Felix Zillicoffer, shot down when he nearsightedly blundered into the Federal lines.

II The Call to Arms

A NEWSPAPERMAN LONG REMEMBERED the mood in an encampment of Northern volunteers that he visited in May, 1861. "There was not one man in a hundred that believed there would be any war or fighting," he wrote. "All were unanimous in the conviction that the South would not fight, and that if the North put armies in the field, the terrified secessionists would hasten to seek shelter from the storm they had invoked. It was a picnic, a pleasure-trip, a triumphal jaunt through Dixie, with flying banners and beating drums, with all the pleasure of a free excursion, sightseeing, new faces and places. . . ." At about the same time a Georgia woman was watching the local young men march off to war. "Every soldier, nearly, had a servant with him," she recalled, "and a whole lot of spoons and forks, so as to live comfortably and elegantly in camp, and finally to make a splurge in Washington when they should arrive there, which they expected would be very soon indeed. That is really the way they went off; and their sweethearts gave them embroidered slippers and pin-cushions and needle-books, and all sorts of such little et ceteras. . . ."

So it was across the land as Americans prepared to fight a civil war, the reality of which was then entirely unimaginable. This chapter examines what might be called the mechanics of that process—the training camps and parade grounds, the various branches of service, the commissary establishments, and other aspects of military administration.

Arranging this particular Century Collection material in a topical manner is a departure from the exclusively chronological framework of *Battles and Leaders.* As the historian Henry Steele Commager remarks, "The distinguished warriors and statesmen who contributed to that magnificent series addressed themselves, on the whole, to the battles themselves; after all, who would ask a Sherman or a Longstreet to write about the commissary?" Thus Plates 43, 50, and 52, showing the Army of the Potomac in its 1863-64 winter quarters, appeared in *Battles and*

PLATE 28   *George R. Halm*   15-INCH GUN

Leaders to illustrate post-Gettysburg campaigning. Other plates illustrated *Century* articles after *Battles and Leaders* was published.

As he was in the opening chapter, Walton Taber is well represented here; four of his pictures (Plates 33, 48, 49, and 53) are original illustrations. Two pictures by Harry Fenn (Plates 37 and 46) are of special interest. Fenn was an Englishman who migrated to the United States in the mid-1850's and spent several of the war years studying painting in Italy. His many illustrations for the popular *Picturesque America* (1872-74) established his reputation as a landscape artist, and for the next several decades every leading magazine regularly carried his work. Fenn's drawings have their own distinctive character, whatever their source (in this case photographs). He is the most skilled of the artists represented in this collection; of the entire corps of artists who worked on *Battles and Leaders*, only Winslow Homer and Joseph Pennell would outrank him.

Many pictures in this chapter derive from wartime photographs. The drawing on the facing page, for example, is taken from Alexander Gardner's picture of a great 15-inch Columbiad that guarded Washington. And with one exception, all of them deal with the Federal armies; the exception is ex-Confederate Allen Redwood's group portrait, *Confederate Types* (Plate 55). This was inevitable, given the great mass of Northern source material and the limited number of Southern wartime pictures. In illustrating battle action the *Century* editors made a considerable effort to balance their presentation, commissioning such Southern artists as Redwood and William L. Sheppard and giving many pictures a Confederate or at least a "neutral" perspective (see Plates 8, 22, and 27 in Chapter One); but this was less easy to do in nonaction situations. In fact, however, it did not make that much difference. A Confederate army's winter quarters looked much the same as a Federal army's. The camps on the following two pages could easily have been located below the Mason-Dixon line; the pontoon bridges in Plate 46 could have been laid by Lee's engineers instead of Burnside's; and the cavalrymen in Plate 52 might be mistaken for Jeb Stuart's troopers. This, of course, is not true of commissary and supply scenes; the only time Johnny Reb ever saw such magnificence was when he captured a Yankee supply depot. With that qualification, then, the scenes in this chapter can be said to fairly represent both North and South answering the call to arms.

PLATE 29 *Edwin J. Meeker* CAMP BURGESS, BOWLING GREEN, KENTUCKY

PLATE 30 *Edwin J. Meeker* CAMP OF THE 40TH NEW YORK, ALEXANDRIA, VIRGINIA

PLATE 31 *Walton Taber* CAMP DENNISON, CINCINNATI

As the raw levies assembled, the first need was places to put them.
Seemingly overnight, camps sprouted everywhere. The Camp Burgess
view (Plate 29) is taken from a lithographed drawing by Ohio
Private Alfred Mathews. The Rebels had originally held Bowling Green,
and on the hill is a fort they constructed. Camp Dennison (Plate 31)
was one of Ohio's chief mobilization centers. The wooden barracks
were thrown up by the first troops dispatched there. Plates 30
and 32 are both based on diary sketches—which have apparently dropped
from sight—by the 40th New York's Robert K. Sneden. John Sedgwick
commanded the brigade to which Sneden's unit was assigned.

PLATE 32 *Edwin J. Meeker* HEADQUARTERS OF GENERAL SEDGWICK

PLATE 33   *Walton Taber*   THE AWKWARD SQUAD

PLATE 34   *Walton Taber*
PARADE OF THE 110TH PENNSYLVANIA INFANTRY

Taber's *The Awkward Squad* is a graphic example of the challenge faced by Civil War drill sergeants. To reveal the mysteries of close-order drill to totally unlettered farm boys, officers had each one tie a tuft of hay to his left foot and straw to his right, and chants of "Hay-foot, Straw-foot!" echoed across the parade grounds. "Straw-foot" soon became the tag for any raw recruit. Eventually all the awkward squads, drilled and properly armed and uniformed, became soldiers and finally veterans, like the infantrymen in Plate 34. These Pennsylvanians, who posed for photographer Alexander Gardner at Falmouth, Virginia, in the spring of 1863, saw action in all of the Army of the Potomac's major campaigns from Fredericksburg to Appomattox.

PLATE 35   *Walton Taber*   PARADE OF THE 3RD PENNSYLVANIA ARTILLERY

"The first thing in the morning is drill, then drill, then drill again. Then
drill, drill, a little more drill. Then drill, and lastly drill. Between
drills, we drill and sometimes stop to eat a little and have a roll-call."
So wrote a disgruntled Pennsylvanian in 1862, and it was a common enough gripe.
Yet to drill meant to learn by rote, and more so than in modern armies,
a Civil War army short on such rote was utterly helpless. Simply to go from
marching order to fighting order demanded promptly executed maneuvers. The
tasks of loading single-shot weapons, of attacking in mass formation, of holding
a line under intense artillery fire all required troops with a certain sense of
automatic response. Drill, too, was supposed to impart martial pride, particularly
by means of dress parades and mass reviews. The Pennsylvania gunners
above are on parade at Fortress Monroe, on the Virginia peninsula, in 1862.
The battalion at right was stationed at a prison camp at Sandusky Bay on Lake Erie.

PLATE 36   *Walton Taber*   THE HOFFMAN BATTALION, JOHNSON'S ISLAND

PLATE 37 *Harry Fenn* PROVOST-MARSHAL'S OFFICE, CORINTH, MISSISSIPPI

Wherever Federal armies reached into the South they unintentionally trampled out the institution of slavery. In occupied territory such as Corinth, Mississippi, at left, fugitive slaves flooded into the Union lines, and any army on the march was trailed by swarms of blacks seeking freedom first and beyond that they knew not what. The slave family below forded the Rappahannock to keep pace with John Pope's Army of Virginia as it retreated northward on the eve of the Second Battle of Bull Run. The army perforce had to try to feed and shelter this mass of people, and it soon put the able-bodied men to work building fortifications and doing camp chores (just what many of them had been doing for the Confederate army before they escaped). Finally this manpower was tapped more directly and the black man entered the Union army. Fenn's water color follows a George Armstead photograph; the Taber drawing, an Alexander Gardner photograph.

PLATE 38   *Walton Taber*
FUGITIVE SLAVES FORDING THE RAPPAHANNOCK

PLATE 39 *Walton Taber* UNION ARMY COOK

Few things concerned Rebel or Yankee more than the quality of rations, yet few things got less attention from army administration. Early in the war, food was issued in company lots, and how it got from there into the men's stomachs was up to the men. Later, with organization, came the assignment of company cooks, but any talent they demonstrated for preparing food was usually coincidental. The cook in Plate 39 is an impressed contraband. Plates 40 and 41 reveal private initiative at work; the sturdy outdoor oven and the importation of a real stove (as well as the elaborated Sibley tent dwellings) indicate winter quarters. Plate 42 is the commissary's bakery tent. A sketch by Frank Schell of *Leslie's* is the source of Hogan's drawing; the others are after Gardner or Brady pictures.

PLATE 40 *Thomas Hogan* CAMP OVEN

PLATE 41   *Walton Taber*   CAMP OF THE 153RD NEW YORK INFANTRY

PLATE 42   *Walton Taber*   COMMISSARY TENT

PLATE 43   *J. D. Woodward*   THE SHEBANG AND POST OFFICE, BRANDY STATION, VIRGINIA

The larger drawing in Plate 43 is the Army of the Potomac's military post office at 1863-64 winter quarters. It was claimed in 1864 that a letter mailed in Boston would reach a man in the Petersburg trenches in four days. At top is a field office of the U.S. Sanitary Commission (tagged the "shebang" for its many services—"the whole shebang"), a private organization that took up government slack in such areas as military hygiene, health care, medicine, and decent clothing. In Plate 44 are views of an enormous Federal supply dump for the Petersburg siege and an elaborate regimental commissary. Across the lines Lee's food situation was grim. "It is hard to maintain one's patriotism on ashcake and water," one of his men wrote.

PLATE 44   *Edwin J. Meeker*   COMMISSARY DEPOT AND HEADQUARTERS, PETERSBURG, VIRGINIA

Civil War military engineering offered the contradictory promise of rapid troop movements on the one hand and of static, positional warfare on the other. Speed records for constructing or reconstructing railroad bridges became a commonplace. The span below, near Fredericksburg, was cobbled together in 40 hours by Federal engineers to help supply Grant's 1864 campaign. Both armies were highly adept at pontoon bridging. Plate 47 shows one such bridge, on the Bull Run battlefield. The left wing of the Army of the Potomac crossed the Rappahannock in the Battle of Fredericksburg on the twin spans opposite, built under fire by Burnside's engineers. Material shortages hampered Confederate engineering efforts, but in field fortification the Army of Northern Virginia was unsurpassed—perhaps because Robert E. Lee began his military career as an engineer.

PLATE 45   *Edwin J. Meeker*   MILITARY RAILROAD BRIDGE OVER POTOMAC CREEK

PLATE 46   *Harry Fenn*   PONTOON BRIDGE OVER THE RAPPAHANNOCK

PLATE 47   *Walton Taber*   PONTOON BRIDGE OVER BULL RUN

PLATE 48   *Walton Taber*   TELEGRAPHING IN THE FIELD

The telegraph brought about a revolution in military communications, not only between Richmond or Washington and the armies in the field, but within the armies themselves. Grant wrote that when his army went into camp or field position during the Petersburg campaign, in each brigade "a mule loaded with a coil of wire would be led to the rear" to link up with higher command. "Thus, in a few minutes longer time than it took a mule to walk the length of its coil, telegraphic communication would be effected between all the headquarters of the army." These drawings were done to illustrate an 1889 *Century* article on the military telegraph.

PLATE 49   *Walton Taber*   LINEMAN, MILITARY TELEGRAPH

PLATE 50 *Walton Taber* ARMY FORGE. BRANDY STATION, VIRGINIA

In the cavalry arm the Confederates had a solid edge over
their enemy. For scouting and for screening an army's
movements Jeb Stuart's troopers were incomparable,
and not until late in the war did the Federal cavalry begin
to catch up. The Yankee trooper below "stands to horse";
above is a Yankee blacksmith at work. Both drawings
are after Gardner photographs. Plate 52, after a Timothy
O'Sullivan photograph, shows a cavalry outfit in winter
quarters. A veteran of the war's biggest cavalry fight,
at Brandy Station in June of 1863, the 18th Pennsylvania
would also see action at the Battle of Yellow Tavern,
on May 11, 1864, where Stuart was mortally wounded.

PLATE 51 *Walton Taber* UNION CAVALRYMAN

PLATE 52   *Walton Taber*   CAMP OF THE 18TH PENNSYLVANIA CALVARY

PLATE 53   *Walton Taber*   FALL OF THE LEADERS

From the war's first shot to the last the Federal artillery was outstanding. It had more and better guns than the Rebels, and more top-flight artillerists.
Taber illustrates here an incident at the Battle of Fredericksburg, when Captain John Hazard's Rhode Island battery went to the aid of beleaguered infantry.
"Hazard took his battery out in gallant style," General Darius N. Couch recalled.
"Men never fought more gallantly, and he lost a great many men and horses."

"On the basis of the whole war record
it cannot be said that the common soldier
of one side was any better or any worse
fighter than the one who opposed him,"
writes historian Bell Irvin Wiley, the
leading chronicler of Johnny Reb and Billy
Yank. "They were both Americans, by
birth or adoption, and they both had the
weaknesses and the virtues of the people
of their nation and time." Often the
soldiers themselves sensed these basic
underlying similarities. A New Yorker,
writing home about fraternizing with Rebels
on the picket line, remarked that they
usually ended their chats "by mutually
wishing we had let those who made the
quarrel be the very ones to fight. . . . We
would restore the Union tomorrow and
hang both cabinets at our earliest
convenience afterwards." The Billy Yank
at left fought in the 14th New York
at First Bull Run. Redwood's drawing is
based on wartime observation as a staff
officer in the 55th Virginia infantry.

PLATE 54   *Walton Taber*   A UNION VOLUNTEER

PLATE 55 *Allen C. Redwood* CONFEDERATE TYPES

III War on the Western Rivers

OLD GENERAL SCOTT had proposed the plan when the war was young, to much loud derision from the amateur strategists who were sure that a quick march on Richmond by the national army would be sufficient to scatter the secessionists and snuff out rebellion. Winfield Scott was gone now, pushed into retirement, Bull Run had at least partially sobered up the amateurs, and in the spring of 1862 the plan was going to be tried. It was, in fact, a very sound plan, and ultimately it would be the blueprint for Northern victory. Scott's idea was to enforce a rigorous blockade of the Confederacy while exerting continuous pressure all around the perimeter "so as to envelop the insurgent states and bring them to terms with less bloodshed than by any other plan." (The critics, amused at the notion of unleashing the massive Federal power to coil around and envelop the tiny mouse of rebellion, had tagged it the Anaconda Plan.) The key thrust, said Scott, should be made in the Western theater, along the Mississippi River, "to clear out and keep open this great line of communication." Geography was solidly behind his logic, for whichever side controlled the great rivers—the Mississippi, the Cumberland, the Tennessee—was a long way toward controlling the entire Mississippi Valley.

The major Federal campaign in the West that began in February, 1862, is the theme of this chapter. (McClellan's simultaneous offensive against Richmond will be examined in Chapter Four.) The coverage opens with the construction of the Union fleet of ironclad gunboats, the taking of Forts Henry and Donelson, and the terrible battle at Shiloh. The scene then shifts to the parallel drive down the Mississippi itself, climaxed by the savage "fleet action" fought in full view of the citizens of Memphis. Finally, there is Farragut's capture of the South's largest city, New Orleans, and his abortive effort to seize Vicksburg and open the entire river. (Plate 56 is the maintop of Farragut's flagship.)

The campaign achieved much, yet fell exasperatingly short—and so the war was prolonged. In that summer of 1862 Vicksburg was ripe for the taking, its defenses meager compared to what they soon became. Confederate forces in the

PLATE 56 *Walton Taber* MAINTOP OF THE "HARTFORD"

62

West were in disarray, hardly a match for Halleck's huge army massed at Corinth, Mississippi. But the Federal command on the spot lacked the killer instinct to crowd the enemy into a corner and annihilate him. It was a pattern that would become all too familiar to Abraham Lincoln.

In illustrating this campaign the *Century* editors made good use of the artistic flair of Henry N. Walke, who as captain of the Yankee gunboat *Carondelet* was in the thick of the action. Walke had served in the old navy in the Mexican War, and his surviving drawings and water colors of that conflict reveal him as an artist of talent. He continued his sketching habit in the Civil War, and following his retirement he wrote *Naval Scenes and Reminiscences of the Civil War* (1877) and illustrated it with his drawings. It may be these reproductions that were utilized by the *Century* artist corps, but if so, considerable artistic license is evident. It is possible that as a contributor himself to *Battles and Leaders* Walke loaned his original wartime sketches to the artists. In any event, Walke's originals have since disappeared, and these Century Collection pictures are certainly the best, and perhaps the only, extant record of them.

One *Century* artist who utilized the Walke sketches was Harry Fenn (Plates 59 and 69), but the most frequent users were Frank H. Schell and Thomas Hogan. Schell was a combat artist for *Frank Leslie's*, which published over 200 of his pictures, and several pen-and-ink drawings based on his wartime sketches appear in this book—the title-page illustration, for one. After the war Schell headed *Leslie's* art department and went into an illustrating partnership with lithographer Hogan. Sometimes Schell and Hogan worked in pen-and-ink (Plates 70 and 88), but their most distinctive pictures are a series of large water colors (averaging some two feet by three feet) of Mississippi River naval actions. Four of them are reproduced here.

An illustrator who makes his first appearance in this chapter is J. O. Davidson, one of the leading nautical painters of the day. As his set of New Orleans pictures indicates, he frequently worked in tempera and made use of *Century* consultants, who were to insure accuracy or, as in Plate 80, at least point out his mistakes. But it was fair to say that Davidson "knows our ships," as a contemporary critic put it, "as no other artist knows them," and not surprisingly the editors went to him often for the *Battles and Leaders* naval sections.

PLATE 57   *Theodore R. Davis*
BUILDING GUNBOATS AND MORTAR BOATS

By January, 1862, thanks to the driving energy of a St. Louis boatbuilder named James B. Eads, the Federals possessed a powerful Western river squadron of ironclad gunboats. Theodore Davis, who returned from his Southern tour via the Mississippi Valley, sketched a pair of these vessels (above), of a design perfected by naval constructor Samuel H. Pook and called "Pook's Turtles," under construction at Carondelet, Missouri. Two mortar boats— floating platforms for huge 13-inch mortars—are visible at left.

PLATE 58   *Rufus F. Zogbaum*   HEADQUARTERS IN THE FIELD

PLATE 59   *Harry Fenn*   GUNBOATS AT FORT DONELSON

The Turtles' first test came early in February at Fort Henry on the
Tennessee River, and they had sparkling success; after a short
bombardment the fort surrendered to flotilla commander Andrew Foote.
It was different a week later at Fort Donelson on the Cumberland.
In Plate 59 Fenn, working from a sketch by gunboat captain
Henry Walke, depicts the flotilla's attack. Donelson's gunners
riddled the ironclads and forced their retreat. It was left to
Grant to capture the fort—Zogbaum's sketch shows his officers
conferring—and on February 16 he did so, taking over 10,000 Rebels.

PLATE 60 *Theodore R. Davis*
ARMY TRANSPORTS AT THE CAIRO LEVEE

The jumping-off place for Federal operations in the Western river war was Cairo,
Illinois, at the confluence of the Mississippi and Ohio rivers; whether
campaigning down the Great River or into Tennessee via the Cumberland and
Tennessee rivers, which enter the Ohio less than 60 miles upstream, they
started here. Davis' water color is from sketches he made there late in 1861.
At center is the St. Charles hotel, "the only hotel of any consequence in
that mud-hole," a newspaperman reported. It was a tough, wild town, he went
on, where whiskey "overflowed everything, filled everything, pervaded everything."

In mid-March Grant's army was at Pittsburg Landing, on the Tennessee River close
to the Mississippi line, camped around a rude country church called Shiloh.
He had some 40,000 men with him, and would continue on southward as soon
as 35,000 more under General Don Carlos Buell arrived from Nashville. Confederate
General Albert Sidney Johnston, desperately pulling together troops at Corinth,
Mississippi, 20 miles to the south, was determined to strike before the odds
against him became too long. The result was the great Battle of Shiloh,
the first major combat of the Civil War and a sobering shock to anyone who
still believed in picture-book wars. In Sheppard's nighttime scene below, Rebel
officers direct a slave-labor battalion. The siege guns in Plate 62 formed
the last Federal line of defense at the battle's crisis point. Waterhouse's
battery (after an eyewitness sketch) was squarely in the path of Johnston's army.

PLATE 61   *William L. Sheppard*   SLAVES CONSTRUCTING EARTHWORKS, CORINTH, MISSISSIPPI

PLATE 62   *Walton Taber*   SIEGE BATTERY, PITTSBURG LANDING

PLATE 63   *Edwin J. Meeker*   WATERHOUSE'S BATTERY, SHILOH

At first light on Sunday, April 6, a sparkling
spring day, yelling Rebels came spilling
out of the thickets around the Shiloh meetinghouse. Redwood depicts them charging
into a campful of surprised Yankees commanded
by General Benjamin Prentiss. The Federals,
Prentiss' men among them, reeled back.
Very few on either side had seen any combat or
had much training, and the fight was a brutal,
disorganized slugging match. Prentiss managed
to rally his troops and some remnants from
other commands in a patch of woods and briars
soon called the Hornet's Nest. Grant told
them to hold at any cost. For long hours
they beat back repeated Confederate charges
(during one of which General Johnston was
mortally wounded) until they had no strength
left and had to surrender. But Prentiss'
stand won Grant what he needed most—time.

PLATE 64   *Allen C. Redwood*   THE BATTLE OF SHILOH

A.C. Redwood - 84

Plate 65 shows the country lane—the so-called "sunken road"—that meandered through the Hornet's Nest. Prentiss' Yankees, supported by a few guns, hold the road line; John Marmaduke's Confederates are at right. The source of Odgen's drawing was a cyclorama painting of Shiloh. (Only two Civil War examples—picturing Gettysburg and Atlanta—of this once-popular art form have survived.) During the struggle for the Hornet's Nest, Grant was establishing a last-ditch line covering Pittsburg Landing; and finally, as evening came on, this line stopped the Rebels. That night, during a violent thunderstorm, some 20,000 of Buell's troops came ashore to brace the Union army (Plate 66). The next day the fighting resumed, with the Federals doing the attacking. They retook part of the ground they had lost the day before, and at last the Rebels, now badly outnumbered, pulled back to Corinth. Grant's army was too spent to pursue. It has been estimated that about 100,000 men took some part in the two-day Battle of Shiloh; in round figures, one out of four was killed, wounded, or missing.

PLATE 65   *Henry A. Odgen*   THE HORNET'S NEST

PLATE 66 *Thure de Thulstrup* BUELL'S TROOPS ARRIVING AT PITTSBURG LANDING

PLATE 67   *Walton Taber*   BYPASS CHANNEL ABOVE ISLAND NUMBER TEN

The drive southward along the Tennessee was only one arm of the Union campaign in the West in the spring of 1862; a parallel advance pushed down the Mississippi. The northernmost Confederate strong point on the river, Columbus, Kentucky, had been outflanked and made untenable. Federal attention now focused on a string of citadels beginning with Island Number Ten, and ingenuity came into play. While mortar boats lobbed massive shells into the Rebel defenses (Plate 68), a navigable waterway was hacked through bayous at a point where the river nearly doubled back on itself, and Island Number Ten was bypassed. In Plate 67 Taber illustrates the novel underwater saw used to clear the channel. Shallow-draft transports could use this bypass, but the gunboats drew too much water. Commander Henry Walke of the *Carondelet* volunteered to run the Rebel batteries to show that it could be done; and did so, in a spectacular nighttime exploit amidst lightning flashes and thundering Confederate guns (Plate 69). On the same day the Battle of Shiloh ended, Island Number Ten surrendered. The next target was Fort Pillow, shown in Plate 70. Except for the Taber, the drawings on these two pages are from Walke's sketches.

PLATE 68   *Edwin J. Meeker*   MORTAR BOATS SHELLING ISLAND NUMBER TEN

PLATE 69   *Harry Fern*   THE "CARONDELET" PASSING ISLAND NUMBER TEN

PLATE 70   *Frank H. Schell and Thomas Hogan*   IRONCLADS AT FORT PILLOW

PLATE 71   *Frank H. Schell and Thomas Hogan*   ATTACKING CONFEDERATE BATTERIES AT WATSON'S LANDING

As part of the operation to seal off Island Number Ten (the tenth Mississippi island counting south from the mouth of the Ohio), batteries guarding the Confederates' escape route were to be silenced. *Carondelet*, aided by *Pittsburgh*, which had also run the Island Number Ten gantlet, undertook this task. The two gunboats, *Carondelet* in the lead, are shown pounding one of the enemy works. This water color and the two that follow are based on Walke sketches.

On May 10, as a mortar boat sheltered behind Plum Run Bend shelled Fort Pillow, a Rebel flotilla made a quick sortie and scored heavily. The Union craft are to the left. Gunboat *Cincinnati* (center) is being rammed by the *General Price* (partially obscured by her consort, the *General Van Dorn*, foreground). *Cincinnati* had already been rammed by the *General Bragg* (listing, right), and would be rammed a third time; both she and gunboat *Mound City* had to be run aground to keep from sinking.

PLATE 72   *Frank H. Schell and Thomas Hogan*   THE BATTLE OF PLUM RUN BEND

PLATE 73   *Frank H. Schell and Thomas Hogan*   THE BATTLE OF MEMPHIS

A month later the Federals took their revenge. Following the Rebel evacuation
of Fort Pillow, Captain Charles H. Davis' ironclad fleet, braced by
rams of its own, advanced on the railroad center of Memphis. On June 6
an outgunned Confederate squadron steamed out to defend the city and was
massacred; only the *General Van Dorn* (whose stern is visible at far left)
escaped. The Rebel vessels are shown in full retreat, pursued by the Federals
in the distance. At left center is the *General Bragg*, later captured. The
two stricken Confederate craft at the right were victims of the Yankee rams.

After Shiloh the Union commander in the West, Henry Halleck, massed no less than three armies—some 100,000 men—and began an advance on Corinth, Mississippi, where Beauregard's Rebel army of some 50,000 effectives was encamped. Meeker's drawing, after a lithographed sketch by Private Alfred Mathews, shows an Iowa regiment fording one of the innumerable streams in the area. "Old Brains" Halleck was a bookish soldier utterly dominated by caution. He had never commanded troops in combat—and never would—and was far more interested in capturing Corinth than in bringing Beauregard to battle. Entrenching at every pause, flooding his flanks with scouting forces, Halleck required 26 days to march 20 miles.

PLATE 74   *Edwin J. Meeker*   HALLECK'S ARMY ON THE MARCH TO CORINTH

PLATE 75 *Walter Fenn* CORINTH DWELLINGS

Corinth was a railroad junction of no little importance to the shrinking
Confederate position in the West, and Beauregard had hoped to defend it. But he
was frustrated by a lack of manpower, and the decision was made to evacuate.
The Corinth houses opposite (as laid out for *Battles and Leaders*) were sketched
from postwar photographs. Number 1 was in turn the headquarters of Confederate
Braxton Bragg, Halleck, and, in 1864, Confederate John Bell Hood. Beauregard
made his headquarters in number 2, Grant in 3. Union General William Rosecrans
directed the Battle of Corinth in October, 1862, from number 4, and the body
of Albert Sidney Johnston lay in state after Shiloh in number 5. Private
Mathews' lithograph of his Ohio regiment entrenching on the road to Corinth
is the source for Plate 76. Confusing Halleck with theatrics (much shuffling of
trains, much cheering of "reinforcements"), Beauregard slipped away unscathed.
The Federal host settled down in Corinth and let the initiative slip away.

PLATE 76 *Edwin J. Meeker* BUILDING BREASTWORKS BEFORE CORINTH

PLATE 77   *J. O. Davidson*   CONFEDERATE RAM "STONEWALL JACKSON"

Still a third Federal striking force was assigned to operate in the Mississippi Valley in that spring of 1862, this one aimed at New Orleans. Its cutting edge was David Farragut's squadron of powerful deepwater cruisers, advancing upriver from the Gulf. New Orleans itself was virtually undefended, stripped of troops by the crisis farther north; it had to depend on Forts Jackson and St. Philip on the lower river and on a makeshift "river defense" squadron. Typical of the squadron was the *Stonewall Jackson* (above), a steam tug fitted with a single gun and "armored" with cotton bales. The rugged *Louisiana* (below) could have been a real threat to Farragut's vessels, but her power plant was unfinished; she was towed downriver and tied up by the forts, nothing more than a floating battery. Beyond the forts and the fleet, the Rebels could only harass the Yankees, as the snipers in Redwood's sketch are doing.

PLATE 78   *Walton Taber*   CONFEDERATE IRONCLAD "LOUISIANA"

PLATE 79   *Allen C. Redwood*   AN INCIDENT IN THE DEFENSE OF NEW ORLEANS

PLATE 80 *J. O. Davidson* THE "GOVERNOR MOORE" RAMMING THE "VARUNA"

PLATE 81 *J. O. Davidson* FORT ST. PHILIP UNDER ATTACK

PLATE 82   *J. O. Davidson*   THE "GOVERNOR MOORE" IN FLAMES

In mid-April mortar boats began lobbing 220-pound shells into Forts Jackson and
St. Philip. They kept at it for six days, and tough old Farragut grew impatient;
finally he determined to run the forts. In the early morning of April 24
the fleet got under way. The forts opened a rapid fire, the cruisers
replied with their broadsides, and the mortar boats added voice to the
cannonade. A Northern officer likened it to "all the earthquakes in the
world and all the thunder and lightning storms together." Every Federal ship
was hit, flagship *Hartford* 32 times (she also briefly ran aground and was
briefly set ablaze by a fire raft), but finally the squadron was safely through.
Now it was engaged by the river defense vessels. In Plate 80 the *Varuna*,
the only Union ship lost in the operation, is rammed and pounded
by the *Governor Moore* (left) and the *Stonewall Jackson*. (*Battles and Leaders*
used only a central detail from this painting, for the two rams were actually
side-wheelers; a consultant, Captain Beverley Kennon of the *Governor Moore*,
apparently caught the error.) Farragut's cruisers put a quick end to the
battle. In Plate 82 the *Governor Moore* is ashore, gutted and afire, victim
of the *Pensacola* (foreground). In the right background is the sunken *Varuna*.
The other Union vessels are (from left) the *Oneida*, *Pinola*, and *Iroquois*.

PLATE 83   *J. O. Davidson*   FARRAGUT'S SQUADRON AT NEW ORLEANS

PLATE 84   *Thure de Thulstrup*   TAKING DOWN THE STATE FLAG, NEW ORLEANS

PLATE 85   *J. O. Davidson*   Taking the Surrender of Forts Jackson and St. Philip

The day after passing the forts, Farragut's fleet
dropped anchor before New Orleans. Commissioned to
illustrate the scene, J. O. Davidson wrote the *Century*'s art
editor to describe his composition (Plate 83): "I show
the fleet steaming up in a body, the Mississippi
and Hartford in the lead. The city front and levees in
flames. A crowd waving Confederate flags at the
fleet and a rain storm over all." Despite the defiance,
the helpless city had to surrender. Thulstrup records the
scene at City Hall when Louisiana's flag was lowered.
The two Confederate forts below the city were also
helpless. The Fort Jackson garrison mutinied, and
on April 28 David Dixon Porter, left behind to keep an
eye on the forts, accepted their surrender aboard
the gunboat *Harriet Lane*, as depicted in Plate 85.

Following his seizure of New Orleans,
Farragut was ordered to complete the job of
opening the Mississippi; he was to steam
upriver, capture Vicksburg, and link up with
Davis' gunboat squadron. In Washington
it looked easy, but Farragut was doubtful.
His big cruisers might run the Vicksburg
batteries, just as they had passed the
New Orleans forts, but this would actually
accomplish little. The navy's guns could
not reduce Vicksburg, nor could it be
isolated as Forts Jackson and St. Philip had
been; troops were needed to take the city,
and Farragut had too few of them for the job.
Nevertheless, by June 28 most of his Gulf
Squadron, after a sharp fight, was above
Vicksburg—and Vicksburg was no closer to
surrender. In late July, sped along by
the embarrassing affair of the *Arkansas*
(overleaf), Farragut headed back to New
Orleans before low water stranded his
squadron upriver. In another Schell-Hogan
water color after a Walke sketch, the Union
ships, led by the big sloops *Hartford* and
Richmond, blaze away at the *Arkansas* (right)
as they steam south of Vicksburg.

PLATE 86   *Frank H. Schell and Thomas Hogan*   FARRAGUT'S SQUADRON AT VICKSBURG

The career of C.S.S. *Arkansas* lasted 24 highly eventful days. The half-built ironclad had been towed far up the Yazoo River to escape capture, and there a determined lieutenant, Isaac N. Brown, took charge and completed her against appalling odds. *Arkansas* was decidedly homemade, her armor railroad rails and her machinery shaky, but she was deadly, and on July 15 she took on the entire Federal fleet at Vicksburg. Brown first steered *Arkansas* into a contest with Henry Walke's *Carondelet* (Plate 88), and the Union gunboat got the worst of it. Then he steamed straight through the Yankee fleet, causing considerable damage and much mortification. Later, *Arkansas* suffered engine failure and had to be blown up (Plate 89), but by then the South's grip on Vicksburg was secure.

PLATE 87   *Walton Taber*   UNION WARSHIPS "MISSISSIPPI" AND "WINONA"

PLATE 88   *Frank H. Schell and Thomas Hogan*   "CARONDELET" VS. "ARKANSAS"

PLATE 89 *J. O. Davidson* DESTRUCTION OF THE "ARKANSAS"

IV The Peninsula Campaign

AS STRATEGICALLY IMPORTANT as the campaigns in the West might be, it was what went on in the Eastern theater that captured the attention and dominated the headlines. As a consequence, the opening of McClellan's 1862 spring campaign, for which the old Bull Run slogan, "Forward to Richmond," was revived, was awaited with intense interest. "Little Mac" had spent the months since Bull Run equipping and training and polishing his army, and he did the job well; had the military of that day included a Training Command, George McClellan would have been superbly qualified for the post. Yet he was slow approaching action—and he would prove slower still in action. There was much argument in Washington about whether to march on Richmond overland or make a waterborne end run, and how best to protect the capital in the meantime. McClellan's plan for the water route, landing on the peninsula southeast of Richmond, at last prevailed, but the defense-of-Washington question was never clearly resolved; and then Stonewall Jackson confused the matter even further by his threatening maneuvers in the Shenandoah Valley.

Despite such uncertainties, the tools to end the rebellion were in McClellan's hands that spring, and the following pages illustrate what he did with them. Like the simultaneous offensive in the West, the Peninsula campaign came exasperatingly close to total success. In the end, perhaps, it came down to the fact that McClellan was a man harboring deep doubts about himself; thus half-blinded, he never saw the true measure of the army he commanded. Lee, with his uncanny insight into the mind of his opponent, took full advantage of that weakness.

The Northern papers mobilized to cover the campaign. Winslow Homer of *Harper's Weekly* made one of his rare wartime excursions into the field, but the star performer for *Harper's* was Alfred R. Waud. Waud, an Englishman who had studied at the Royal Academy before emigrating in 1850, was a veteran at the business of newspaper illustration. Early in 1862 he left the *New York Illustrated News*, and the Peninsula campaign was his first for *Harper's*. At 33 Waud was senior to most of the war artists—Theodore Davis, for example, was 22, and

PLATE 90   *William H. Shelton*   A TEMPTING BREASTWORK

Edwin Forbes of *Leslie's* was 23—but none could match him in vigor and presence. He was described by a fellow war correspondent as "blue-eyed, fair-bearded, strapping and stalwart, full of loud, cheery laughs and comic songs, armed to the teeth, jack-booted, gauntleted, slouch-hatted . . . continually vaulting on [his] huge brown horse, and galloping off full split, like a Wild Horseman of the Prairie." But the hard going on the Peninsula would get even Waud down. Soon after the Seven Days' battles that ended the campaign, he complained of something he labeled "billious remittent fever" picked up from "exposure to the damned climate in cussed swamps &c."

The half-dozen Wauds reproduced here are finished versions or elaborations of his pictorial reporting for *Harper's*. The bulk of his work for the *Battles and Leaders* series was done in pen and ink, but he also produced an occasional water color in this period, to which he obviously devoted more care. In fact, it would be hard to find a single picture that is more symbolic of the entire Peninsula campaign than Waud's water color of Federal reinforcements crossing the gloomy Chickahominy River (Plate 110).

Of the 30 plates in this chapter, a sizable proportion, 19, are based on eyewitness sketches. Two of them (Plates 102 and 106) are by an ex-Confederate soldier, William L. Sheppard. The 29-year-old Virginian, who had studied art in New York and Paris before the war, served in the Richmond Howitzers during this campaign, sketching whenever he found a free moment. Sheppard remained in the Army of Northern Virginia right through to its disbandment at Appomattox. In the postwar years he was in demand not only as a newspaper artist and book illustrator, but also as the unofficial chronicler of the Confederate soldier.

Seven of the plates stemming from eyewitness reporting have as their source an extensive illustrated wartime diary, of at least four volumes, kept by Robert K. Sneden, a topographical engineer in the 40th New York. Little is known of Sneden's life beyond his wartime experiences, which included more than a year spent in a total of nine Confederate prison camps, including notorious Andersonville. The fate of his diary is a mystery. After it was utilized by the artists for *Battles and Leaders* in the 1880's, it seems to have disappeared. As a result, the 35 Century Collection drawings credited to this source may be the only surviving record of these Sneden sketches.

When the plan for McClellan's spring offensive was finally formulated, its designated starting point was Fortress Monroe, a sturdy masonry pile three decades old at the tip of the peninsula formed by the James and York rivers. Plate 92, showing the fort as it looked just before the war, was taken from a lithograph. Its faculties included the Hygeia Hotel (foreground), which served as a military hospital during the Peninsula fighting; at the right is the wharf detailed in Davis' Plate 93. Davis was at the fort that spring on assignment from *Harper's*. A few miles inland was the village of Hampton, burned in August, 1861, by order of Confederate General John Magruder. He gave the order, he said, after learning that Ben Butler, commandant at Fortress Monroe, intended to billet fugitive slaves there. Robert Sneden's sketch is the source for Plate 91.

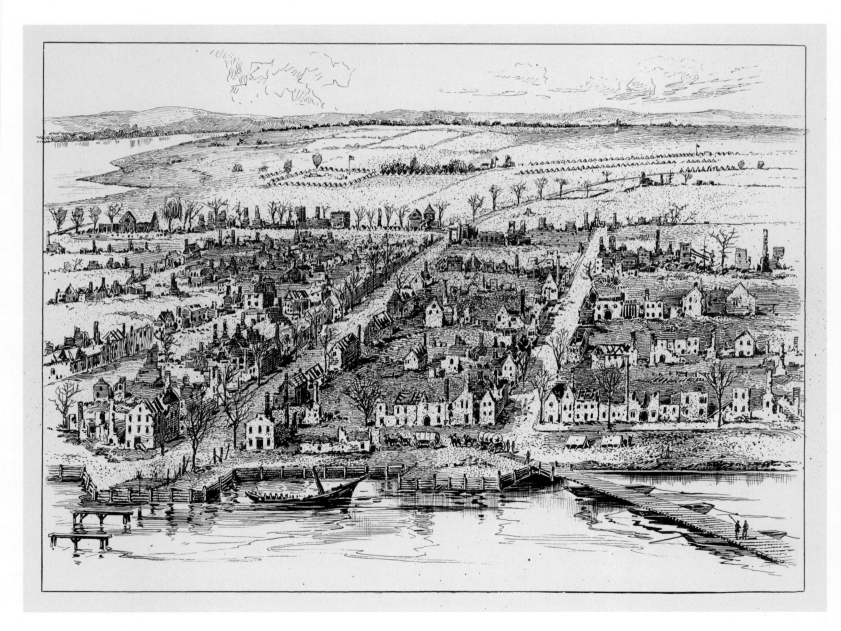

PLATE 91   *Edwin J. Meeker*   THE RUINS OF HAMPTON, VIRGINIA

PLATE 92   *Walton Taber*   FORTRESS MONROE

PLATE 93   *Theodore R. Davis*   QUARTERMASTER'S DOCK, FORTRESS MONROE

PLATE 94   *J. O. Davidson*   REMODELING THE "MERRIMACK"

McClellan's campaign plan was nearly demolished by C.S.S. *Virginia*.
The famous Southern ironclad had begun life as the steam frigate
Merrimack, burned and scuttled when the Federals abandoned the
navy yard at Norfolk early in the war. The Rebels raised her and, as
Davidson shows above, constructed an iron-plated citadel on her
berth deck. On March 8 the *Virginia* steamed into Hampton Roads and
mangled the Federal blockading squadron. That night, fortuitously, the
Monitor arrived from New York; in Plate 95 Davidson depicts
her with the *Minnesota*. The next day the ironclads fought
to a draw, and the Union grip on Hampton Roads was re-established.

PLATE 95   *J. O. Davidson*   ARRIVAL OF THE "MONITOR" AT HAMPTON ROADS

PLATE 96 *Edwin Forbes* THE BATTLE OF CROSS KEYS

After the neutralization of the *Virginia* permitted McClellan's
offensive to begin, its progress was deeply affected by what happened
in the Shenandoah Valley. On orders from General Lee, Jefferson
Davis' military adviser, Stonewall Jackson was dispatched to create
a strategic diversion in the Valley. He was wholly successful,
sidetracking substantial strength from McClellan in one of the dazzling
campaigns of the war. Forbes shows the climax of the operation:
slipping between two converging Federal columns, Jackson turned and
whipped them both—at Cross Keys (above) and Port Republic—then
joined the army facing McClellan. This was the first battle Forbes
covered for *Leslie's*. He had trouble getting close to the action, so he
simply sketched Yankee guns firing and troops marching to the fight.

101

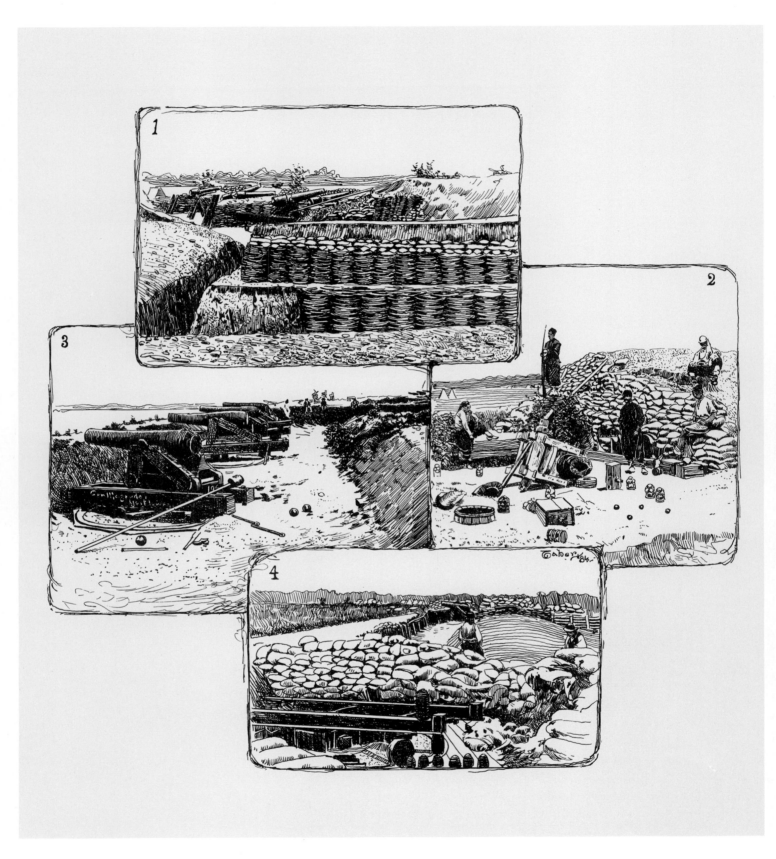

PLATE 97 *Walton Taber* FORTIFICATIONS AT YORKTOWN

Early in April the Army of the Potomac, 85,000 strong, began its drive up the Peninsula. It was a brief advance; coming up against General Magruder's entrenchments at Yorktown (held by 15,000 men, although Federal Intelligence divined available Rebel strength at six times that total), McClellan determined on war by siege. It took him a month to get his siege train—some 71 pieces, ranging up to 8-inch rifles and 13-inch mortars—into position to open fire; on the eve of the scheduled bombardment the enemy pulled out. Plate 98, after Sneden's sketch, shows one of the 15 Federal batteries built before Yorktown. These ten-ton mortars were the largest in the Federal arsenal; none fired a shot. The scenes on the opposite page are based on Gardner photographs taken after the Rebel withdrawal. Number 1 is a Union battery of powerful rifled cannon. The others are views of the Confederate lines, showing heavy guns the Rebels were unable to take away with them.

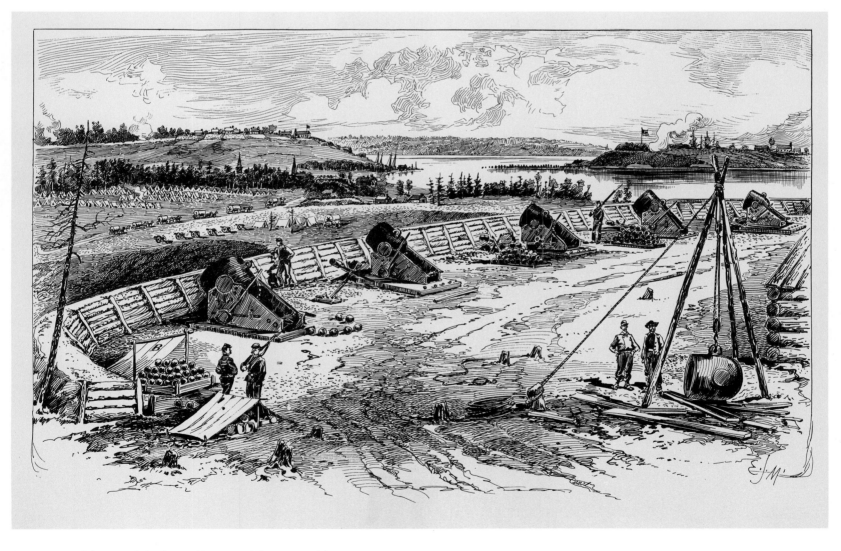

PLATE 98   *Edwin J. Meeker*   BATTERY NUMBER 4, YORKTOWN

Meeker's Plates 99 and 100 are based on sketches in
the Sneden diary. Sneden's New York regiment was assigned
to General Samuel Heintzelman's 3rd Corps; the general's
headquarters below, set up next to a steam-powered
saw mill, are seen against a backdrop of neat encampments.
In Plate 100 the Federals entering historic Yorktown
on May 4 file past the commanding general's headquarters
(center background). "The success is brilliant," wrote
McClellan. But the Rebels had gained the time to organize
and reinforce their army before Richmond, Joe Johnston
was on the scene to take charge, and McClellan's critics in
Washington were in full voice about his slow progress.
Through May the Army of the Potomac slogged steadily
toward Richmond in heavy rains that turned the roads to
mudholes (Plate 101). McClellan assured Lincoln, "I firmly
believe we shall beat them"—providing he got more troops.

PLATE 99   *Edwin J. Meeker*   HEINTZELMAN'S HEADQUARTERS BEFORE YORKTOWN

PLATE 100 *Edwin J. Meeker* UNION TROOPS ENTERING YORKTOWN

PLATE 101 *Walton Taber* FORWARD TO RICHMOND

PLATE 102   *William L. Sheppard*   CONFEDERATE SKIRMISHERS

Both these drawings are the work of men who witnessed the
Peninsula campaign. Sheppard's Richmond Howitzers were
in the pull-back from Yorktown, and he described the
incident above as a Rebel skirmish line being pushed back
by Yankees advancing through the orchard in the distance.
Meanwhile, on the other side of the lines, Alf Waud
was covering the campaign for *Harper's*, to whom he
sent a sketch of Rebels being chased out of Mechanicsville,
northeast of Richmond, late in May. When he took on
the *Battles and Leaders* assignment, however, Waud placed the
fleeing Confederates, as he imagined them, against a
background taken from an 1865 photograph of the village.

PLATE 103   *Alfred R. Waud*   CONFEDERATE RETREAT THROUGH MECHANICSVILLE

PLATE 104   *Harry C. Edwards*   FEDERAL OBSERVATION BALLOON

An aspect of the campaign that attracted much comment was Professor Thaddeus S. C. Lowe's aerial reconnaisance squadron. In the drawing above, after Sneden, one of the professor's two hydrogen balloons soars aloft near McClellan's headquarters. As the shellbursts suggest, the Rebels tried hard to shoot down the snoopers, bringing up one of their accurate English Whitworth rifled guns, but they scored no hits; anti-aircraft gunnery was too new an art. Plate 105 is the landing at White House plantation, some 25 miles from Richmond. This was to be the main supply base for McClellan's planned siege of the capital, for here the Peninsula's single railroad, the Richmond & York River, crossed the Pamunkey, and only by water and rail could his siege train be brought forward; the big guns were too heavy to be moved by road. The thrust of the Federal drive on Richmond, therefore, was along the railroad. White House, the home of Rebel cavalryman W. H. F. Lee, second son of Robert E. Lee, was burned during the Federal "change of base" in June. The inset is Waud's view of the ruins.

PLATE 105   *Alfred R. Waud*   WHITE HOUSE, PAMUNKEY RIVER

PLATE 106   *William L. Sheppard*   RICHMOND DEFENSE LINES

PLATE 107 *J. D. Woodward* CHICKAHOMINY SWAMP

As McClellan methodically drove ever closer to the gates of Richmond, Joe Johnston's view of the situation darkened. "We are engaged in a species of warfare at which we can never win," he wrote Lee. McClellan, he went on, planned to "depend for success upon artillery and engineering. We can compete with him in neither." Hurried efforts were made to strengthen the city's defenses. The water color by Sheppard, a native of Richmond, records a section of fortifications near the Richmond-Mechanicsville turnpike. The Confederates had a strong ally, however, in the Chickahominy River, which meandered across the Federal line of advance. It formed a swampy, tangled, confusing barrier; the Woodward drawing above is from a Brady photograph. On May 30, when a spring deluge flooded the Chickahominy, McClellan was caught astride the river, with two of his army corps on one side and three on the other. Seeing his opportunity, Johnston lashed out.

On the last day of May, Johnston struck at McClellan's bridgehead on the Richmond side of the Chickahominy. With the bridges behind them in danger of being washed away by the flooding, turbulent river, these Yankees stood in peril. But nothing went right for the Confederates. Detachments took the wrong roads, and attacks were made piecemeal and behind schedule. The Federals were pushed back around Fair Oaks Station, on the Richmond & York River line, but when the fighting dwindled out at nightfall they had not been broken. The Vanderhoof drawings below of farm buildings that served as Union field hospitals are taken from the Sneden diary. Fenn's water colors in Plate 109 are derived from George Barnard photographs of the so-called "twin houses" in the nearby hamlet of Seven Pines. The lower scene shows an unfinished Federal redoubt. At top is the burying ground for 400 of the Fair Oaks dead.

Farm House - Fair Oaks V⁻ᵃ

Hyers House " " →

Union Hospitals.

PLATE 108   *Charles A. Vanderhoof*   FIELD HOSPITALS, FAIR OAKS

Fair Oaks
Rear view of old houses.
Graves of 400 soldiers.

Front view of same

PLATE 109   *Harry Fenn*   THE FAIR OAKS BATTLEFIELD

One reason Johnston's attack achieved
less than he hoped was the fact that the
isolated Union bridgehead was reinforced
in spite of the appalling conditions.
McClellan ordered General Edwin Sumner to
get troops over the Chickahominy, but
his engineers warned him that the bridges
were unsafe and impossible to use.
"Bull" Sumner may have been an old
regular without a jot of imagination,
but he was exactly the man for this job.
"Impossible?" he bellowed. "Sir,
I tell you I *can* cross! I am ordered!"
Waud's water color shows Sumner's men
tramping across the nearly swamped
"Grapevine" bridge spanning the river.
The next day, June 1, the Rebel attack
was renewed without result, and the
fighting ended in stalemate. Yet Fair
Oaks had a profound effect on the war, for
Joe Johnston was one of the 4,700 Rebel
wounded. Robert E. Lee was named in
his place to head the force that was now
known as the Army of Northern Virginia.

PLATE 110   *Alfred R. Waud*   SUMNER'S CORPS CROSSING THE CHICKAHOMINY

One of Lee's strongest traits as a soldier was an unswerving determination to seize the initiative. Learning from Jeb Stuart that the Federal right flank was insecurely anchored, Lee quickly brought Stonewall Jackson from the Valley and prepared to strike that flank, threatening not only a sizable piece of McClellan's army but also his railroad supply line and thus his whole strategic plan. On June 25 began the famous Seven Days. The tavern at Old Cold Harbor was on the axis of Lee's offensive. Near Dr. Gaines' gristmill a spectacular charge by Hood's Texas Brigade pushed the Federals into retreat; the mill was destroyed by Sheridan's cavalry in 1864. Plate 113 illustrated the growing Stonewall Jackson legend. At Gaines' Mill he personally seized a whole squad of Yankees, who ruefully acknowledge their captor as they are led off.

PLATE 111   *Walton Taber*   OLD COLD HARBOR TAVERN

PLATE 112   *Walton Taber*   RUINS OF GAINES' MILL

PLATE 113   *Allen C. Redwood*   CAPTURED BY STONEWALL JACKSON

The Seven Days was actually a single rippling week-long
battle that extended from northeast of Richmond to
well southeast of the capital. McClellan was forced to get
his army to a new supply base on the James River, and
Lee tried to bring him to a decisive battle before he could
get there by cutting through the Federal line of march
from the flank. One such attack took place at the village
of Glendale on June 30; Plate 114, based on the Sneden
diary, depicts Union reinforcements massing around a corps
headquarters as the fighting rages in the background.

PLATE 114   *Charles A. Vanderhoof*   THE BATTLE OF GLENDALE

PLATE 115 *Alfred R. Waud* DESTRUCTION OF AN AMMUNITION TRAIN

Alf Waud was everywhere that week, filling his sketchbook
with scenes of the fast-moving campaign for *Harper's*.
This water color shows the Federals running a burning,
exploding munitions train into Chickahominy Swamp; once
their rail link was cut they could only take whatever
could be moved by road. On July 5 Waud summarized his
experience for a friend as "Seven days almost without food
or sleep, night and day being attacked by overwhelming masses
of infuriated rebels thundering at us from all sides."

PLATE 116   *Alfred R. Waud*   ENGAGEMENT AT WHITE OAK BRIDGE

Waud's remark about "overwhelming masses of infuriated rebels" was echoed by the Union high command; the phrase "attacked by greatly superior numbers" appears more than once in McClellan's dispatches. Lee's army was, in fact, smaller than McClellan's, but the Northerner never wavered in the belief that he was hugely outnumbered. Thus he argued that the move to the James (a "change of base," he termed it) should be considered a victory, for the army—and thereby the country—had been saved. Indeed, it was a skillful enough maneuver, with the Yankee artillery particularly distinguishing itself. In Waud's drawing, an elaboration of a sketch he sent to *Harper's*, a battery of rifled guns holds off Jackson's corps at a crossing of White Oak Swamp on June 30. Still, in a week's time the Army of the Potomac had been pushed more than 20 miles from Richmond's suburbs, and McClellan's strategy for ending the war was in tatters.

PLATE 117   *Thure de Thulstrup*   THE BATTLE OF MALVERN HILL

PLATE 118   *Alfred R. Waud*   BERKELEY, HARRISON'S LANDING

On July 1 Lee made one final effort at a showdown fight.
The Federals were massed on good defensive ground at
Malvern Hill, with artillery posted to sweep every approach.
Lee's attack, when it came, was marred by confusion
and poor staff work—the Army of Northern Virginia was not
yet the smooth fighting machine it would become—but
probably even the best-mounted attack would have withered
before the terrible Yankee artillery. Thulstrup portrays
one of the gun crews that repelled the attack. Malvern
Hill ended the Seven Days, and McClellan safely withdrew to
a heavily fortified position at Harrison's Landing on
the James. Berkeley, the ancestral home of the Harrisons,
was serving as a Union hospital and signal station
when Waud sketched it. Below, Frank Schell of *Leslie's*
shows fugitive slaves adding to the bustle of the great base.

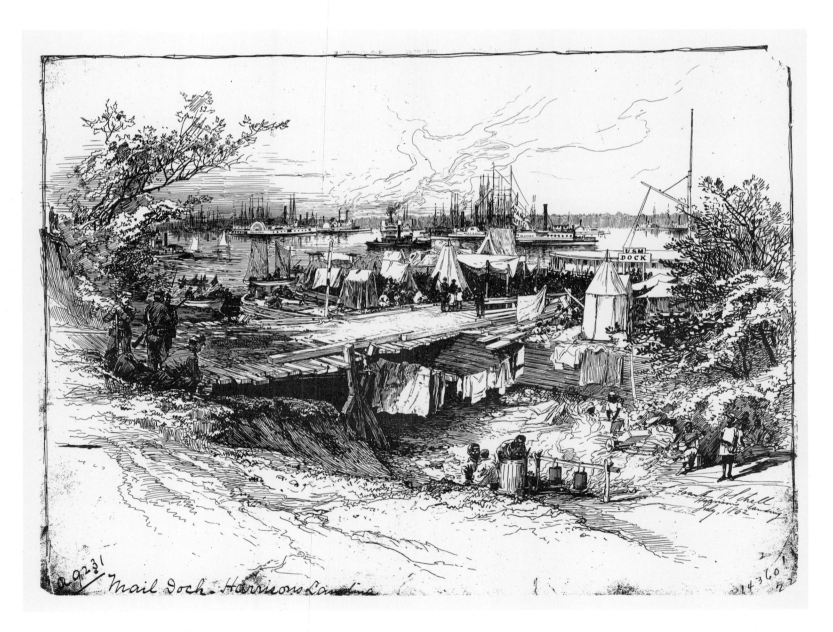

PLATE 119   *Frank H. Schell*   HARRISON'S LANDING

V Confederate Offensive

IN THE SUMMER AND FALL of 1862 the Confederacy rolled to its high-water mark. Hindsight nicely underscores reasons for this sudden turn of events—lackluster, stodgy Federal generalship, imperfect strategic vision in Washington, Robert E. Lee's dynamism—but to contemporaries it was astonishing and incomprehensible. It was hard for a Northerner to see why things ground to a halt in the West when there were 100,000 Yankee soldiers in northern Mississippi and vicinity; it was equally hard to understand the defensive posture of the 100,000-man Army of the Potomac, camped just two dozen miles from Richmond. That was the situation on July 11 when Henry Halleck was appointed general-in-chief of the Northern armies. On paper Halleck's record in the West was a good one; only later would Lincoln discover him for what he was—a competent clerk.

On July 23, when Halleck arrived in Washington to take up his new duties, he found an odd situation. McClellan, at Harrison's Landing, could not resume the offensive because, he said, Lee had 200,000 men on call. (Lee had 70,000; McClellan, an observer noted, "always saw double when he looked rebelward," and in this case he saw triple.) Halfway between Richmond and Washington was John Pope's new Army of Virginia, formed out of the various units that had guarded Washington or chased after Stonewall Jackson in the Shenandoah Valley. The Confederates were squarely between these two armies. It was decided to shut down the Peninsula campaign and ship the troops northward to strengthen Pope.

This decision was no surprise to Lee; he promptly grasped that the sluggish Federal high command was presenting him with the time to act first. The result was his humiliation of Pope at Second Bull Run, which opens this chapter. (The monument pictured in Plate 120 was raised on the Bull Run battlefield in 1865 to commemorate that action.) Without pause Lee turned his army toward the Potomac River fords, determined to carry the war to the North and force a showdown battle. His offensive came to its awful climax along the banks of Antietam Creek

PLATE 120 *Walton Taber* SOLDIERS' MONUMENT, BULL RUN

in Maryland, and half the chapter's pictures are devoted to it. The Confederate offensive in the West, which crested at about the same time, concludes the section.

Antietam and Perryville were lost chances to end the rebellion with a spectacular stroke. The odds were all in McClellan's favor at Antietam; certainly his men exhibited all the courage that was required. In Kentucky Buell missed the chance to overwhelm an overextended Rebel army far from its home base. Now it would be a different and a harder war. The abolition of slavery emerged at last from the shadows to become an avowed war aim. Conscription was a fact in the South and on the agenda in Washington. McClellan and Buell, the cautious captains, were gone, their dismissal ironically made easier by the fact that after their "victories" they suddenly no longer seemed indispensable.

Mathew Brady's photography team came into its own during the Second Bull Run and Antietam campaigns—at Antietam Alexander and James Gardner produced some of the most memorable war pictures ever made—and the *Century* editors made wide use of this resource. Walton Taber worked extensively from these photographs, and also drew two strong original illustrations (Plates 134 and 143).

Edwin Forbes of *Leslie's* also hit his stride covering Lee's offensive. As noted in the commentary with Plate 96, Forbes had trouble covering his first combat assignment. "My ideas of witnessing a battle underwent great change," he later wrote. "To be a spectator was nearly as dangerous as being a participant." But the Second Bull Run and Antietam battles seemed to him "picturesque," for they offered vantage points from which to see wide sweeps of action, and he kept on the move to find fresh perspectives. (He would have agreed with Theodore Davis' observation that most people "seem to have an idea that all battlefields have some elevated spot upon which the general is located, and that from this spot the commander can see his troops, direct all their maneuvers and courteously furnish special artists an opportunity of sketching the scene.") At Second Bull Run Forbes moved particularly fast when Longstreet's Confederates came boiling toward the Henry House Hill, where he was sketching a panoramic view (see Plate 127). At Antietam he captured such key actions as Hooker's charge on the Dunker Church (Plate 135) and the Federal advance over Burnside's Bridge (Plate 137). The Battle of Antietam, Forbes concluded, "was a dramatic and most magnificent series of pictures."

On August 3, 1862, McClellan was ordered to evacuate the Peninsula and come north to aid and comfort Pope's Army of Virginia. But Lee was already on the move, dispatching Stonewall Jackson to give Pope a lesson in generalship. Pope hastily withdrew behind the Rappahannock; Forbes watched the troops cross the river on a military railroad span (Plate 122). Eight days later Jackson was squarely behind Pope, cutting his supply lines and pillaging his base at Manassas Junction. In Plate 123, after Timothy O'Sullivan's photograph, a shoeless Yankee contemplates the wreckage. Jackson moved off to the old Bull Run battlefield, and on August 28 he wiggled the bait by striking at a Federal column near Groveton. In the water color below, the Rebels are in the woods and the Federals are strung out along the Warrenton turnpike at center.

PLATE 121 *Edwin Forbes* THE BATTLE OF GROVETON

PLATE 122 *Edwin Forbes* RETREAT OF THE ARMY OF VIRGINIA

PLATE 123 *Walton Taber* A DISORGANIZED PRIVATE

PLATE 124   *Edwin Forbes*   MARCH OF LONGSTREET'S CORPS THROUGH THROUGHFARE GAP

For several days Pope had been ordering units this way and that, frantically
seeking the elusive Jackson. Now, it appeared, the quarry had been run
to ground, and in his relief he quite forgot about the other half of the Army
of Northern Virginia. While Pope's back was turned, Lee had brought
Longstreet's corps on a wide flank march behind the Bull Run Mountains and into
Thoroughfare Gap (as illustrated above) to link up with Jackson. On the
Bull Run field were familiar landmarks of the struggle of a year earlier. The
Henry House (Plate 126) burned during the first battle; Meeker's drawing is based
on a Gardner photograph. A postwar photograph is the source for Plate 125;
the perspective is from the Union position looking toward the partially
graded roadbed of an abandoned railroad, behind which Jackson posted his troops.

PLATE 125   *Walton Taber*   Jackson's Position at Second Bull Run

PLATE 126   *Edwin J. Meeker*   Ruins of the Henry House

PLATE 127   *Edwin Forbes*   THE SECOND BATTLE OF BULL RUN

On August 29 Pope battered Jackson's line but could not break it. That afternoon the rest of Lee's army arrived and positioned itself on the Federal flank. The next day, still focusing single-mindedly on his tormentor Jackson, Pope renewed the attack, only to see his army splintered by Longstreet's massive flank assault. Forbes' water color is a finished version of his wartime sketch for *Leslie's*. The vantage point looks down on neatly aligned Federal units attacking Jackson late in the second day's fighting. The columns on the slope at left are reserves moving to stem Longstreet's breakthrough.

PLATE 128   *Walton Taber*   HARPER'S FERRY, FROM THE MARYLAND SIDE

PLATE 129   *Walton Taber*   LUTHERAN CHURCH, SHARPSBURG, MARYLAND

McClellan had been in no hurry to turn troops
over to Pope, and few of his men got
into the Bull Run fight. Three days later
Lincoln reluctantly gave McClellan's army
back to him, and Pope's, too; there was
no one else to call on. McClellan wrote his
wife: "under the circumstances no one
else *could* save the country, and I have not
shrunk from the terrible task." The
task was immediate. Lee was not surrendering
the initiative, and by early September he
was across the Potomac and ranging northward.
Jackson pounced on Harper's Ferry, sweeping
up its 12,000-man garrison; in the
foreground of Plate 128 (from Brady's
photograph) is the ruined Baltimore & Ohio
bridge. Learning that a lost copy of
his marching orders was in Yankee hands, Lee
called together his scattered army at
Sharpsburg, where Antietam Creek enters the
Potomac, while Union signalers on nearby
Elk Mountain tracked his moves. Plates 129
and 130 are based on Gardner photographs.

PLATE 130   *Walton Taber*
UNION SIGNAL STATION, ELK MOUNTAIN

Lee's Special Order 191, found by an Indiana private and promptly forwarded to headquarters, showed the pieces of the Confederate army scattered far and wide. Here was McClellan's chance to crush his enemy in detail and assure himself a place in the military textbooks, but caution overwhelmed opportunity.

On September 15 Lee had but 18,000 men assembled on the high ground behind Antietam Creek; across the stream was most of the Federal army, watching. More Rebels came up the next day, and one last division was due September 17; but even then Lee would be outnumbered two to one. The views of the respective commander's headquarters are derived from postwar photographs. McClellan's battle plan called for Hooker to ford the Antietam, depicted by Forbes, preparatory to hitting Lee's flank. September 17 was to be the day of battle.

PLATE 131   *Edwin J. Meeker*   LEE'S HEADQUARTERS, SHARPSBURG

PLATE 132   *J. D. Woodward*   THE PRY HOUSE, MCCLELLAN'S HEADQUARTERS

PLATE 133   *Edwin Forbes*   HOOKER'S CORPS CROSSING ANTIETAM CREEK

PLATE 134 *Walton Taber* UNION CHARGE THROUGH THE CORNFIELD

McClellan's plans were vague—he apparently wanted to strike Lee's flanks simultaneously, exploiting any success that appeared—and his tactical control was all but nonexistent. Thus Antietam followed its own terrible logic. It began with Hooker's assault on the Rebel left, where there was charge and countercharge in farmer Miller's cornfield. "Men, I can not say fell; they were knocked out of the ranks by dozens," wrote a major in the 6th Wisconsin.

PLATE 135 *Edwin Forbes* Charge of Hooker's Corps at the Dunker Church

The Hagerstown turnpike leading into Sharpsburg ran past
the Miller cornfield, and alongside the pike a bit
closer to town was a small whitewashed Dunker meetinghouse
that was the aiming point for several Union assaults.
The troops in Forbes' water color above won a foothold
around the church, only to be knocked back by a vicious
Confederate counterattack. By about 9 A.M. both sides were
fought out in this sector; Lee's line had bent, but
held. "It was never my fortune to witness a more bloody,
dismal battle-field," remembered Joe Hooker, who was among
the wounded. The cornfield and the woods and the clearings
were strewn with windrows of bodies. Hood's Rebel
division, said its commander, was "dead on the field."

When the firing died down in the area of the Confederate left,
Frank Schell of *Leslie's* wandered over the field with
sketchbook in hand. Along the edge of the Miller cornfield,
while a Yankee battery fired in the background, he
sketched this scene and jotted down his impressions. The
Rebel by the large tree, his torn leg in an improvised
tourniquet of corn stalks, called out to him. "For the Lord's
sake get me out of this," he pleaded. The battle was
sure to resume, he said, and "I don't want our own boys to
ride over me." Of the figures at right center Schell wrote,
"A gaunt, tall boy sat with dazed & hopeless expression—
his ankle shattered & near the corpse of his father,
at whose side he had fought since leaving their Georgia home."

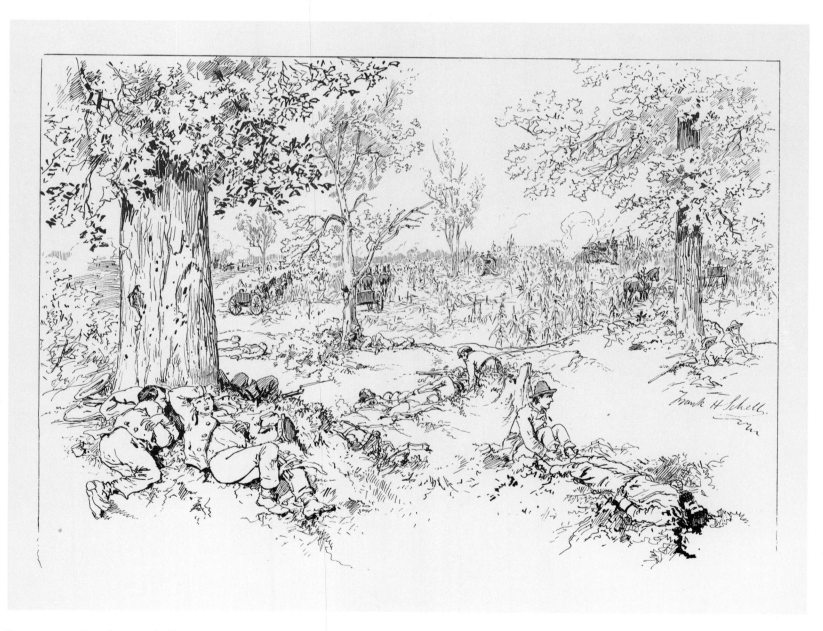

PLATE 136   *Frank H. Schell*   INCIDENT ON THE ANTIETAM BATTLEFIELD

PLATE 137   *Edwin Forbes*   BURNSIDE'S BRIDGE

As the other corps commanders in the crescent of Federal forces took their units into action—attacking piecemeal, for the most part, without coordination from the top—the combat shifted toward the Confederate center. Again it was a close-run thing, but Lee was able to stave off any breakthrough. By now the day was half gone, and over on the Federal left flank Ambrose Burnside was still fussing with the problem of getting across a narrow stone bridge on his front. Finally, under prodding, he had two regiments charge pell-mell over the span; Forbes' water color (Plate 137) of their success is from his eyewitness sketch. Eventually, after more delay, Burnside's troops pressed almost into Sharpsburg itself; the town is visible over the brow of the hill in Forbes' Plate 138. Then a sudden, hard counterattack by A. P. Hill drove them off. Hill had led his men on a grueling forced march from Harper's Ferry, leaving half of them straggling behind, but with the rest arriving at exactly the crucial moment.

PLATE 138   *Edwin Forbes*   BURNSIDE'S ATTACK TOWARD SHARPSBURG

PLATE 139   *Walton Taber*   BLOODY LANE

PLATE 140   *Walton Taber*   THE HAGERSTOWN TURNPIKE

Bloody Antietam was over at last. It was the costliest single day of the Civil War. "No tongue can tell, no mind conceive, no pen portray the horrible sights I witnessed this morning," a Pennsylvanian wrote. Now the photographers arrived to record the human wreckage. These Taber drawings are after pictures by Alexander Gardner or his son, James. The sunken road at the center of Lee's position (Plate 139), where D. H. Hill's men crouched behind a crude breastwork of fence rails, was called Bloody Lane. The section of the Hagerstown pike in Plate 140 borders the Miller cornfield. In Plate 141 is a Rebel gun crew and its limber on the Confederate left. The burial details (Plate 142) trudging across the battlefield in the following days had more than 4,700 bodies awaiting them.

PLATE 141   *Walton Taber*   THE DUNKER CHURCH

PLATE 142   *Walton Taber*   BURYING THE DEAD

PLATE 143 *Walton Taber* CONFEDERATE WOUNDED AFTER ANTIETAM

The Army of Northern Virginia had been terribly mauled, but Lee audaciously held
his lines a full day before taking the roads back to Virginia. With him
went the long wagon trains of wounded. In an article for *Battles and Leaders*
(for which Taber's illustration was done), a Shepherdstown, Maryland, woman
wrote that Rebel wounded from Antietam "filled every building and overflowed into
the country round . . . wherever four walls and a roof were found together."

PLATE 144 *Walton Taber* UNION SOLDIERS, CORINTH, MISSISSIPPI

PLATE 145 *Walton Taber* BATTERY ROBINETTE, CORINTH

PLATE 146 *Harry Fenn* DEPOT AND HOTEL, CORINTH

The Confederate offensive in the West developed out of the
notion of maneuvering around behind the careful Don Carlos Buell
in Kentucky to cut his communications and make him turn
and fight at long odds. So that the Federals to the
west, in Tennessee and Mississippi, would not interfere in the
scheme, the dashing Earl Van Dorn started a drive of his own.
His prime target was the Union force under Rosecrans in
Corinth, Mississippi. Fenn drew Corinth's hotel and depot
(above) from pictures taken in 1862 by a local photographer,
George Armstead. Armstead also posed the Yankees in Plate 144.
On October 3–4 Van Dorn's assault on Corinth failed to
budge the Federals. The redoubt in Plate 145 was at storm
center; Taber's drawing follows a photograph, probably Armstead's.

PLATE 147   *Edwin J. Meeker*   CUMBERLAND GAP

PLATE 148   *Harry Fenn*   FORT MITCHELL, CINCINNATI

In August the twin Rebel columns of Kirby Smith and Braxton Bragg began probing into Kentucky. Their advance forced the Federals out of Cumberland Gap, a vital communications channel; the installations and encampments there are shown in Plate 147. Private Alfred Mathews' lithographed sketch is the source for Plate 148. The troops manning Fort Mitchell had been in the army just a month; as Buell remarked dryly, the Confederate invasion "produced an excitement which was intense in some places, amounting almost to consternation." That consternation was caused in part by the wide-ranging Confederate cavalry, particularly the troopers led by John Hunt Morgan and Nathan Bedford Forrest. Taber's drawing below led off the *Battles and Leaders* coverage of Bragg's campaign.

PLATE 149   *Walton Taber*   CONFEDERATE CAVALRY

PLATE 150　*Harry Fenn*　DEFENSE OF CAGE'S FORD

By late September much of the steam had leaked out of Bragg's offensive; he was not the sort to risk all for all-out victory. On October 8, near the village of Perryville in central Kentucky, the armies of Bragg and Buell finally met. It was a sharp and confusing action that, like Antietam, was a tactical draw but a strategic defeat for the Confederates. Bragg pulled his main army out of Kentucky, trailing cavalry raids and skirmishes behind him. Fenn's water color, after a Mathews sketch, shows one such action. It was fought on the Cumberland River in November between Mathews' Ohio regiment (foreground and at right) and the cavalry and horse artillery of Morgan lieutenant Basil Duke.

VI Yankees and Rebels

WARS THROUGH HISTORY have seldom treated the common soldier to anything but a hard lot. This was certainly his fate in the Civil War, that most brutal of all America's wars. The men in the ranks, Northerners and Southerners alike, stood a good chance of getting shot, captured, or very sick; and considering the state of medicine and the competence of prison-camp administration, any of these eventualities was likely to be fatal. In four years, from all causes, 600,000 to 620,000 Yankees and Rebels died (the statistics are imprecise).

In part, the high-risk factor was a result of the mis-timing of revolutions. One revolution that was well along in the 1860's involved military ordnance. The war's basic arm was the rifled musket, which could consistently kill at 250 yards. The accurate rifled cannon was also on the scene. Yet the compensating revolution in military thinking had not yet begun; infantry tactics still harked back to the days of the old smoothbore musket, which seldom hit anything over 100 yards away. The consequences of this mismatch were frightful casualty lists. Competent health and medical practice was another revolution that arrived too late to help Billy Yank and Johnny Reb. Bacteriology, antisepsis, adequate sanitation, balanced diet—all were as the mysteries of the moon. Observing that all of this was multiplied by the general disorganization inherent in a civil war, one authority concludes that in 1861 the Union and the Confederacy went to battle "with medical capabilities below those of Imperial Rome."

Above all, the Civil War was the most stupendous happening in the young nation's history. No one and no institution was prepared for an upheaval of such dimensions; much had to be improvised and jury-rigged and started from scratch. It was hard enough simply to arm and clothe and transport the man in the ranks; anything that turned out to benefit his general welfare was usually more accidental than calculated.

The war was also the biggest thing that had happened to the men who fought it. At first there was a novelty to military life. "It is fun to lie around, face

PLATE 151   *Walton Taber*   SENTRY DUTY

unwashed, hair uncombed, shirt unbuttoned and everything un-everythinged," wrote a young Yankee. "It sure beats clerking." When it came to pulling duty, a Rebel remarked, "most men objected because they said they did not enlist to do guard duty but to fight the Yankies—all fun and frolic." Attitudes soon darkened and hardened. Yet in spite of everything, morale remained high for a remarkably long time (only in the last winter of the war did the Confederates become demoralized; "the soldiers are badly out of heart," one of them wrote in January, 1865). Faith in a winning general helps explain the morale in Lee's Army of Northern Virginia or Sherman's Army of the Tennessee, but in long-suffering outfits such as the Federal Army of the Potomac or the Confederate Army of Tennessee, a quiet self-pride developed out of the adversity and hard knocks. All in all, the average Civil War soldier was a tough enough character.

On the following pages is a look at the daily life of these men. The opening section deals with such things as living quarters, reveille, pulling duty, punishments, the simple pleasures of camp life. Next is a glimpse of the care (or the lack of it) of the sick and wounded. The chapter concludes with the treatment of POW's. (*Battles and Leaders* did not cover prison camps; the plates on the final six pages were commissioned to illustrate later *Century* articles on the topic.)

As was true of Chapter Two, on military administration, many of these illustrations derived from photographs. The camera excelled at recording the realities of comparatively static camp life, as the *Century* editors were quick to appreciate. Alexander Drake, the magazine's art director, scoured sources in Washington and elsewhere for suitable photographs. "Drake is back, brown, hearty & enthusiastic," Editor Gilder wrote three months before the first of the war articles appeared. "I believe he has done a fine piece of work getting 150 photos . . . which are handy for reference & use." Walton Taber redrew many of the photographs, and produced eight of the chapter's original illustrations. Other source material included sketches by combat artists Frank Schell of *Leslie's* and Theodore Davis of *Harper's*, and the drawings of Private Alfred E. Mathews of the 31st Ohio. Mathews' sketches of camp life and battle scenes in the Western theater, most of them lithographed and distributed by the Cincinnati firm of Middleton, Strobridge & Co., are the most important and accurate of all the wartime lithographs.

Men in winter quarters spent a good deal of time improving on their living accommodations, partly for their own comfort, partly as a hedge against boredom. During the long Petersburg siege, for example, the troopers below built themselves sturdy "stockaded" huts roofed with standard-issue wedge tents. Fireplaces ranged from elaborate brick structures (left) to simple "furnaces" of wood and clay, with provision kegs for chimneys. Such chimneys took fire regularly, and on these occasions, a veteran recalled, "a lively hurrah would run through the camp." The Oneida cavalry had a good war, serving exclusively as headquarters escorts, orderlies, and provost guards. Specialty units like the telegraph corps (Plate 153) usually managed to enjoy many of the amenities of life; few hardships are evident in this pleasant 1864 camp site. The Illinois regiments in Plate 154, stationed at Corinth for more than a year, had time to get comfortable, and their inherited Confederate barracks even included birdhouses. All three drawings derive from photographs.

PLATE 152   *Edwin J. Meeker*   CAMP OF THE ONEIDA CAVALRY, PETERSBURG, VIRGINIA

PLATE 153   *Thomas Hogan*   CAMP OF THE MILITARY TELEGRAPH CORPS, BRANDY STATION, VIRGINIA

PLATE 154   *William H. Drake*   QUARTERS OF THE 52ND ILLINOIS, CORINTH, MISSISSIPPI

PLATE 155 *Frank H. Schell* CAMP OF DURYEE'S ZOUAVES, FORTRESS MONROE

PLATE 156 *Walton Taber* CAMP GOSSIP

PLATE 157 *Walton Taber* HEADQUARTERS OF GENERALS WARREN AND CRAWFORD, PETERSBURG, VIRGINIA

As they have since the time of Xerxes, officers collected
whatever privileges the army offered. Colonels and majors of
newly formed regiments were theoretically elected by the
company officers, but in practice it was usually the man who worked
the hardest to recruit the unit who commanded it. Captains
and lieutenants were elected by the men themselves. It was
not a system designed to bring the best men to the top,
and complaints about incompetence considerably exceeded the normal
level of griping. One Yankee private concluded that officers
"get all the glory and most of the pay and don't earn ten
cents apiece on the average, the drunken rascals." In the end,
the rough-and-ready test of an officer's competence was
how he met the shock of combat. Schell's view of a spacious
headquarters tent is from his 1861 sketch. The convivial officers
in Plate 156 and the farmhouse headquarters in Plate 157 are
from photographs; Gouverneur Warren was an Army of the Potomac
corps commander and Samuel Crawford led one of his divisions.

PLATE 158   *Walton Taber*
DRUMMER BOYS

PLATE 159   *Walton Taber*   REVEILLE

The daily routine of Johnny Reb and Billy Yank was regulated by drum and bugle. The day began, of course, with reveille; Taber's original illustration below depicts the morning call for a cavalry unit in the field. Cavalry and artillery operated with 20 or more daily calls, infantry with perhaps a dozen. In the Union army there was no minimum age limit for drummer boys and buglers until 1864, when the enlistment of those under 16 was halted, and early in the war nine- and ten-year-olds were not uncommon. Ohioan Johnny Clem was probably the most celebrated of the drummer boys. His career began at the age of nine, and by the time he was 12 he was a sergeant whose exploits won him fame as the "Drummer Boy of Chickamauga." Johnny Clem retired in 1916 as a major general. Between playing the calls and performing at dress parades and reviews, these youthful musicians handled a wide variety of camp chores, ranging from barbering to serving on burial details.

Erecting fortifications at
Newport News, June 1861.
4th Mass volunteers (3 minute men)
at work in the trenches

Frank H. Schell
June '61

PLATE 160   *Frank H. Schell*   ERECTING FORTIFICATIONS, NEWPORT NEWS, VIRGINIA

Between campaigns or on garrison duty, soldiers had to fight boredom as much as discomfort, lice, disease, and (in the South) hunger. The worse the camp, the longer the line of sufferers and malingerers who answered morning sick call (Plate 161). Drilling was one method of keeping men busy; another was engineering work. The infantrymen above, of the 4th Massachusetts, were sketched by Frank Schell of *Leslie's* at Fort Butler near Fortress Monroe in 1861. Slaves performed much of this manual labor in the Confederate army, and later in the war contrabands did so for the Union forces. Inevitably, boredom spawned fighting, drunkenness, insubordination, and desertion. A Texan charged with desertion in 1863 was sentenced to "ride astride a wooden horse for fifteen days two hours and a half each day . . . except Saturdays and Sundays—the pole upon which he is to sit to be six inches in diameter." The Yankees in Plate 162 (after a photograph) suffer a similar sentence in occupied Vicksburg.

PLATE 161   *Walton Taber*   SICK CALL

PLATE 162   *Walton Taber*   RIDING THE WOODEN HORSE

"Our chaplain is not very popular," a Union private stationed in
Louisiana confided to his parents. "He hardly ever has any
religious exercises and spends a great part of his time
in New Orleans getting the mail." Like so much else about the
military, the quality of its chaplains varied. Reverend Drake
of the 31st Ohio is preaching to a decent turnout below
(after Private Alfred Mathews' lithographed sketch), but this
was in 1861; war-weariness and growing cynicism would take
a toll of worshipers. Yankees and Rebels alike preferred to
pass the time with practical jokes, theatricals and musicals, or
just playing cards (Plate 165). Sheppard based Plate 164
on his experience in Lee's army. A rabbit chase was considered
high entertainment in both armies, but hungry Confederates
always made sure that a rabbit stew concluded the entertainment.
To supplement their skimpy diets, the Rebels grew proficient
at fishing and trapping; one Texan even had high praise
for roasted armadillo, which he christened "iron clad possum."

PLATE 163   *Edwin J. Meeker*   PREACHING AT CAMP DICK ROBINSON, KENTUCKY

Plate 164   *William L. Sheppard*   A Rabbit in Camp

Plate 165   *Walton Taber*   A Game of Cards

PLATE 166   *Edwin J. Meeker*   Crossing Fishing Creek

PLATE 167   *Alfred R. Waud*   THE FATE OF THE RAIL FENCE

Civil War troops on the offensive perforce became prodigious marchers,
particularly in the Western theater. In Plate 166, after one
of Private Mathews' sketches, Yankees ford a placid Kentucky stream
early in 1862; they would soon engage the Rebels at nearby Logan's
Crossroads. Marchers promptly discovered a ready supply of firewood in
the split-rail fences that lined America's rural roads. "It is
astonishing how rapidly the fences would disappear," a cavalryman wrote.
"They seemed literally to be alive." In the margin of his drawing
above, war artist Waud described a Union officer's attempt to placate
Northern farmers by issuing orders that only top rails could be
taken. With each arriving squad taking the topmost of the rails that
remained, farmers' fences continued to disappear, only more slowly.

PLATE 168   *Thure de Thulstrup*   FIELD HOSPITAL AT SAVAGE'S STATION

PLATE 169   *Walton Taber*   FIELD HOSPITALS, ANTIETAM

One of the war's more chilling statistics is that about two out of
every nine men who served, North and South, did not survive.
This was due primarily to the great advances in weapons and to
the inexactness of the science of medicine. Stupidity compounded
the tragedy. Federal General Don Carlos Buell, for example, was
steadfastly opposed to a medical corps, and a surgeon at
an Antietam field hospital complained to Clara Barton: "I am tired
of this inhuman incompetence, this neglect and folly, which
leave me alone with all these soldiers on my hands, five hundred
of whom will die before daybreak unless they have attention
and I with no light but a five-inch candle." The 2,500 Federal
wounded at Savage's Station on the Peninsula (Plate 168, after
a James Gibson photograph) fell into Confederate hands when
McClellan retreated. Federal surgeons treated Rebel wounded left
behind at Antietam when Lee withdrew; Taber's drawings above of
the makeshift battlefield quarters are from Gardner photographs.

PLATE 170   *J. O. Davidson*   HOSPITAL SHIP "RED ROVER"

On the Mississippi River Hospital boat
D. A. January.

PLATE 171   *Theodore R. Davis*   HOSPITAL SHIP "D. A. JANUARY"

PLATE 172 *Walton Taber* UNION HOSPITAL, FREDERICKSBURG

Those wounded in battle were first examined at forward aid stations.
Their next stop—and often their last—was a field hospital,
where they were sorted with grim efficiency. Men with head or
spinal wounds were put aside to die as quickly as they might while
the doctors turned to those with some chance of surviving. The
most common operation was amputation. Recuperation took place in base
hospitals in the rear areas. The warehouse above served as
a collecting point during Grant's 1864 campaign, when the wounded
came pouring back from the front in unprecedented numbers. In the
West the Federals used hospital ships; Davis' sketch for Plate 171,
of the *January*'s ward patients being entertained, was probably made in
1863. The *Red Rover* (Plate 170), the navy's first hospital ship,
was considered a "floating palace." She boasted "bath-rooms, laundry,
elevator for the sick . . . amputation room, gauze blinds to the windows to
keep the smoke and cinders from annoying the sick, two separate
kitchens, for sick and well, and a regular corps of nurses."

PLATE 173   *Walton Taber*   BURIAL SQUAD, SPOTSYLVANIA COURT HOUSE

Approximately 200,000 Yankees and Rebels died or were mortally wounded in combat, but the Civil War's great killer was disease. Nearly 400,000 died of such things as dysentery, typhoid, pneumonia (the pneumonia death rate among Confederates was 400 per 1,000 cases), and a staggering assortment of other maladies. Davis' drawing below, a finished version of his 1863 sketch, records the funeral of an officer dead of disease. The site is one of several canal projects Grant initiated to try and bypass Vicksburg; in the background are two steam dredges. Battle dead were usually disposed of with less ceremony, often enough in mass graves. The burial detail in Taber's Plate 173 was photographed by Gardner in May, 1864, after the Battle of Spotsylvania. In this period the Army of the Potomac averaged 2,000 battle casualties a day.

PLATE 174   *Theodore R. Davis*   MILITARY FUNERAL, VICKSBURG

A soldier on the firing line had a considerably better chance
to survive than a soldier taken prisoner. Some 60,000 men died in
POW camps, nearly 10 per cent of the war's overall death toll.
No one meant for this to happen; no one in Richmond or Washington
advocated mistreating or killing prisoners. But mixing shortages,
ignorance, incompetence, and red tape with the primitive sanitation
and medical care of the period produced much the same
results. The camp on Ohio's Johnson's Island, in Sandusky Bay
on Lake Erie, was built in 1862 to house captured Rebel officers.
It has a deceptively tidy look in the view below, based on
a guard's sketch (Davies, one of the most celebrated American artists
of the early 20th century, did illustrations in his early days
to make ends meet). There was nothing tidy about the Florence camp
(Plate 176), hastily thrown up late in 1864 to house captives
evacuated from Andersonville when Sherman advanced into Georgia.
Conditions in Florence were as appalling as they had been
in Andersonville. The Richmond warehouse of Libby & Son, ship
chandlers (Plate 177), held Yankee officers; a Gardner
photograph, taken in April, 1865, is the source of Taber's drawing.

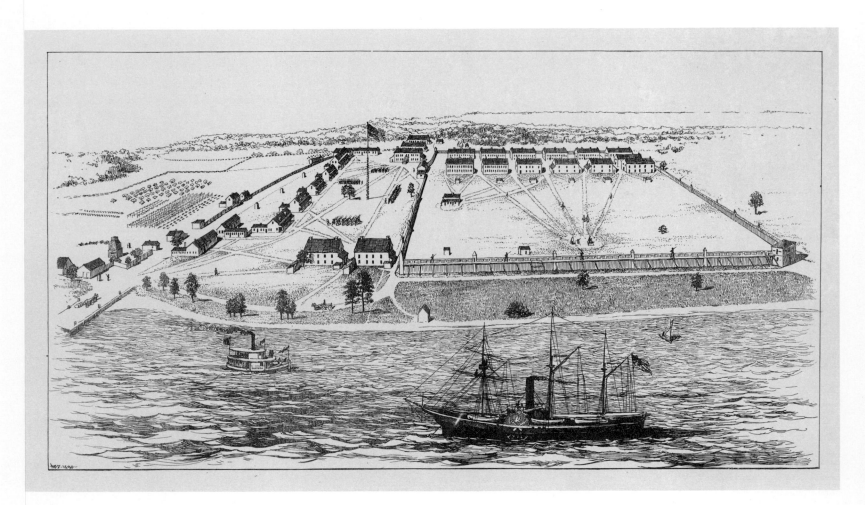

PLATE 175   *Arthur B. Davies*   JOHNSON'S ISLAND PRISONER OF WAR CAMP

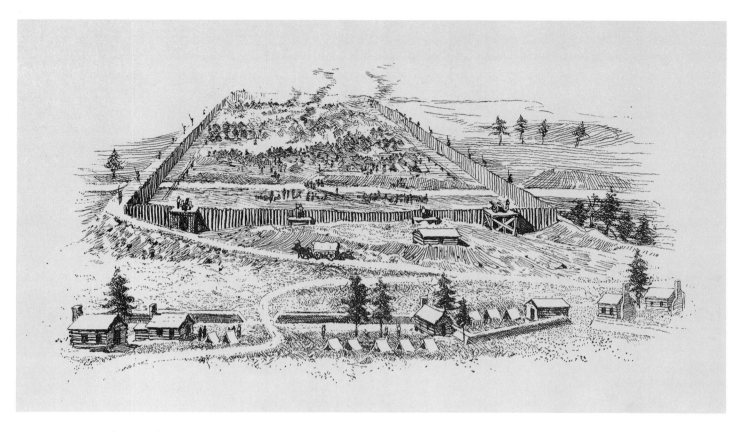

PLATE 176 *Walton Taber* PRISONER OF WAR CAMP, FLORENCE, SOUTH CAROLINA

PLATE 177 *Walton Taber* LIBBY PRISON, RICHMOND

PLATE 178   *Walton Taber*   ISSUING RATIONS, ANDERSONVILLE

PLATE 179 *Walton Taber*
WEARY HOURS, ANDERSONVILLE

The basic problem for the Rebels confined at
Johnson's Island was surviving the winters.
Lake Erie's icy winds drove temperatures
well below zero, and a prisoner recalled that it
"was just the place to convert visitors to the
theological belief . . . that Hell has torments
of cold instead of heat." The deadline
(Plate 180) was one of the standard POW camp
features; anyone stepping across this line
would draw fire from the guards without warning.
Taber's drawings on this page are original
illustrations; Plate 178 is derived from
a photograph taken by A. J. Riddle in August
of 1864. Bread is shown being issued,
but this was a rarity; Andersonville's bakery
was wholly inadequate for the more than
30,000 prisoners jammed into the stockade by
the summer of 1864, and most rations were
issued uncooked. "Received ½ pint meal,
½ teaspoon salt, 3 tablespoons beans for
todays ration," read a prisoner's diary entry
in April, 1864; in time this would seem
comparatively generous. Short rations and
a polluted water supply were the primary causes
of Andersonville's staggering death rate.

PLATE 180 *Walton Taber* THE DEADLINE, JOHNSON'S ISLAND

PLATE 181 *Walton Taber*
COLD QUARTERS, JOHNSON'S ISLAND

Curious civilian visitors were apparently not uncommon at Andersonville (Plate 182); a diarist's entry in March, 1864, reads: "Some of the country people came today to have a look at us terrible Yankees." Plate 183 is taken from an A. J. Riddle photograph. The camp covered 26 acres, including the deadline strip (at far right) and a three-acre swamp. Shelter was minimal, and the latrines drained into the stream that served as the primary water supply. When Riddle's picture was made in August, 1864, Andersonville's death rate had reached 100 a day, and in its one year of operation it killed 13,000 men. Because it was the biggest camp, Andersonville was the deadliest; but, in fact, every POW camp, North as well as South, was a deathtrap.

PLATE 182 *Walton Taber* VISITORS AT ANDERSONVILLE

PLATE 183 *Walton Taber* ANDERSONVILLE STOCKADE

VII Blockading the South

THE CONFEDERACY'S LONG AND INTRICATE coastline—some 3,500 miles—posed a major challenge to both contestants. For Southerners it meant a great many places to bring in from overseas armaments and medicines and the thousand and one other items sorely needed to wage war, yet at the same time it was an enormous length of coastline to defend. For Northerners the challenge was to find enough ships to blockade not only the major ports but the complex of sounds and inlets and river mouths that make up so much of this coastline, while at the same time acting offensively to force the Rebels to disperse their strength as widely as possible. This chapter examines facets of the blockade: the assaults on the forts and fortifications, from the North Carolina sounds to Mobile and Galveston, that guarded the South's main channels to the outside world; Rebel blockade runners and commerce raiders such as the *Alabama*; Southern counterattacks and countermeasures, including ironclad rams and various "infernal machines"; and the evolving naval revolution that effected almost every aspect of the blockade. It was a contest in which the North held most of the cards. The Rebels countered with ingenuity and boldness, but these were not enough. In the war's closing months Mrs. Chesnut, the Charleston diarist, called the blockade a "stockade, which hems us in with only the sky open to us."

The *Century* editors found that illustrating naval actions posed problems different from those of the other war papers. With fewer "hard" sources such as photographs and wartime lithographs to draw upon, they utilized original illustrations and redrawn amateur sketches by eyewitnesses; more than half the plates in this chapter fall in these categories.

Nine pictures are by J. O. Davidson, the specialist in naval illustration, but not all were done for *Battles and Leaders*. Plates 201-203, showing the Rebel raiders *Florida* and *Tallahassee*, illustrated an 1898 *Century* series on commerce raiding written by former Confederate naval officers. Even though his pictures were to be converted to woodcut reproductions, Davidson was more at home painting in tempera than drawing in line. Sending off one of his paintings to the *Century* art

PLATE 184   *Alfred R. Waud*   SAILOR ON PICKET DUTY

director, he wrote: "I tried . . . it in pen and ink in various ways, but finding them unsatisfactory had to resort at the last moment to the more certain medium. . . ."

Xanthus Smith makes his first appearance in this chapter. Smith was a 22-year-old artist (and ex-medical student) in Philadelphia when the war began, and he promptly enlisted in the navy. As a captain's clerk and later as a staff aide he apparently found sufficient time to sketch, and he had more than sufficient subject matter. He was aboard Du Pont's flagship *Wabash* at Port Royal and Fort Pulaski (Plates 194-197), saw the fighting at Charleston in 1863 (Plate 217), and was with Farragut's squadron when it blasted its way into Mobile Bay in 1864 (Plate 222). After Appomattox, Smith returned to Philadelphia and produced a number of highly regarded paintings of Civil War naval battles (and several land actions as well). These oils are panoramic in scope, whereas the pen drawings he did for *Battles and Leaders* are smaller and more intimate in scale. Smith continued to paint well into the new century, dying in 1929 at the age of 90.

Among the amateur artists whose work *Century* collected was Horatio L. Wait, a navy paymaster who saw service in the Yankee squadrons blockading Charleston and Mobile, and who, like Smith, found the leisure to fill up sketchbooks. He lent them to the illustrators of an article on the blockade he wrote for *Century* in 1898. They have apparently since disappeared; like the Walke and Sneden wartime sketches, the Century Collection copies may be the only record of Wait's originals. (Waud's drawing, opposite, is believed to be based on a Wait sketch.)

The newspaper special artists were called on once again. Waud's Confederate "infernal machine" (Plate 185) was based on his experiences as a *New York Illustrated News* artist in 1861, before he switched to *Harper's Weekly*. Frank Schell of *Leslie's* and his lithographer-partner Thomas Hogan are represented by four drawings, including one based on a wartime sketch by their old standby, Henry Walke (Plate 200). Theodore Davis' views of Fort Pulaski (Plate 198) and of Charleston (Plate 218) stem from his travels for *Harper's*.

To ensure accuracy, *Battles and Leaders* depended heavily on consultants when dealing with naval topics. These experts included Charles Olmstead, Confederate commandant at Fort Pulaski, Thornton Jenkins, captain of U.S.S. *Richmond* in Farragut's Gulf Squadron, and John McIntosh Kell, Raphael Semmes' first officer on board both his famous commands, *Sumter* and *Alabama*.

A much-feared Confederate naval weapon was the underwater mine, or torpedo, as it was known in that era. Meeker's Plate 187 shows an array of these "infernal machines" and methods of delivering them, after sketches by Horatio Wait of the Union navy. Number 1 is one of the diminutive torpedo boats called Davids that the Rebels sent against the Union fleet besieging Charleston in 1863. These steam-powered craft were armed with spar torpedoes. Numbers 3 and 6 are torpedo boats of more fanciful design. Number 2 is a free-floating torpedo, triggered by a contact fuze, made from a modified beer keg. A fixed spar torpedo is shown in number 4; the "volcano" torpedo (number 7) was a similar device affixed to pilings. Both exploded on contact with a ship's hull. Numbers 5 and 8 are types of contact fuzes. One of the Confederacy's first torpedo designs is depicted in Plate 185. The explosive in the 6-foot metal cylinder was set off by a slow-burning fuze. Waud's drawing is from a sketch he made in June, 1861. The Union tug in Plate 186 (after Wait), with a "torpedo rake" poised over her bow, sweeps for mines in the Stono River near Charleston in 1863.

PLATE 185   *Alfred R. Waud*   FISHING TORPEDOES OUT OF THE POTOMAC

PLATE 186   *Edwin J. Meeker*   TUG "PLATO" SEARCHING FOR TORPEDOES

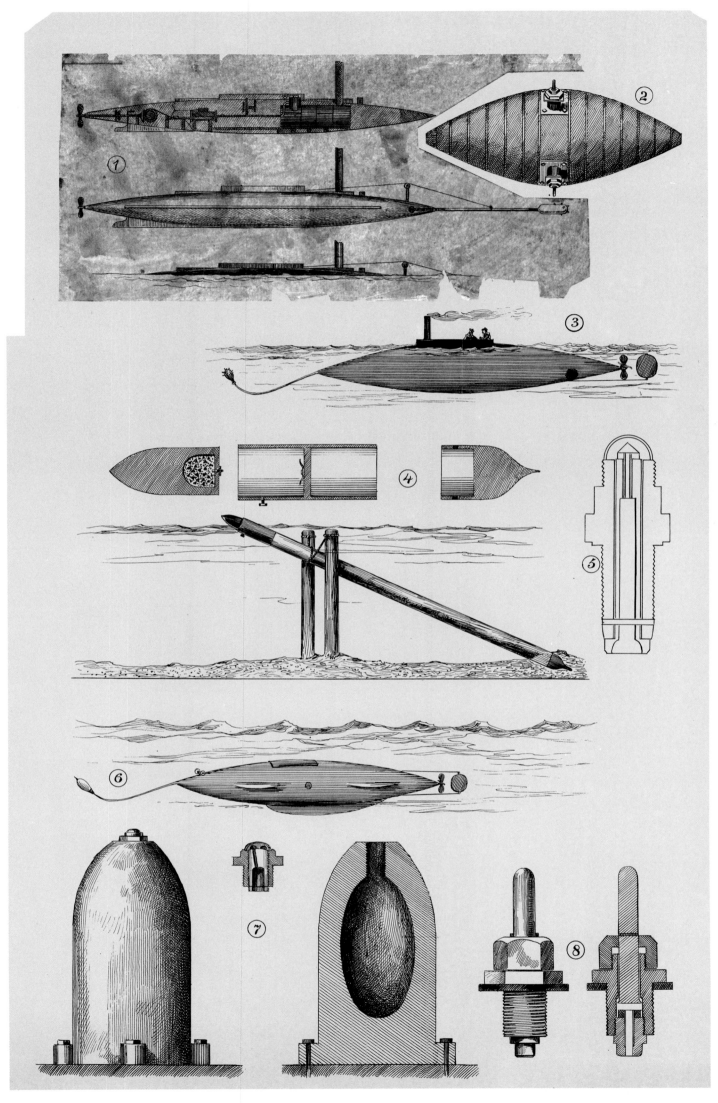

PLATE 187 *Edwin J. Meeker* CONFEDERATE TORPEDOES AND TORPEDO BOATS

The South's resources were greatly strained by the effort to protect its long coastline against Federal incursions. Typical of the Rebel coastal batteries was the one sited to fire at Fort Pickens in Pensacola Harbor (Plate 189); the cannon are old Columbiads of War of 1812 vintage. Taber's drawing is based on an 1861 photograph. His original illustration below portrays an abortive Confederate attempt to gain the initiative in North Carolina's coastal waters. In October, 1861, a Southern force assaulting Cape Hatteras was counterattacked and, as shown here, driven back to its boats. This demolished, wrote a Federal officer, "an elaborately conceived plan on the part of the enemy to . . . destroy Hatteras Light and recapture the forts of the inlet."

PLATE 188   *Walton Taber*   CONFEDERATE RAIDERS, HATTERAS ISLAND

PLATE 189 *Walton Taber*
CONFEDERATE WATER BATTERY, PENSACOLA

OVERLEAF: The Union campaign to win
the North Carolina sounds began in earnest
early in 1862, when a joint army-navy
striking force seized Roanoke Island, which
dominates both Albemarle and Pamlico sounds.
The Yankees went on to capture several
of the state's ports, including New Berne;
Schell's water color shows gunboats
shelling Fort Thompson, which guarded
the town. This is an example of
how the *Battles and Leaders* editors sought
illustrative balance by calling for
pictures with a Confederate perspective.
Schell covered the New Berne expedition, and
Leslie's ran his sketch of Fort Thompson
after its capture. For *Battles and Leaders*
he drew a nearly identical picture, but
added Rebel gun crews, smoke spurting from the
gunboats, and bursting shells, and exchanged
the Stars and Bars for the Stars and Stripes.

PLATE 190 *Frank H. Schell* THE BOMBARDMENT OF FORT THOMPSON

PLATE 191 *Thomas Hogan* FORT MACON AFTER ITS SURRENDER

To finally ensure Federal control of North Carolina's inland waters
required the taking of Fort Macon, a sturdy old masonry work near Morehead
City that dominated the southern approaches to Pamlico Sound. Sapping
commenced in March, 1862; by late April siege guns were emplaced and
the bombardment began. After ten hours of pounding, the fort surrendered.
Schell of *Leslie's* was on hand to sketch the victors inspecting their prize,
and his partner Hogan used those sketches to make the views above. The
Federals had already firmly established themselves farther down the Atlantic
seaboard. In November, 1861, an expedition had descended on Port Royal
Sound, near Beaufort, South Carolina. Plate 192 shows a rifled gun in one
of the defending forts. The homes in Plate 193 were requisitioned
by the Yankees; atop the house in the upper drawing is a signal station.

PLATE 192   *Xanthus Smith*   A Battery at Fort Beauregard

PLATE 193   *T. F. Moessner*   Federal Headquarters, Beaufort, South Carolina

PLATE 194   *Xanthus Smith*   U.S.S. "WABASH"

PLATE 195   *Xanthus Smith*   HILTON HEAD, SOUTH CAROLINA

Port Royal Sound, some 60 miles south of Charleston
and 30 north of Savannah, is a spacious harbor
sheltered by Hilton Head and Phillips islands.
If the blockade was to be enforced, the Union would
need just such a base, and the navy went all
out to take it with the biggest flotilla it had ever
assembled. His victory, wrote Flag Officer
Samuel Du Pont, was "more complete and more brilliant
than I ever could have believed." Xanthus Smith
did these drawings from his wartime sketches. The
big steam frigate *Wabash* was Du Pont's flagship, and
the sloop-of-war *Vandalia* was rear ship in the
line of battle. The base at Hilton Head, with its
busy wharves and warehouses, is shown as it
looked in 1863, with the monitor *Weehawken* at left.

PLATE 196   *Xanthus Smith*   U.S.S. "VANDALIA"

Hulking Fort Pulaski, at the mouth of the Savannah River, was manned by a military garrison of one when Georgia troops seized it in January, 1861, two weeks before the state seceded. Four months later Theodore Davis, in company with Russell of the London *Times*, toured Fort Pulaski and sketched it for *Harper's*. The upper drawing in Plate 198 derives from that visit, but the middle drawing was labeled "not Pulaski" (far right) by Colonel Charles Olmstead, the fort's commander; it appears that Davis mistakenly turned to one of his 1861 sketches of Fort Sumter when making this view. A year later he returned to watch Fort Pulaski pounded into ruins. The lower drawing in Plate 198 shows one of the big siege mortars being sighted. Pulaski surrendered on April 11, and the blockade was drawn tighter. Smith's Plate 197 pictures the exterior damage. Rifled cannon were primarily responsible for the breaches in the 7-foot-thick walls.

PLATE 197   *Xanthus Smith*   FORT PULASKI AFTER ITS SURRENDER

WANTED.

Tybee Light

Fort Pulaski
Mouth of Savannah river
May 61.

Theo R. Dav

Mounting Guns on The
of Fort Pulaski
Fort Pulaski.
Says Gl
who

Bombardment and Breaching of Fort Pulaski
Lieut. Horace Porter directing The   April 11th 1862.
Mortar fire

PLATE 198   *Theodore R. Davis*   VIEWS OF FORT PULASKI

PLATE 199   *Alfred R. Waud*   BLOCKADE RUNNERS

The Civil War on the high seas entangled the Federal navy in two
contests—one against swift and elusive blockade runners, the other
against wide-ranging Confederate commerce raiders warring on
American-flag merchantmen. Waud's drawing above is a composite view
of typical types of blockade runners. They are (from left) *Neptune*,
Vesta, and *Alliance*, derived from Horatio Wait's sketches
made following their capture. Plate 200 pictures the raider
Florida running the blockade off Mobile in September, 1862. Built
in Liverpool under the direction of Confederate naval agent James Bulloch,
the *Florida* was unarmed and her crew stricken with yellow fever when
she raced into the haven of Mobile. The drawing is based on a sketch by
Henry Walke, who had been transferred from the Western rivers to
a blue-water command. Early in 1863 *Florida* broke out of Mobile and
ranged across the Caribbean and Atlantic taking prizes. Her
career ended in October of 1864. She was at anchor in a Brazilian
port when the captain of the pursuing Federal cruiser *Wachusett*
rammed and captured her (Plate 201) in defiance of the neutrality laws.

PLATE 200   *Frank H. Schell and Thomas Hogan*   THE "FLORIDA" RUNNING THE BLOCKADE

PLATE 201   *J. O. Davidson*   THE "WACHUSETT" RAMMING THE "FLORIDA"

Barante Suliote

PLATE 202   *J. O. Davidson*   THE "TALLAHASSEE" BURNING THE "ADRIATIC"

Tallahassee   Pilot boat

These Davidson pictures illustrated an 1898 *Century*
article on the eventful cruises of the raider
Tallahassee written by her commander, John Taylor Wood.
A converted blockade runner commissioned in
July, 1864, *Tallahassee* terrorized coastal shipping
from New Jersey to Maine. One of Wood's early
prizes was the packet *Adriatic* (Plate 202), taken
off Long Island. Her 170 passengers were put aboard
the bark *Suliote*, at left; at the far right is
a captured pilot boat that Wood used to decoy his
victims. A few weeks later the Maine bark
Glenarvon, out of Glasgow with a cargo of iron, was
seized and scuttled (Plate 203). Wood ruefully
admitted this might have been a mistake; one
of *Glenarvon*'s passengers was a Down Easter matron
who "came on board scolding and left scolding.
Her tongue was slung amidships and never
tired. . . . When she left us to take passage in a
Russian bark, she called down on us all the
imprecations that David showered on his enemies."
Tallahassee's escapes were legendary. She survived
the war, but the sealing of the last Confederate
ports by early 1865 left her a ship without a
country; at the war's end she was stranded in Liverpool.

PLATE 203   *J. O. Davidson*   THE SCUTTLING OF THE "GLENARVON"

The *Century* war papers included, in the April, 1886, issue, an account
entitled "Life on the *Alabama* by One of the Crew," one P. D. Haywood.
It was not particularly complimentary to either the crew of the celebrated
Confederate commerce raider or to her captain, dashing Raphael Semmes.
These three Taber drawings, made "from sketches by the author,"
illustrated the narrative. Plates 204 and 206 picture *Alabama* sailors
seeking relief from their boring lot (Aracas Keys were "desolate
sandbanks" in the Caribbean). Whenever a prize was taken, Haywood noted,
the boarding party "rushed below like a gang of pirates" (Plate 205).
Three issues later the *Century* editors printed Haywood's reply
to their request for his nautical background. It was a gaudy enough tale—
Charleston-born but raised in England, Royal Navy service in the
Crimea, free-lance gallantry in the Indian Mutiny and for the
Chinese navy in the Taiping Rebellion—but did nothing to allay
growing suspicions. In the issue of March, 1887, the editors
acknowledged that they had been hoaxed. "P. D. Haywood," they
told their readers, "was not a seaman on the Confederate cruiser
[he turned out to be James Young of Philadelphia, a convicted forger],
though . . . he assured us he was, and furnished references which seemed to
be satisfactory." The hoaxer then claimed that his anecdotes came
from a real *Alabama* sailor, but "unable to attach any importance
to that statement," the editors dropped the account from *Battles and Leaders.*
Out of 230 contributors they had uncovered a single bad apple.

PLATE 204   *Walton Taber*   DIVERSION ON DECK

PLATE 205   *Walton Taber*   LOOTING ABOARD A PRIZE

PLATE 206   *Walton Taber*   CHRISTMAS ON ARACAS KEYS

197

The *Alabama* was another of the Liverpool-built raiders contracted for by Confederate naval agent Bulloch. For two years *Alabama* crisscrossed the world's oceans taking Yankee prizes—65 in all, valued at more than $6 million. By June, 1864, however, the strains were beginning to show; as Semmes later wrote, "Her commander, like herself, was well-nigh worn down." He took *Alabama* into Cherbourg for a much-needed refit. The Federal screw steamer *Kearsarge* arrived to stand sentinel outside the harbor, and Semmes promptly challenged. On June 19 the two ships met well out in the Channel, with some 15,000 Frenchmen crowding the shoreline to watch. On the back of this painting is a critique by John McIntosh Kell, Semmes' onetime first officer. Kell suggested Davidson make a few corrections, mainly in the armament of the *Alabama* (right), and concluded, "otherwise the picture is very good."

PLATE 207   *J. O. Davidson*   "ALABAMA" VS. "KEARSARGE"

PLATE 208 *Walton Taber* "Kearsarge" Gun Crew

Alabama had sunk the only Federal warship lost in battle
on the high seas, sending U.S.S. *Hatteras* to the bottom off
Galveston in January, 1863, but against *Kearsarge* she
was overmatched. The two vessels were about the same size,
but *Alabama* and her machinery were badly worn, and
she could not match the punch of the *Kearsarge*'s two 11-inch
Dahlgrens. Taber's drawing above shows one of these
pivot guns in action, and Plate 209 pictures the havoc they
caused. The *Kearsarge*'s well-drilled gun crews pumped
shot after shot into the Rebel raider, and in an hour
it was over; with his ship settling fast, Semmes surrendered.
Davidson's Plate 210 depicts the *Alabama*'s death throes.

PLATE 209   *Michael J. Burns*   THE "ALABAMA" TAKES A HIT

PLATE 210   *J. O. Davidson*   THE "ALABAMA" SINKING

This action-packed scene, painted from descriptions by an eyewitness (who enthusiastically wrote on the back of the picture, "the best illustration I have ever seen"), records a tidy Confederate triumph over the blockade. On the first day of 1863 a pair of Texas "cottonclad" steamers pounced on the Union squadron holding Galveston. One of them rammed the revenue cutter *Harriet Lane*, as seen here, and a boarding party took the ship. Galveston was soon once again in Confederate hands. "It was eight o'clock, the victory was won, and a New Year's gift was made to the people of Texas," a Rebel soldier proudly recalled.

PLATE 211   *J. O. Davidson*   Boarding the "Harriet Lane" at Galveston

John Ericsson's *Monitor* drove the Union navy full steam ahead into the developing revolution at sea—but only after she had proved herself in battle. When the *Monitor* was under construction, wrote navy secretary Gideon Welles in his diary, "many naval men and men in the shipping interest sneered at her as a humbug." Soon squat, turret-armed ironclads were being turned out at a rapid pace. The first ordered were of the *Passaic* class, essentially a refined version of *Monitor*; *Lehigh* (Plate 213) is an example. She saw action at Charleston (overleaf). Ericsson sought to advance the naval revolution a step further with a truly oceangoing ironclad, the *Dictator* (below). She was longer than the navy's biggest wooden steam frigates and mounted two 15-inch guns in a revolving turret, but her design was imperfect. A buoyancy problem cut her speed and cruising range, making *Dictator* less handy for most assignments than the smaller, shallow-draft ironclads.

PLATE 212   *J. O. Davidson*   THE IRONCLAD RAM "DICTATOR"

PLATE 213   *Walton Taber*   CREW OF THE MONITOR "LEHIGH"

PLATE 214 *J. O. Davidson* THE "MONTAUK" BEACHED FOR REPAIRS

In April, 1863, Union monitors steamed into Charleston Harbor with orders to knock out
Fort Sumter. They failed, and took a fearful pounding. *Montauk* (shown above after an
earlier action) was hit 14 times, *Weehawken* (Plate 217), 53 times. That summer the Yankees
emplaced guns on Morris Island in the harbor. The Parrott rifles in Plate 216 fired
30-pound shells. In the Marsh Battery below was a massive 8-inch Parrott, the "Swamp Angel."
After 35 shots at Charleston the piece exploded and dismounted itself, as shown here.

PLATE 215 *Walton Taber* THE MARSH BATTERY, MORRIS ISLAND

PLATE 216   *Walton Taber*   BATTERY HAYS, MORRIS ISLAND

PLATE 217   *Xanthus Smith*   DAMAGE TO THE "WEEHAWKEN"

German Church   Masonic Hall Waverly Hotel   Baptist Church   Pavilion Hotel

The decision to turn siege guns on Charleston was symbolic of the growing callousness
cloaking the war. The Federals notified General Beauregard that unless Charleston and the
harbor defenses were evacuated, they would open fire from "easy and effective range of the
heart of the city." When there was no response, the Swamp Angel began to fire shells
filled with "Short's Solidified Greek Fire," a primitive incendiary. Davis' view of the damage
done before the gun burst is probably based on sketches he made there after Charleston's fall.

Market.

St Peter
Church

Charleston
Hotel

Circular Ch.

Ruins. South Carolina Institute.
or Secession Hall

E. Meeting Street

Charleston under Fire. August 1863
with from the Mills House —

PLATE 218   *Theodore R. Davis*   CHARLESTON UNDER FIRE

Illustrated here are two Confederate counterattacks on the blockade of North Carolina's sounds. On February 2, 1864, John Taylor Wood, who would later command the raider *Tallahassee*, boarded and burned the Yankee gunboat *Underwriter* (Plate 219) at New Berne. But a simultaneous infantry assault on the town failed. The Confederates had more success three months later. Their powerful ironclad ram *Albemarle* (Plate 220) attacked the guard ships at Plymouth, ramming and sinking one gunboat and clearing the way for the port's recapture. A Federal counterattack on May 5 led to the pitched battle shown in Plate 221, after an eyewitness sketch by Yankee sailor Alexander C. Stuart. U.S.S. *Sassacus* rammed the ironclad, but succeeded only in crippling herself. *Albemarle*'s end came in October. Lieutenant William Cushing daringly conned a small steam launch through a galling fire to explode a spar torpedo under the ironclad's hull, sending her to the bottom (Plate 221, inset).

PLATE 219   *J. O. Davidson*   CONFEDERATES BURNING THE GUNBOAT "UNDERWRITER"

PLATE 220   *M. H. Hoke*   BUILDING C.S.S. "ALBEMARLE"

PLATE 221   *Walton Taber*   THE FATE OF THE "ALBEMARLE"

PLATE 222 *Xanthus Smith*
"RICHMOND" AND "LACKAWANNA"

Admiral Farragut wanted to take Mobile as he had taken New Orleans—
running its guardian forts with his deep-water cruisers,
challenging any Rebel flotilla that appeared—and on August 5, 1864,
he got his chance. It was a savage fight. The drawing above,
after Smith's wartime sketch, shows two of the big Federal screw sloops
stripped for action. In Plate 224 is the most formidable of the
works guarding Mobile Bay as it looked after its capture. A monitor
attacks a smaller fort in Plate 223. The surrender of the Rebel
ironclad *Tennessee*, after a gallant fight, sealed Farragut's triumph.

PLATE 223 *Frank H. Schell* FORT POWELL, MOBILE BAY

PLATE 224 *Charles A. Vanderhoof* FORT MORGAN AND LIGHTHOUSE, MOBILE BAY

PLATE 225 *Walton Taber* RUINS OF FORT FISHER

With Mobile Bay sealed off, the blockade at last had a stranglehold
on the Confederacy; the only remaining major port open to blockade
runners was Wilmington, North Carolina. In December, 1864, a
"grand naval and military expedition" challenged Wilmington's Fort Fisher,
a rambling earthen fortification far more resistant to shelling
than the old-fashioned works of brick and stone like Forts Morgan
and Pulaski. With ineffectual Ben Butler in charge, the grand
expedition accomplished nothing. "Send me the same soldiers with another
general, and we will have the fort," Admiral David Dixon Porter
wrote Grant. He was sent capable General A. H. Terry, and in
January the Federals captured Fort Fisher and closed the South's last
door to the outside world. These drawings, after O'Sullivan
photographs, show the results of Porter's overwhelming bombardment.

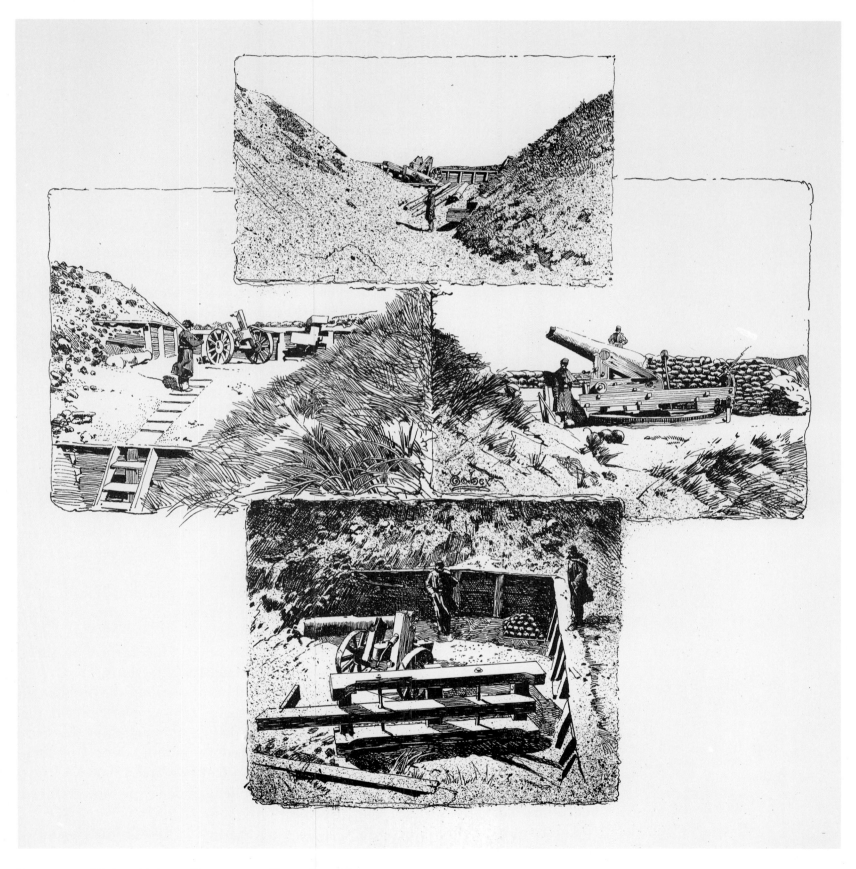

PLATE 226   *Walton Taber*   DISMOUNTED GUNS, FORT FISHER

VIII   The Turning Point

IN A SINGLE DAY, July 3, 1863, within a period of approximately six hours, the course of the Civil War turned forever against the Confederacy. At about ten o'clock that morning two Rebel officers entered Grant's siege lines at Vicksburg under a flag of truce and presented a request for surrender terms; and in the late afternoon, a thousand miles to the east, the survivors of Pickett's Charge drifted back across the smoky fields in front of Cemetery Ridge and Lee knew that he had lost the battle at Gettysburg. It took time for the impact of these two widely separated events to sink in, but their implications became clear all too soon. A few days later an official in the War Department in Richmond, having digested the news, wrote in his diary that the previous week had been "one of unexampled disaster since the war began. We are *almost exhausted*." President Jefferson Davis was moved to admit that "we are now in the darkest hour of our political existence."

The reversal of Lee's fortunes came suddenly. The story presented on the following pages opens with his decisive repulse of the Federals at Fredericksburg the previous winter. In May, in the most brilliantly conducted battle of his career, Lee demolished a fresh enemy offensive at Chancellorsville. Emboldened by these victories, he invaded the North, only to be checkmated at Gettysburg.

In the West the pattern was different. Grant had been worrying the problem of Vicksburg for months, trying this scheme and that one, coming ever closer to the scheme that would succeed. His final approach was bold and imaginative (his generals said foolhardy): a thrust deep into enemy territory, without supply or communication lines, dependent primarily on speed. In just two and a half weeks he cut Vicksburg off from food and reinforcement, put it under siege, and regained his communications. Vicksburg's fall became only a matter of time.

The Century Collection coverage of the three battles in the Eastern theater is dominated by Edwin Forbes of *Leslie's* and by former Rebel soldiers Allen Redwood and William Sheppard. Forbes produced a serial set of water colors of the Chancellorsville campaign, of which five are reproduced here. Two pieces from a

PLATE 227   *Theodore R. Davis*   WOODEN MORTAR, VICKSBURG

Gettysburg series also appear (Plates 242 and 243); they were done in pencil, perhaps as studies for a set of etchings he was contemplating. All seven pictures, of course, derive from his wartime sketches.

Redwood and Sheppard were on these battlefields as well, storing away the impressions that would become drawings and paintings in the postwar years. Sheppard's pictures were admired in the North as well as the South, and Plate 235 is based on one of at least three paintings he did for a former Yankee officer in the 29th Pennsylvania. Redwood's letter to the *Century* art editor, quoted in the commentary with Plate 244, offers a glimpse of how the *Battles and Leaders* illustration program operated. It is a rare glimpse; the letter's edges are charred, testimony to a fire in the *Century* offices in 1888 that destroyed much of the company's correspondence dealing with the war papers.

The pictures of the Vicksburg campaign include ten by Theodore Davis of *Harper's*, and they show him at the top of his form. Davis lacked great artistic skill, but as a pictorial reporter he was among the best of the "specials." His drawings of siege warfare at Vicksburg are detailed and informational; Plates 253 and 259, in particular, have strong documentary qualities. He had as well a sense of the visual anecdote, as witness the drawing opposite. Lacking small mortars for the close-in work of trench warfare, Grant's handy Westerners invented their own, boring out sections of hard gum-tree logs for 6- or 12-inch shells and banding them with strips of iron. As Davis wandered the network of Federal trenches one of these curious pieces and its insouciant gunner caught his eye.

Like Alf Waud, Davis was gregarious and enthusiastic, and he won the respect of the fighting men. He traveled with Grant's staff during the Vicksburg campaign and was frequently in the midst of the action—once his horse was shot out from under him—and on such occasions he admitted that he hurried his sketching. "Probably my note-book of General Grant's Vicksburg campaign contains some of the very queerest specimens of hasty memoranda," he remarked.

In 1889 Davis wrote "How a Battle is Sketched" for *St. Nicholas,* the Century Company's young people's magazine. For illustration he submitted several of his Vicksburg sketches, two of which appear here. Plate 250 is, by Davis' testimony, a copy of his original, but Plate 251 is a leaf from his campaign sketchbook—one of the few Century Collection drawings that is a wartime original.

General Ambrose Burnside, brought forth to replace
McClellan as head of the Army of the Potomac, is remembered
for his splendid side-whiskers and for his disastrous
direction of the Battle of Fredericksburg. On that chill December
day in 1862 his troops charged repeatedly, with incredible
bravery, across an open plain against a Rebel position
that was impregnable; staring at the bloody pageantry, Lee was
moved to his famous remark: "It is well that war is so
terrible, or we should grow too fond of it." Burnside
made his headquarters in the Phillips House (below), on the
north bank of the Rappahannock opposite Fredericksburg;
the photograph from which this drawing was made was
taken two months later when the house burned. Redwood was
with the Army of Northern Virginia at Fredericksburg,
where he observed the Mississippians in Plate 229 keeping up
a harassing fire on the Federal engineers building
pontoon bridges across the river just before the battle.

PLATE 228 *Walton Taber* THE PHILLIPS HOUSE

PLATE 229   *Allen C. Redwood*   CONFEDERATE SHARPSHOOTERS, FREDERICKSBURG

PLATE 230 *Edwin Forbes* ABANDONING WINTER CAMP, FALMOUTH

Spring, 1863, brought the Army of the Potomac a new
general and fresh hope. Both were badly needed.
Veterans remembered the winter of 1862-63 as the worst
of the war. Military administration was a shambles.
In the winter quarters at Falmouth, opposite
Fredericksburg, desertions and deaths from disease
rose alarmingly. Morale dropped alarmingly. "As far as
I can judge from what I have heard, there is very
little zeal or patriotism in the army now," a
Massachusetts private wrote. "The men have seen so much
more of defeat than of victory & so much bloody
slaughter that all patriotism is played out." Another
concluded: "The whole thing is roton to the
core." In late January "Fighting Joe" Hooker took
command. Hooker had not won his nickname for paperwork,
yet he proved to be an able military housekeeper.
Conditions improved quickly and dramatically, and in
late April a new campaign was launched to a
fanfare of optimism. Plate 230 pictures the Federals
leaving their stripped winter quarters and burning
surplus supplies. Below, the Rappahannock is crossed
at Kelly's Ford, upstream from Fredericksburg,
in an effort to outflank the Army of Northern Virginia.

PLATE 231   *Edwin Forbes*   CROSSING THE RAPPAHANNOCK

PLATE 232   *Charles A. Vanderhoof*   THE CHANCELLOR HOUSE

PLATE 233   *Edwin Forbes*   READING HOOKER'S ADDRESS TO THE ARMY

PLATE 234   *Edwin Forbes*   MEETING JACKSON'S FLANK ATTACK, CHANCELLORSVILLE

By April 30 Joe Hooker had a good part of his army encamped at the hamlet of
Chancellorsville, in a thick and gloomy woodland known locally as the
Wilderness. He made his headquarters at the Chancellor House, the one imposing
structure for miles around. Plate 232 is taken from a sketch by
Robert Sneden of the 40th New York; the inset pictures its subsequent fate
at the hands of the armies. That evening General Order Number 47 was read to
the troops, as depicted by Forbes in Plate 233. "The operations of the
last three days have determined that our enemy must either ingloriously fly,
or come out from behind their defences and give us battle on our own ground,
where certain destruction awaits him," Hooker announced. But Lee
would not follow that script. He did come out from behind his defenses, but the
battle he gave was on ground of his own choosing, not Hooker's. On
May 2 he sent half his army, under Stonewall Jackson, on a long flanking march,
and that evening Jackson demolished the exposed Union right wing.
Forbes' water color above shows Yankee artillerists trying to stem this assault.

Under Shelling in the Wilderness.

PLATE 235   *William L. Sheppard*   UNDER FIRE AT CHANCELLORSVILLE

W. L. Sheppard

His devastating flank attack left Lee
calling the tune for the remainder of the
Chancellorsville campaign. As Hooker
would later acknowledge, "to tell
the truth, I just lost confidence in
Joe Hooker." The next day, despite the
loss of Stonewall Jackson, mortally
wounded by his own men in a confusing
nighttime skirmish, Lee severely
pressed the Federal positions around
Chancellorsville. These troops
of the 29th Pennsylvania, covering
the Chancellor House, endure an artillery
barrage. Sheppard's water color
derives from a painting he did for
Captain W. L. Stork of the regiment.

PLATE 236   *Walton Taber*   THE STONE WALL, FREDERICKSBURG

Hooker had left John Sedgwick and 40,000 men to threaten Fredericksburg, and
his last aggressive move of the battle was to order Sedgwick to push
aside the 10,000 Rebels holding the town and advance against the rear of Lee's
army at Chancellorsville. Sedgwick had a stiff time of it, for the Rebels
held the same line—behind a stone wall at the foot of Marye's Heights—
that had stymied Burnside the previous December. Finally, however,
the Confederates were driven out; Taber's drawing above was taken from Brady's
photograph of the position. Lee was equal to the new threat. Holding
Hooker pinned at Chancellorsville, he hit Sedgwick at Salem Church and
drove him from the field. The church (Plate 237, after a postwar photograph)
still bore bullet scars 20 years later. During the fighting the dry
underbrush in the Wilderness caught fire, and in Plate 238 Forbes portrays
the efforts of Yankees to save wounded comrades caught between the battle lines.

PLATE 237   *Walton Taber*   SALEM CHURCH

PLATE 238   *Edwin Forbes*   RESCUING WOUNDED FROM THE BURNING WOODS

PLATE 239   *Allen C. Redwood*
CONFEDERATES ON THE MARCH TO GETTYSBURG

As he had done after Second Bull Run, Lee held
the initiative by invading the North.
In Plate 239 Redwood depicts his Rebel comrades
at a river ford. The Army of the Potomac,
now led by George Meade, its fifth commander in
less than a year, pursued into Pennsylvania,
and on July 1-3 the two armies fought their
epic battle at Gettysburg. In Plate 240 Waud
shows a key moment in the second day's
fighting: Hood's Rebels overrunning the rocky
jumble known as the Devil's Den. Soon thereafter
Federal artillery singlehandedly halted
a Confederate breakthrough. Taber's Plate 241
follows a sketch by a Union artillerist.

PLATE 240 *Alfred R. Waud* THE DEVIL'S DEN, GETTYSBURG

PLATE 241 *Walton Taber* GOING INTO ACTION UNDER FIRE

PLATE 242   *Edwin Forbes*   CONFEDERATE ASSAULT ON CEMETERY HILL

Special artist Forbes arrived late for the Battle of
Gettysburg, and saw only a part of the sprawling action.
However, he spent two days after the fighting ended
carefully exploring the battle sites and listening to many
eyewitness accounts. These two pencil drawings derive
from his field studies and the drawings he sent
off to *Leslie's*. The Cemetery Hill action above took place
late on the second day, when there was the bitterest
sort of hand-to-hand fighting among the guns on the crest
of the hill before Jubal Early's Confederates were
finally repulsed. The Yankees holding the hill were dug in
around the elaborate entrance gate to the town cemetery.

On July 2 Lee made a concerted effort to seize rocky
Culp's Hill, the right-hand anchor of Meade's line, but
could not break the Federal grip on the position. The next
morning this struggle resumed; Forbes' drawing shows
Rebel skirmishers at the base of the hill, preliminary to
the main assault (overleaf). In the next days Forbes
examined the slopes of Culp's Hill and the rest of the field,
and was appalled. "The sight was ghastly," he recalled;
"everything bore the mark of death and destruction . . .
the earth was torn and plowed by the terrible artillery
fire, and under fences and in corners, and anywhere that
slight shelter offered, the dead lay in dozens . . ."

PLATE 243   *Edwin Forbes*   CONFEDERATE ASSAULT ON CULP'S HILL

"Since I saw you last, I have been thinking of your request that I should think of some Gettysburg subjects,' & I give you the result of said cogitation," wrote Allen Redwood to *Century* art editor Lewis Fraser in 1886. Redwood had served in Lee's army at Gettysburg, and he described one subject he wanted to attempt as "the attack upon Culp's Hill, the morning of July 3d, by Steuart's Brigade. Gen. Steuart & many of his command live here [in Baltimore] & I have several friends among them with whom I visited this spot in '76 & made a sketch of the ground. . . ." Fraser agreed to the proposal, and this water color was the result. Pickett's celebrated charge dominated the third day at Gettysburg, overshadowing the fact that some of the most bitter fighting of the entire battle took place that morning on the slopes of Culp's Hill. But Steuart's assault, like all those that preceded it, could not dislodge the Federals. When his attempt to crack Meade's center later in the day also failed, Lee realized that the gamble for a decisive victory was lost. On July 4 his army was on the roads back to Virginia.

PLATE 244   *Allen C. Redwood*
STEUART'S BRIGADE AT CULP'S HILL

PLATE 245 *Frank H. Schell* Confederate Gunboat, Bayou Teche

Events in the West also built toward a climax in the spring of 1863 as Grant
evolved the strategy that would win Vicksburg. Covering the campaigns
along the Mississippi for *Leslie's* were Frank and Fred Schell. In Plate 245
Frank depicts a Union attack on the steamer *Cotton* on Bayou Teche,
in Louisiana, preparatory to a drive up the Mississippi toward Port Hudson.
At Vicksburg Admiral David Dixon Porter's squadron cleared for action.
Fred Schell's water color shows the big armored steamer *Blackhawk*,
Porter's flagship, and a pair of the Yankee shallow-draft ironclad gunboats.

The "Osage"

The "Choctaw"

PLATE 246   *Fred B. Schell*   FEDERAL WARSHIPS ON THE MISSISSIPPI

PLATE 247   *Frank H. Schell and Thomas Hogan*   FARRAGUT PASSING THE PORT HUDSON BATTERIES

To win control of the stretch of river between Vicksburg and Port Hudson,
Farragut determined to run his cruisers past Port Hudson's guns. On the night
of March 14, 1863, he made the attempt, painted here from a Walke drawing.
Farragut's vessels are (from left) flagship *Hartford*, *Mississippi*, and *Richmond*,
with gunboat *Genesee* lashed alongside. Only *Hartford* and a gunboat made
it; *Mississippi* ran aground and was destroyed, and damage forced the others to
turn back. Still, the Federals now blockaded 250 more miles of the river.

237

PLATE 248 *J. O. Davidson* PORTER PASSING THE VICKSBURG BATTERIES

By April Grant had his final plan for taking Vicksburg well
begun. He marched his army down the west bank of the
Mississippi and ordered Porter to run transports and gunboats
past the citadel; this would enable him to transport
his army across the river and, as he later wrote, "secure a
footing upon dry ground on the east side of the river
from which the troops could operate against Vicksburg."
Davidson's paintings depict Porter's vessels passing the city
on the night of April 16. Plate 248 follows a sketch
by Confederate Colonel S. H. Lockett, the engineer in charge
of Vicksburg's defenses. In Plate 249 the flotilla
is below the city; in the right foreground Sherman is rowed
out to confer with Porter aboard the *Benton*. Porter
was there to stay. His underpowered gunboats would be unable
to make their way safely upstream past Vicksburg's guns.

PLATE 249   *J. O. Davidson*   PORTER'S FLEET BELOW VICKSBURG

PLATE 250   *Theodore R. Davis*   THE BATTLE OF CHAMPION'S HILL

PLATE 251   *Theodore R. Davis*   AN INCIDENT IN THE VICKSBURG CAMPAIGN

PLATE 252   *Harry Fenn*   CONFEDERATE LINES, VICKSBURG

Grant's campaign against Vicksburg included a swift drive inland from the
river that cut the city's railroad lifeline at Jackson, Mississippi,
a fierce clash at Champion's Hill, and with the envelopment of the city, the
re-establishment of his supply line. Traveling with the Yankees was
Theodore Davis, and on the opposite page are two of what he called his
"memorandum sketches," done hastily under fire. In Plate 250, which
Davis described on the back as a "fac simile" of his wartime original, a Union
battery is at left and a column of Confederate prisoners is at right.
Plate 251 is a page from one of Davis' Vicksburg sketchbooks. Yankee
and Rebel officers investigating the identity of two parallel marching columns
open fire on each other. "When, presently, we saw these horsemen firing
their revolvers at one another," Davis wrote, "we knew that those were not our
troops marching over there, and made arrangements accordingly." On
May 18 Grant's troops arrived at Vicksburg, to face the zigzag of redoubts
and entrenchments visible in Fenn's drawing above, after a photograph.

One day after reaching Vicksburg, Grant launched a sudden assault in the hope of catching the Rebels unready. But they were ready and waiting. "We did all mortal man could do— but such slaughter!" exclaimed a Union officer. A second assault three days later also failed, and Grant had to be content with sapping operations to tighten his grip on the city. The "mole holes" in Davis' drawing sheltered the Yankee sappers advancing trench lines and digging tunnels against the 3rd Louisiana Redan, described by a besieger as "the most formidable redoubt on the entire line."

The White House (Sherley I think) at Entrance of McP

PLATE 253   *Theodore R. Davis*   FEDERAL LINES, VICKSBURG

saps Vicksburg - July 1st 63 —

It seemed that everyone in and around Vicksburg—Rebel and Yankee, civilian and soldier—went burrowing underground to escape the constant shelling and the sniping. "The whurrur of the paret shells is frightful the whize of the minie ball has an undescrubeable affect where you heer [one] you know it has passe you, but heave a dread of the next one," an itinerant Vicksburg dentist wrote in his diary. A woman added, "We are utterly cut off from the world, surrounded by a circle of fire." These two Davis drawings are based on sketches he made shortly after the surrender. Fenn's Plate 256, based on 1880's photographs, shows siege scars remaining after 20 years.

PLATE 254   *Theodore R. Davis*   EFFECTS OF SHELLFIRE, VICKSBURG

PLATE 255   *Theodore R. Davis*   THE CONFEDERATE RIDGE BATTERY

DOUBLE CAVE IN THE 'RIGBY HILL

Sky parlor Hill. A signal station
during the siege. Taken while Tele-
-phone pole was being erected.

Vicksburg

cave near machine shop Vicks[...]

PLATE 256   *Harry Fenn*   SCENES IN VICKSBURG

In late June a detachment of Yankee ex-coal miners drove a tunnel under the principal Confederate redoubt, mined it with over a ton of gunpowder, and on June 25 set off the mine. In Fenn's drawing below, the White House that is a feature of Plate 253 is visible by the trees on the ridge line at right. Plate 258 shows Federal troops holding the crater scooped out by the mine's explosion. They got no farther, however; suspecting a mining operation, the Confederates had constructed back-up entrenchments and were quickly able to seal off the break in their line. Both of these plates are based on Private Mathews' lithographed sketches. Grant wrote a testimonial for Mathews' views after the siege, saying he did "not hesitate to pronounce them among the most accurate and true to life I have ever seen."

PLATE 257   *Harry Fenn*   EXPLOSION OF THE VICKSBURG MINE

PLATE 258 *Harry Fenn* THE FIGHT IN THE CRATER

Davis' drawing sums up much of what the
Vicksburg siege was like—the ragged, cut-up
terrain, the complex of burrowing trench
lines (the saps), the never-ending mortaring
and sniping, the boredom, the death.
How close the opposing lines came is
dramatized by the flags in the center
background. As his captioning indicates, this
is the area of the June 25 mine explosion.
But what Davis could not show was the hunger
and deprivation in Vicksburg. Huddled in
caves and cellars, trying to survive on peas
and mule meat and worse, Vicksburg's civilians
were the real victims of the siege.
"I do not think people who are physically
brave deserve much credit for it; it
is a matter of nerves," a woman wrote in her
diary on June 25. "I first seemed to
realize that something worse than death might
come; I might be crippled, and not killed . . .
That broke down my courage . . . this horrible
place; I cannot stay; I know I shall
be crippled." There were rumblings of mutiny
from the starving soldiers in the trenches.
On July 3 John Pemberton, Vicksburg's
commander, asked Grant for surrender terms.

PLATE 259   *Theodore R. Davis*
THE LAST DAY OF THE VICKSBURG SIEGE

from Wooden mortar   Entrance   Shells from mortar   Sharp Shooters -   Shermans 15 Corps

enmorter   of mine   Crater of   Boats -   Court House -   Batteries
                   June 26th Explosion   Ransoms Atak -   Smiths attack

Last days in the Saps in front of Vicksburg.

July 2d '63 -

It was under the oak tree shown at left, as Davis points out in his well-captioned view, that Grant and Pemberton first met to discuss the surrender of Vicksburg. (Davis portrayed himself standing next to the tree, busy with his sketchbook.) Souvenir hunters later moved in on the tree. "It was but a short time before the last vestige of its body, root, and limb had disappeared," Grant noted. July 4 was the official date of the surrender, and in Plate 261 Davis shows the first Federal division that marched into the city. General John Logan is the central figure in the group of horsemen at right center; behind him are Confederate troops with arms stacked. Soon thereafter Grant reached Pemberton's Vicksburg quarters (Plate 262). Nearly 30,000 Rebels laid down their arms in Vicksburg, but, more importantly, the Confederacy was split. With Port Hudson's surrender four days later, the Mississippi River—what old General Scott had called that "great line of communication"—was in Federal hands.

PLATE 260   *Theodore R. Davis*   GRANT AND PEMBERTON DISCUSS TERMS

Logan's Division Entering

Logans Division Entering by the Jackson Road
...burg July 4th '63

PLATE 261   *Theodore R. Davis*   LOGAN'S DIVISION ENTERING VICKSBURG

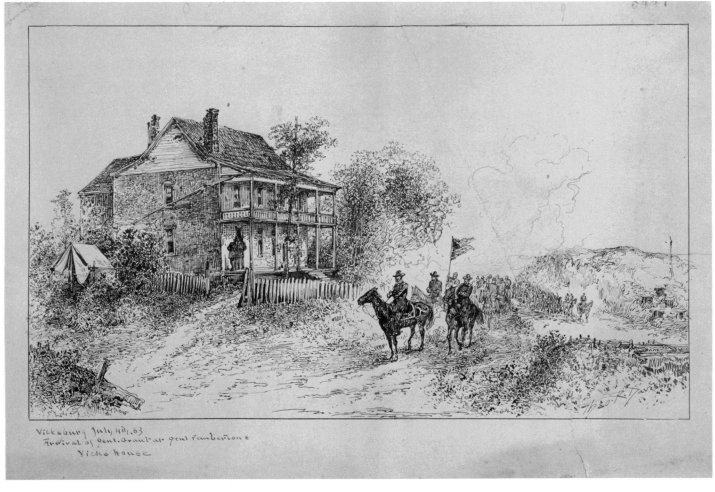

Vicksburg July 4th, 63
Arrival of Genl. Grant at genl Pemberton
Vick's House

PLATE 262   *Theodore R. Davis*   GRANT'S ARRIVAL IN VICKSBURG

IX Gateway to the Deep South

TO THE DEVISERS OF grand strategy in Washington and Richmond, Chattanooga, Tennessee, was one of the most important places on the map. This was a railroad war, and here lines from the four points of the compass came together—the East Tennessee & Georgia from Lynchburg, Virginia; the Western & Atlantic from Atlanta; the Memphis & Charleston from the Mississippi Valley; the Nashville & Chattanooga from northern Tennessee. Chattanooga was the Confederacy's main artery linking East and West; much of the logistical support for Southern efforts to hold the Mississippi Valley and build a defensive line in Kentucky (and later in central Tennessee) funneled through Chattanooga. The South, in other words, could not afford to lose the city. In Northern hands it would be a gateway; from there, said Charles A. Dana of the War Department, "the heart of rebellion was within reach." He meant Georgia, the South Atlantic seaboard, the interior of the Carolinas.

Right at the start, when the Union went on the offensive in the West in the spring of 1862, there was a plan for a "flying column" from the Grant-Buell-Halleck operations to reach out and seize Chattanooga; and a detachment did, in fact, get within 30 miles of the city. The chapter opens with the behind-the-lines part of that operation—the Andrews Raid or, as it is better known, the Great Locomotive Chase. The raiders' attempt to isolate Chattanooga by cutting its key railroad line was an eye-catching bit of derring-do, and that quality is reflected in the Taber drawings overleaf. "As a military operation it meant little," an authority writes of the Great Locomotive Chase; "as an adventure story it ranks high."

As it turned out, there were no shortcuts to Chattanooga. The Federals' moves were tied to their railroad supply lines, and they had no help from the ironclads that had been so useful in the Western river war; navigation on the Tennessee was blocked by the rapids at Muscle Shoals in northern Alabama. At the turn of the year Rosecrans tried his hand. He and Bragg met in a brutal slugging match at Murfreesboro, and Private Mathews' regiment, the 31st Ohio, was there. Mathews' sketches are the basis for Plates 267 and 269.

PLATE 263 *Walton Taber* UMBRELLA ROCK, LOOKOUT MOUNTAIN

The balance of the chapter examines the final operations around Chattanooga in the fall of 1863, and includes the futile Confederate attempt to retake Knoxville in November. The *Century* editors had some difficulty illustrating Chickamauga, the largest and bloodiest of all the battles in the West. *Harper's Weekly* may not have had a special artist there at all, and although J. F. E. Hillen of *Leslie's* was on hand to sketch the fighting, he died shortly after the war. This left the editors without a wartime artist to call upon and with little source material except the few photographs taken at the scene. They did commission an original illustration from Taber (Plate 273), and it is a good visual summation of that bitter struggle in the Georgia woods.

Chickamauga was a sudden explosion at the climax of a series of swift maneuvers, but subsequently the Federals spent two uncomfortable months, from late September to late November, penned in Chattanooga; then their spectacular breakout smashed all Rebel hopes of ever retaking the city. Theodore Davis was on the scene for *Harper's*—so far that year he had already covered Grant's Vicksburg campaign and the joint army-navy operation at Charleston—as was the ubiquitous Private Mathews, and both are represented here.

Following the publication of two Chattanooga articles in *Century* for May, 1887, the editors received a letter from one H. E. Brown of Bethlehem, Pennsylvania. Brown explained that he had witnessed the entire Battle of Lookout Mountain from a vantage point where "the whole field was before me" and had made sketches of the scene. He added that during the campaign he picked up a little money "being a sort of auxilliary to a staff artist of Harpers"—Theodore Davis, no doubt. Brown was invited to submit his drawings of the action, and the two of them that appeared in the *Battles and Leaders* volumes are reproduced here as Plates 283 and 284.

Chattanooga's amphitheater-like setting exercised a considerable attraction on the sketch artists and photographers, and the great bulk of Lookout Mountain, rising more than a thousand feet above the twisting Tennessee River to dominate the entire landscape, appears in several of the illustrations. Plate 263 opposite was drawn from a photograph taken on the crest of the mountain after its capture. The panoramic view reproduced as Plate 274, extensively captioned by the artist, identifies the key geographical features that so strongly influenced the campaign.

PLATE 265 *Walton Taber*
THE ANDREWS RAID: CONFEDERATES IN PURSUIT

PLATE 264 *Walton Taber*
THE ANDREWS RAID: CLEARING THE TRACK

On April 12, 1862, at Big Shanty, Georgia, 22 Yankee raiders
hijacked the Western & Atlantic's Atlanta-to-Chattanooga
night mail train, and the Great Locomotive Chase was
on. James J. Andrews' "romantic and adventurous plan" was
to burn several Western & Atlantic bridges, severing
Chattanooga's chief rail life line, and with a less persistent
pursuit it might have worked. On foot, by handcar and
switch engine, finally aboard the freight locomotive *Texas*, the
Rebels kept coming. Taber's drawing above perfectly
captures the spirit of the chase. Each new confrontation was
more hair-raising than the last; in Plate 264 the
Rebels push clear a burning boxcar cut loose inside a covered
bridge (an event overdramatized by the author of the
Battles and Leaders account; this ploy by the raiders was
actually a fizzle). The Yankees then abandoned the
stolen *General* and fled (Plate 266). All of them were caught,
and eight, including Andrews, were hanged as spies.

PLATE 266 *Walton Taber* THE ANDREWS RAID: ABANDONING THE "GENERAL"

PLATE 267   *Edwin J. Meeker*   FEDERAL REINFORCEMENTS AT MURFREESBORO

In the last week of 1862 the Army of the Cumberland, under Rosecrans, pushed south from Nashville to test the Confederacy's grip on Chattanooga and eastern Tennessee, and on the final day of the year, along Stone's River outside Murfreesboro, it was challenged by Braxton Bragg's Army of Tennessee. The Murfreesboro fight, which spilled over into the new year, was proportionally one of the bloodiest contests of the Civil War: of just over 75,000 engaged, nearly 25,000 were casualties. The battle scenes reproduced here are from Private Mathews' sketches. Bragg's assault bent the Union right flank back on the rest of the army, and Plate 267 shows Yankee reserves moving up into the line. Plate 269 offers a longer view of the pushed-back Union flank; this was the position that finally held. Vanderhoof's drawings of battlefield features are taken from postwar photographs. Bragg's battered army withdrew, but the equally battered Federals did not resume the offensive for six months.

PLATE 268   *Charles A. Vanderhoof*   ROSECRANS' HEADQUARTERS AND OVERALL'S CREEK

PLATE 269   *Walton Taber*   THE FEDERAL RIGHT, MURFREESBORO

William Rosecrans was the sort of general who wanted every man and mule
in place before he would move; but when he finally did move,
after heavy prodding from Washington, he neatly and bloodlessly
maneuvered Bragg out of his blocking position, then into
Chattanooga, then right out of the city. Bragg was looking for a fight,
however, and now he had Longstreet's veterans from Lee's army.
On September 19-20, 1863, at Chickamauga Creek a dozen miles southeast
of Chattanooga, was fought "the great battle of the West." The
Ross House was the headquarters of General Gordon Granger, who marched
Union reserves to the sound of the guns and salvaged Rosecrans'
army. The Lee House, at Crawfish Spring, Georgia, was headquarters
for Rosecrans before the battle and a field hospital during it.
The maneuvering armies struck sparks at Lee and Gordon's Mills on
Chickamauga Creek, shown as it was rebuilt after the war.

PLATE 270   *Harry Fenn*   THE ROSS HOUSE

PLATE 271 *Walton Taber* THE LEE HOUSE

PLATE 272 *Walton Taber* LEE AND GORDON'S MILLS

The country bordering Chickamauga Creek
was mostly a dark and tangled woodland, with
few roads or clearings; this Taber
illustration suggests why a Union officer
termed Chickamauga "a mad, irregular battle,
very much resembling guerrilla warfare
on a vast scale, in which one army
was bushwhacking the other." Neither side
gained much in the first day's fighting,
but on the second day Longstreet struck a gap
in the Union line, ably exploited it,
and sliced off a third of the Federal army,
sending it flying for Chattanooga. The rest
of the Yankees, under George Thomas,
managed to hold their ground long enough to
prevent defeat from becoming rout;
that was the day Thomas became the "Rock of
Chickamauga." The Federals were soon
bottled up in Chattanooga. Charles Dana,
a War Department observer on the scene,
wired Washington: "Chickamauga is as fatal
a name in our history as Bull Run."

PLATE 273   *Walton Taber*   CONFEDERATE BATTLE LINE AT CHICKAMAUGA

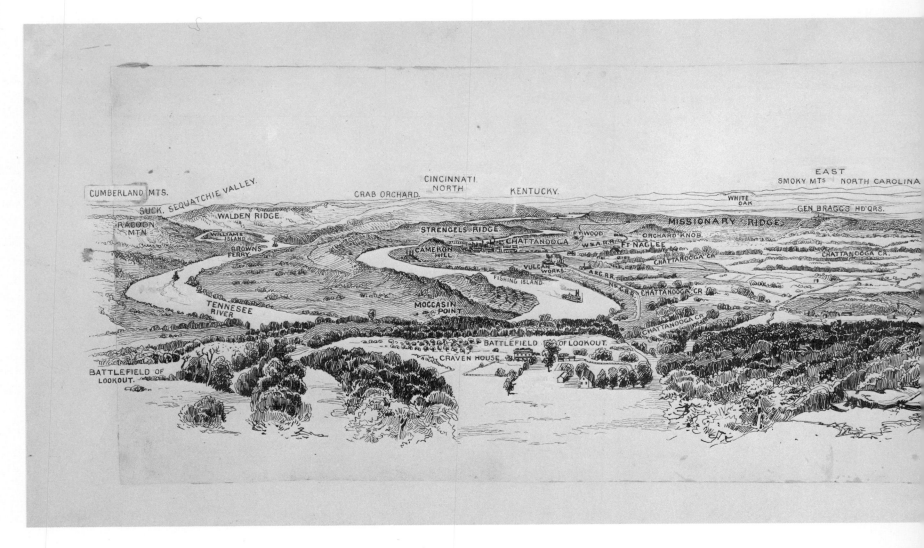

PLATE 274 *Edwin J. Meeker* PANORAMA OF THE CHATTANOOGA AREA

The Army of the Cumberland was safe enough from attack in Chattanooga—
Plate 276, after a Mathews sketch, pictures a section of the sturdy Federal
entrenchments, with Lookout Mountain in the background—but it was in
imminent peril of being starved into surrender. Bragg did not need to surround
the city to besiege it; by holding the heights overlooking Chattanooga,
he dominated its only practicable supply lines. In the panorama above,
after a lithograph, the high ground west, south, and east of the city runs
from Lookout Mountain (the persepctive from which the view was taken) around
to Missionary Ridge (right background); the Rebel guns controlling
the loop in the Tennessee River (left) cut both the river and rail supply routes
into the city. The one alternative was a tortuous 60-mile wagon road
over Walden's Ridge (left background), through country so barren that
the teams had to haul all their own forage, leaving little space for supplies.
Soon the Walden's Ridge road was choked with hundreds of dead mules and
stranded army wagons, and the Federals in Chattanooga were on half-rations.

PLATE 275   *Walton Taber*   ARMY WAGON

PLATE 276   *Edwin J. Meeker*   ARMY OF THE CUMBERLAND, CHATTANOOGA

Washington was galvanized by the Army of the Cumberland's plight. Grant took overall command in the West, Thomas replaced Rosecrans, and reinforcements—Sherman with 17,000, Hooker with 20,000 from the Army of the Potomac—were ordered to Chattanooga. And Thomas' men got to work on a new Tennessee River supply route. On a dark night in late October, as drawn below by Davis, 1,500 men under William Hazen, using bridge pontoons as assault boats, drifted quietly downstream past the Rebel outposts and captured Brown's Ferry (see Plate 274). After assembling a pontoon bridge at the site, the Federals had themselves a makeshift but workable supply line.

2267   WANTED.

Hazens Lodgement Browns Ferry
Oct. 27th 1863 Opening the Cracker Line To Chattanooga.

PLATE 277   *Theodore R. Davis*   HAZEN'S ASSAULT ON BROWN'S FERRY

PLATE 278 *Walton Taber* THE STEAMBOAT "CHATTANOOGA"

The Yankees' so-called Cracker Line began downstream at the
railhead at Bridgeport, Alabama. Supplies traveled by steamboat to
Kelley's Ferry, where the river made a nearly unnavigable loop,
then by wagon across the base of that loop to the pontoon bridge at
Brown's Ferry and on to Chattanooga. The key to the Cracker Line was
the little steamer *Chattanooga*, shown here unloading forage
at Kelley's Ferry. She was an improvisation—a steam engine, boiler,
and stern wheel mounted on a flat-bottomed, scow-like hull—
cobbled together at Bridgeport in record time. Now, observed Lincoln,
the Army of the Cumberland could once again "board at home."

PLATE 279   *Edwin J. Meeker*   FORT STANLEY, KNOXVILLE

Bragg was confident enough of his grip on the Federals
in Chattanooga to undertake a simultaneous operation aimed at
Burnside's force occupying Knoxville, astride the South's
only direct rail connection between Chattanooga and Virginia.
It was President Davis who suggested that Longstreet
might be assigned "to the task of expelling Burnside," and
Bragg was entirely agreeable. Longstreet was enraged
at the failure to exploit the Chickamauga victory, and Bragg
was glad to be rid of him. By mid-November Longstreet's
two divisions from the Army of Northern Virginia were
laying siege to Knoxville, and at the end of the month he
ordered an assault. These views, both based on photographs,
show redoubts in the Knoxville lines. At Fort Sanders,
the focus of Longstreet's attack, the ditch in front of the
parapet became a killing ground; the assault. said a
Union officer, was "an utter and disastrous failure."
Longstreet and his men were soon on their way back to Virginia.

PLATE 280   *Walton Taber*   FORT SANDERS, KNOXVILLE

Moccasin Point. Moccasin Point Military Road.

Chattanooga.

PLATE 281   *Harry Fenn*   LOOKOUT MOUNTAIN

PLATE 282   *Walton Taber*   GENERAL HOOKER AND HIS STAFF

Crest of Lookout, M^t.   looking south along Loo

Once the supply situation in Chattanooga was stabilized, Grant assembled an offensive. By the end of the third week of November it was ready; Thomas' artillery horses were sufficiently recruited to move his guns, and the Sherman and Hooker contingents were in place. The Confederate line was strongest in the center, on Missionary Ridge, so Grant would attack both flanks while Thomas' Army of the Cumberland exerted enough pressure on Missionary Ridge to keep Bragg from reinforcing his right or left. Sherman's Westerners from the Army of the Tennessee would hit the Rebel right. Joe Hooker's Easterners from the Army of the Potomac would strike at Lookout Mountain, the left anchor of Bragg's line. In Plate 282 Hooker and his staff prepare for the battle (the general stands at right, wearing a sword); the drawing above, also from a photograph, views Hooker's objective from the same spot. The main Rebel defense lines ranged across the slopes of the mountain.

Bridging Lookout Creek preparitory to the assault

PLATE 283   *H. E. Brown*   BRIDGING LOOKOUT CREEK

For sheer spectacle the Battle of Chattanooga was unique.
The winning of Lookout Mountain on November 24 became
the "Battle above the Clouds," commemorated in romanticized
paintings and lithographs, but the actual fighting
took place below any clouds. Brown, whose drawings are
based on what he described as "sketches both topographical
and of men in action drawn at the time," was in one of
the divisions making the attack. The Yankees above are crossing a
stream at the base of the mountain before the assault.
The main Rebel resistance was as shown in Plate 284, around
the Craven House at left center. A squad later scaled
the rugged palisade, and next morning's dawn dramatically
revealed the national colors flying at Lookout's crest.

BATTLE of LOOKOUT MOUNTAIN Nov. 24. 1863

(3 P.M. At the first point that any marked resistance was shown.
when our advance was 100 yds beyond the house the contest closed
and at about 9 P.M.)

H.E.BROWN.

PLATE 284   *H. E. Brown*   THE BATTLE OF LOOKOUT MOUNTAIN

PLATE 285   *Walton Taber*   U.S. MILITARY BRIDGE AT CHATTANOOGA

The Chattanooga campaign rose to its melodramatic climax on November 25, when the men of
the Army of the Cumberland took matters in their own hands and without orders stormed
up Missionary Ridge to rout the surprised Rebels. Bragg's army limped off into Georgia.
The Yankees at last had a solid hold on Chattanooga, and they proceeded to turn it
into a springboard for operations against the Deep South. Railroads leading into the city
were repaired, full-time steamboat service was resumed, and engineers constructed
this long span across the Tennessee; Taber's view is from a photograph taken in March, 1864.

X Grant Takes Command

IT HAD TAKEN THREE YEARS, but at last, in the spring of 1864, strategic direction of the Federal war effort was given over to someone who knew how to get the job done. On March 10 Ulysses S. Grant, newly minted as a lieutenant general, was designated general-in-chief of the Union armies. There did not appear to be anything very special about Grant—one lofty Army of the Potomac officer called him "stumpy, unmilitary, slouchy and western-looking; very ordinary, in fact"—yet he possessed a clear and uncluttered vision of the task before him. The Confederacy could exist only so long as its two principal field armies existed. Grant would mass as many of the North's resources as possible against these armies, and attack them simultaneously.

Joe Johnston's Army of Tennessee he assigned to his trusted Western lieutenant, Sherman. Sherman's orders were "to move against Johnston's army, to break it up, and to get into the interior of the enemy's country as far as you can, inflicting all the damage you can against their war resources. . . ." Lee's Army of Northern Virginia was his own assignment. Using the Army of the Potomac as a bludgeon, Grant intended to fight and crowd and pressure Lee unceasingly until one or the other of their armies broke.

In neither East nor West did events and timetables go as Grant had planned them, but in his larger plan he never wavered. This chapter deals with the shaping of the pattern for ultimate Northern victory. In Virginia Grant smashed at Lee repeatedly, from the Wilderness through Spotsylvania and Cold Harbor to Petersburg, producing casualty lists that were staggering. By the end of the summer Lee was nowhere near beaten, yet he was pinned in the defenses of Petersburg, unable to move. After a brief look at the disastrous Red River campaign—the expedition that Grant was too late to stop—the chapter examines Sherman's operations in Georgia that led to his capture of Atlanta on September 1.

The Century Collection illustrations of these campaigns offer clear evidence of

PLATE 286 *Walton Taber* LOOKING FOR A FRIEND

how different a war it had become. Battles such as Shiloh, where the troops had disdained digging trenches and rifle pits and instead stood in ranks to deliver their volleys, seemed part of another war. Now the men dug in without orders, digging with whatever came to hand (Plate 299). Log and dirt entrenchments like those in Plate 293 scarred the Virginia countryside from the Rapidan to Petersburg, and a Yankee with Sherman remarked that a vast area of northern Georgia "was cut up by earthworks almost as thick as furrows in a ploughed field."

Offensive tactics, however, had changed little; masses of men were still ordered to charge elbow to elbow, as they did at Cold Harbor and Kennesaw Mountain and in the battles around Atlanta. Veterans became excellent judges of how this or that frontal attack would fare, and their enthusiasm varied accordingly. One of Sherman's army commanders, John Schofield, later wrote: "The veteran American soldier fights very much as he has been accustomed to work his farm or run his sawmill; he wants to see a fair prospect that it is going to pay." At Cold Harbor a good many Yankees judged that the prospect for profit was not there, and before the battle they carefully wrote out their names and addresses on slips of paper and pinned them to their uniforms so their bodies could be identified.

The newspaper special artists and the photographers dutifully reported the sprawling grim ranks of redoubts and entrenchments. George N. Barnard, a Brady-trained photographer hired by the army's topographical engineers to illustrate the engineering feats of both sides, recorded the Confederate works in northern Georgia and around Atlanta, and his pictures are the basis for over half of the chapter's coverage of Sherman's campaign; the balance is the work of Theodore Davis, who would spend the remainder of the war traveling with Sherman. Davis attempted few panoramic views of the battles he witnessed. He focused instead on such things as the scene at field headquarters (Plates 322 and 323) or on the small dramas of the battlefield (Plate 319).

In Virginia Forbes and Alf Waud continued to travel with the Army of the Potomac, while William Sheppard and Allen Redwood were in the Confederate ranks during these 1864 battles. Like Davis' coverage of the Vicksburg siege, Waud's Petersburg drawings are highly reportorial. His picture of snipers (Plate 302) and his view of the mine explosion (Plate 305), both based on sketches he sent to *Harper's*, are rich in the details of life in the siege lines.

PLATE 287   *Charles A. Vanderhoof*   FORT RAMSAY, UPTON'S HILL, VIRGINIA

PLATE 288   *Charles A. Vanderhoof*   WARRENTON JUNCTION, VIRGINIA

The armies of Lee and Meade were rebuilt only slowly
after their Gettysburg ordeal. Moving to center stage was
the battle for Chattanooga, and both generals had to
send reinforcements west. By October, 1863, although
outnumbered three to two, Lee felt ready to attempt an offensive.
Meade sparred cautiously, refusing to be drawn into battle,
and Lee was forced into the grim awareness that his
Army of Northern Virginia was simply too weak to make a
bold dash northward. The scenes opposite are based on
Robert Sneden's diary sketches made that fall. Fort Ramsay
was an outpost of the Washington defense system; at
right is a signal tower. Lee pulled back, destroying the
Orange & Alexandria as he went; in the view of
Warrenton Junction, on the railroad, piles of ties burn as
Meade's troops march in slow pursuit. An offensive
by Meade in November also came to nothing, and the armies
went into winter quarters. When Grant took overall
command in March he kept Meade on, but determined to travel
with the Army of the Potomac and hold the reins. His
1864 spring offensive got under way in May, and Edwin Forbes
was along. The scene below was sketched west of Fredericksburg.

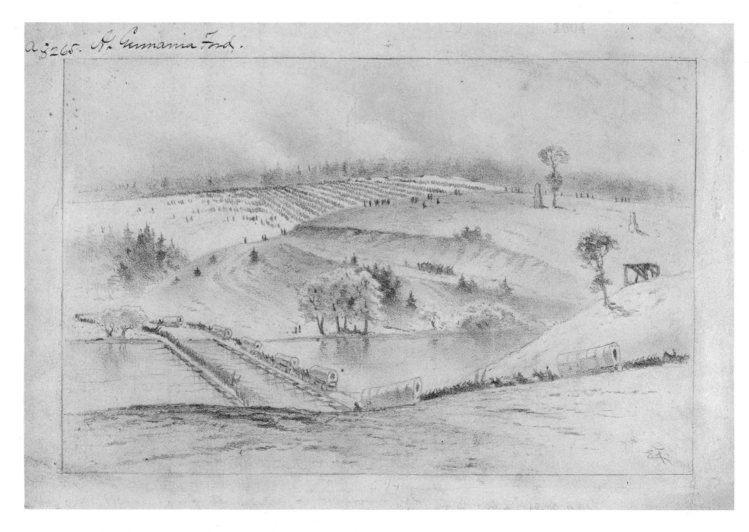

PLATE 289   *Edwin Forbes*   GERMANNA FORD ON THE RAPIDAN

PLATE 290 *Walton Taber* THE WILDERNESS TAVERN

The Rebels had wintered well to the west of Fredericksburg, and Grant's plan was to slice quickly between them and Richmond. Once again, however, Robert E. Lee exercised his disconcerting habit of doing the unexpected. He sent his army driving straight into the Federals in the heart of the tangled Wilderness, expecting the miserable fighting ground to neutralize the Yankee edge in men and guns. The Wilderness Tavern in Plate 290, after a postwar photograph, stood at the junction of the region's two main roads and was at the center of the Union position throughout the battle. Longstreet sought to emulate Jackson's success of the year before, and his flanking attack on the position sketched below very nearly succeeded before Hancock's men finally held. During the Wilderness battle the troops came upon breastworks and grisly relics from 1863's Chancellorsville fight (opposite).

PLATE 291 *Edwin Forbes* HANCOCK'S CORPS ON THE BROCK ROAD

PLATE 294 *Walton Taber* SPOTSYLVANIA COURT HOUSE AND TAVERN

In the Battle of the Wilderness the Federals lost over 17,500 men and the Rebels only
7,500. A Hooker or a McClellan would have retreated across the Rapidan and regrouped.
But before the campaign began, Grant had left a message for Lincoln: "If you see the
President, tell him, from me, that, whatever happens, there will be no turning back"; and
he was as good as his word. On the night of May 7 the Yankees pushed on, still trying
to outflank the Rebels. Lee beat them to the crossroads hamlet of Spotsylvania Court House
and dug in. The views of his entrenchments in Plate 293 are based on photographs.
Plate 295 derives from a sketch Forbes made on May 10, during an all-out Federal assault.

PLATE 295 *Edwin Forbes* FEDERAL ARTILLERY AT SPOTSYLVANIA

PLATE 296   *Walton Taber*   FEDERAL WOUNDED ON THE GROUNDS OF THE MARYE HOUSE

Spotsylvania was a slaughter pen. "Rank after rank was riddled by shot and shell and bayonet-thrusts, and finally sank, a mass of torn and mutilated corpses," a Yankee wrote. Casualties flooded rear areas in unprecedented numbers. The Marye House in Fredericksburg, a rest stop for wounded in transit, was photographed in May by Brady or an assistant. In 1862 Burnside had come to grief trying to storm this high ground called Marye's Heights.

PLATE 297   *Allen C. Redwood*   CONFEDERATE WORKS, CHESTERFIELD BRIDGE

PLATE 298   *Alfred R. Waud*   THE ATTACK OF SMITH'S CORPS, COLD HARBOR

PLATE 299   *Alfred R. Waud*   ENTRENCHING AT COLD HARBOR

After nearly two weeks at Spotsylvania, Grant renewed his turning movement, angling to get between the Rebels and their capital. Lee matched each move, and the armies constantly ground against each other as they maneuvered southeastward toward Richmond. Plate 297, after Gardner's photograph, depicts trench lines covering a crossing of the North Anna River. By June 1 they were at Cold Harbor, where, two years earlier, Lee had launched his first offensive, the Seven Days. The perspective of Plate 298 is from behind the Union lines at Cold Harbor on June 1. Wounded trickle back from the firing line; at right is a column of Rebel prisoners. In Waud's drawing above, Yankees hurriedly dig in with bayonets and tin plates. On June 3 Grant's frontal assault at Cold Harbor cost 7,000 men in less than an hour.

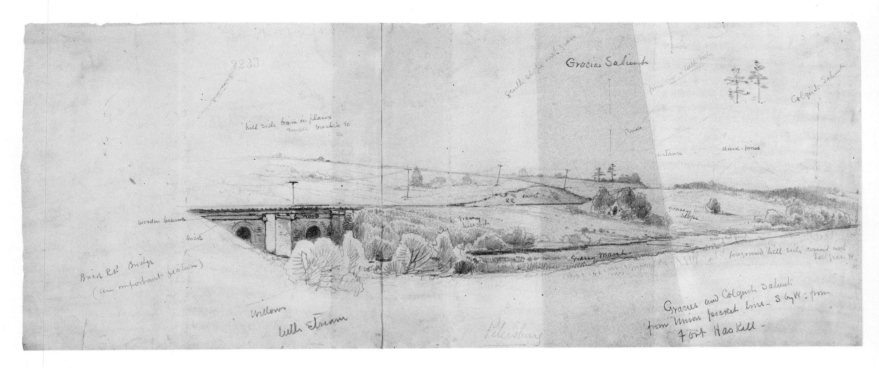

PLATE 300   *J. D. Woodward*   THE PETERSBURG BATTLEFIELD

PLATE 301   *Walton Taber*
UNION BATTERY, PETERSBURG

Cold Harbor was Grant at his worst. The next move was Grant at his best. Behind a deft screen, he pulled out of Cold Harbor and sent his army driving straight past Richmond, across the Peninsula, across the James, and on to Petersburg, the railroad center 25 miles south of Richmond that supplied the capital—and Lee's army. But W. F. Smith, commanding Grant's advance guard, muffed the glittering opportunity. On the evening of June 15 "Petersburg . . . was clearly at the mercy of the Federal commander," said its defender, General Beauregard. For nearly 72 hours the Yankees continued to fumble; then Lee got his army into Petersburg and the chance was gone. Plate 300 is an 1886 field study of the terrain near the Norfolk & Petersburg railroad where Beauregard held off these early Federal attacks. The Gracie and Colquitt salients formed part of the Rebel line. The siege of Petersburg now began. Plate 301 is after a Timothy O'Sullivan photograph; the civilian at right center is Mathew Brady.

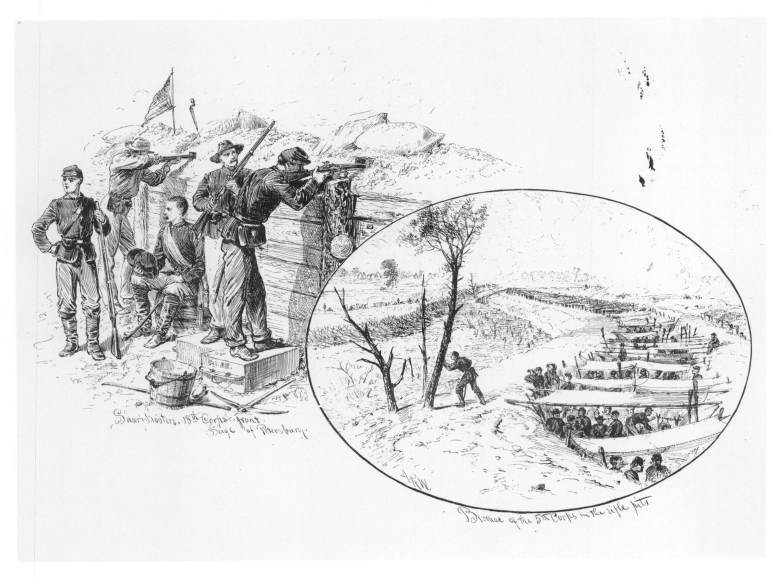

PLATE 302 *Alfred R. Waud* IN THE FEDERAL LINES AT PETERSBURG

PLATE 303 *Walton Taber* BATTERY WAGON

"We have never before used the Spade as we have this summer," wrote a Federal officer from Petersburg in late June. "In any two days of the campaign we have constructed more works than were thrown up by us two years ago during the whole time we were in front of Richmond." The siege was proof of the growing dominance of rifle and shovel. Waud did the original sketches for Plate 302 in July, 1864. According to him, snipers (left) typically fired through a "wooden tube widening outwards like a miniature embrasure buried in the crest of the rifle pit and protected by sandbags"; his second drawing depicts the shelters the troops rigged against the broiling Virginia sun. A telegraphic network was soon laid behind the lines, and Plate 303 shows one of the battery wagons that powered it. The never-ending sapping operations were often done behind the protection of a sap roller (Plate 304), constructed of basketwork mats woven thickly enough to stop enemy shellfire.

PLATE 304   *Alfred R. Waud*   A SAP ROLLER

PLATE 305   *Alfred R. Waud*   EXPLOSION OF THE PETERSBURG MINE

The 48th Pennsylvania was stationed where the opposing Petersburg lines were closest together, facing a Rebel redoubt whose gunners and sharpshooters made life miserable. Many men in the 48th had been coal miners in civilian life, and the idea grew among them to tunnel under the enemy works and blow them up. Henry Pleasants, their colonel, and a mining engineer by profession, took up the tunnel idea enthusiastically. "That God-damned fort is the only thing between us and Petersburg, and I have an idea we can blow it up," he told fellow officers. After more than a month of hard digging and of solving endless problems by brilliant improvisation, Colonel Pleasants and his men had completed a 510-foot tunnel and mined it with four tons of powder. Waud witnessed this scene in the early morning hours of July 30. The explosion, he wrote, came "with a muffled roar . . . as from the eruption of a volcano—which it much resembled—[and] upward shot masses of earth, momently illuminated from beneath by the lurid flare." His drawing also depicts the artillery barrage that opened to support the follow-up assault.

PLATE 306   *Alfred R. Waud*   THE BATTLE OF THE CRATER

Sheppard's Plate 307 shows part of the carnage created by the mine, which blew a huge gap in Lee's lines. But again the Army of the Potomac's officer corps failed miserably. Burnside, in overall command, spearheaded the assault with a poor division led by a general whose courage came out of a bottle. The leaderless troops milled around, gawking at the crater, and were torn apart by a counterattack. Waud's drawing above pictures black reinforcements joining the battle. The artifacts at right were drawn in 1887 in a battlefield museum.

PLATE 307   *William L. Sheppard*   THE CRATER AFTER THE EXPLOSION

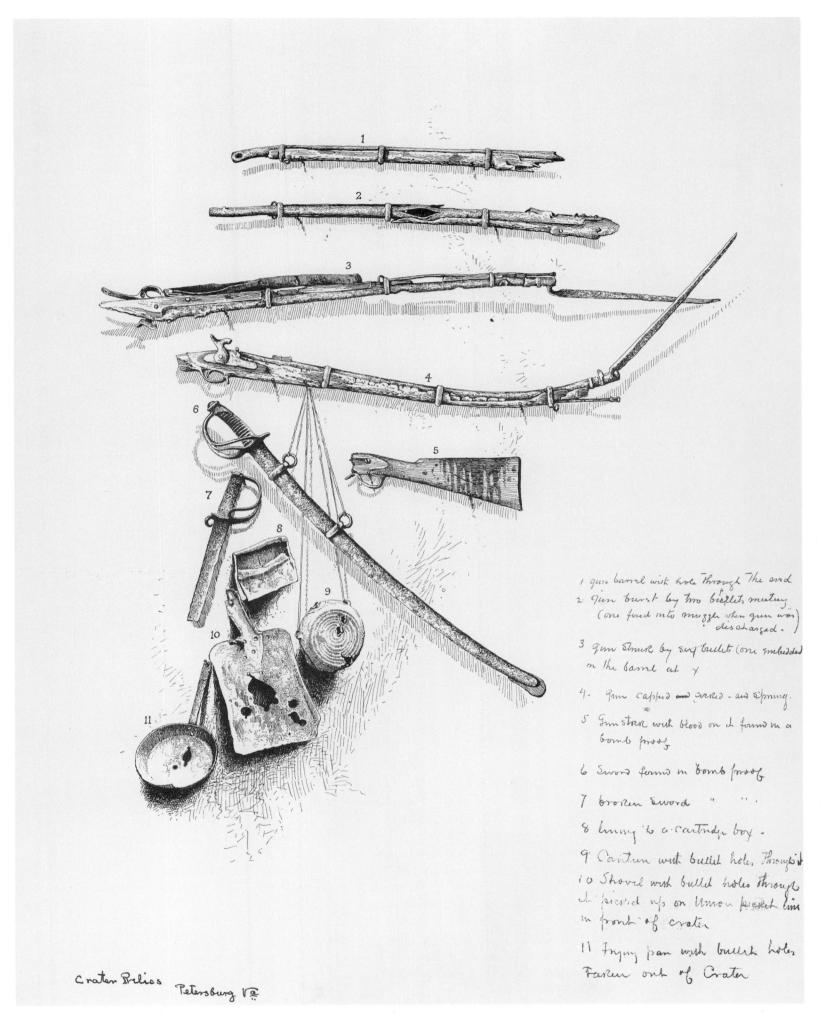

1 gun barrel with hole through the end

2 gun burst by two bullets meeting
(one fired into muzzle when gun was)
discharged.

3 gun struck by six bullets (one embedded
in the barrel at x

4- gun capped and cocked - and sprung.

5 Gun stock with blood on it found in a
bomb proof

6 Sword found in bomb proof

7 broken Sword " " "

8 lining to a cartridge box -

9 Canteen with bullet holes through it

10 Shovel with bullet holes through
it picked up on Union picket line
in front of crater

11 Frying pan with bullet holes
Taken out of Crater

Crater Relics   Petersburg Va

PLATE 308   *J. D. Woodward*   RELICS OF THE CRATER

PLATE 309 *Edwin J. Meeker* CONFEDERATE LINES BEFORE PETERSBURG

By late summer the landscape around Petersburg was barren and blasted,
featureless except for military landmarks of the sort visible in these pictures.
Thousands of soldiers burrowed in the earth, extending lines, deepening
trenches, strengthening "bomb-proofs." Stifling heat and dust alternated with
sudden thunderstorms that left the terrain foul with standing water.
Life in the trenches combined danger and discomfort, boredom and disease.
The Confederate works had proved impregnable to frontal assault, and
Grant turned to the painfully slow task of inching his lines westward to try to
throttle Lee's communications. If he had failed in all his efforts
to destroy Lee, he had succeeded in putting that superb offensive instrument,
the Army of Northern Virginia, permanently on the defensive. "However
bold we might be, however desperately we might fight, we were sure in the end
to be worn out," wrote the Confederate artillerist E. P. Alexander in
his postwar memoirs. "It was only a question of a few months, more or less."

PLATE 310   *Allen C. Redwood*   IN THE TRENCHES

295

PLATE 311   *William L. Sheppard*   UNDER FIRE, PETERSBURG

This water color by ex-Confederate artillerist
William Sheppard pictures the impact of a
hit on a Rebel battery during one of the routine
Federal bombardments. Mortar shells, with their
sputtering fuzes, were usually perfectly visible to
their intended victims. In the fall of 1864 an
Alabamian in Lee's army wrote home to describe
mortar fire: "The mortars are thrown up a great
height and fall down in the trenches like throwing
a ball over a house—we have become very
perfect in dodging them and unless they are thrown
too thick I think I can always escape them
at least at night." In a heavy barrage—when, as
another of Lee's men put it, the "shells fly
by as thick as bats in a summer night"—the troops
sheltered in trenches or bomb-proofs like
the one in the foreground of Sheppard's painting.

PLATE 312   *Frank H. Schell and Thomas Hogan*   PORTER'S FLOTILLA STARTING UP THE RED RIVER

Side-show operations were anathema to Grant, but he took command too late to stop the biggest side show of them all: the 1864 Red River campaign in Louisiana. Plate 312 shows David Porter's powerful squadron leading the way on March 12. Over 40,000 troops were also involved in this vaguely defined effort to stifle the trans-Mississippi Confederacy, open the way to Texas, and appropriate the Red River Valley's cotton crop. The expedition had no trouble taking Fort De Russy (Plate 314, from a sketch made after its capture) near Alexandria, but there was trouble enough waiting upriver. At Sabine Crossroads near Mansfield (the home town of the private in Plate 313) the Rebels inflicted a sharp defeat on the invaders and the expedition beat a hasty retreat, very nearly losing Porter's gunboats in the process. "And thus ended the Red River expedition, one of the most humiliating and disastrous that had to be recorded during the war," wrote a gunboat captain.

PLATE 313   *Henry A. Ogden*   A LOUISIANA PRIVATE

PLATE 314   *Charles A. Vanderhoof*   FORT DE RUSSY, RED RIVER

PLATE 315　*Walton Taber*　ALLATOONA PASS, GEORGIA

On May 7, 1864, as Grant's soldiers struggled through the Virginia Wilderness, Sherman marched south to challenge Joe Johnston in Georgia. Sherman commanded three armies: McPherson's Army of the Tennessee, Thomas' Army of the Cumberland, and Schofield's Army of the Ohio—100,000 men in all. Johnston, who had replaced Bragg, could muster some 60,000 troops. It would be a very different campaign from the bloody slugging match in Virginia. Sherman and Johnston were maneuverers, and northern Georgia offered them the room to maneuver. All three of these drawings are based on photographs by George Barnard. At Resaca Sherman found the enemy's lines too imposing and resorted to a flanking march, a pattern he repeated throughout the campaign. By May 20 Johnston had pulled back behind the Etowah River, 35 miles north of Atlanta, to a strong position in the defile of Allatoona Pass, on the Western & Atlantic. The Rebels wrecked the railroad as they withdrew, and the Yankees rebuilt it as they advanced.

PLATE 316   *Walton Taber*   THE RESACA BATTLEFIELD

PLATE 317   *Edwin J. Meeker*   CONFEDERATE DEFENSES AT ETOWAH BRIDGE

Stymied at Allatoona Pass, Sherman swung his entire force
off to the west on a long flanking march, and Johnston had
to pull back to avoid being trapped. The two armies came
together once more around a country meetinghouse
called New Hope Church, 25 or so miles northwest of Atlanta.
Both Rebels and Yankees were by now highly adept at
throwing up earthworks like those in the drawing below,
after a Barnard photograph. Such positions, Sherman found,
were "as dangerous to assault as a permanent fort,"
and he complained that no sooner were the Confederates driven
from one line of works than they had a new line built
and manned. Theodore Davis was at this point traveling with
the Army of the Cumberland, and his drawing at right
again reveals his talent for capturing the visual anecdote.

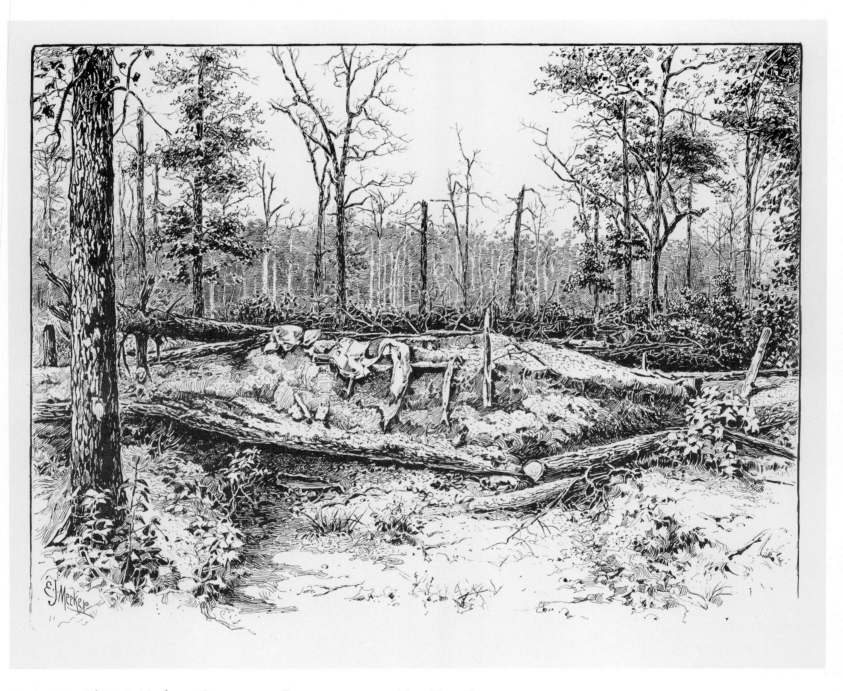

PLATE 318   *Edwin J. Meeker*   CONFEDERATE ENTRENCHMENTS AT NEW HOPE CHURCH

An Incident
Battle of New Hope Church
Bad fix for a
Confederate
Sharp shooter

PLATE 319   *Theodore R. Davis*   An Incident at New Hope Church

PLATE 320   *Edwin J. Meeker*   THE DEFENSES OF ATLANTA

PLATE 321 *Walton Taber* CONFEDERATE GUNNERS

Although Joe Johnston's army was his primary target,
Sherman considered the city of Atlanta, with its foundries,
rolling mill, munitions factories, supply warehouses,
and railroad connections, a worthwhile secondary target.
"What tremendous defences of Atlanta the rebs had!" wrote
one of Sherman's staff of the 10-mile ring of works.
"Forts, breast-works, ditches, *chevaux-de-frise* . . . and
stockade on flank, inapproachable by musketry and protected
by ground, etc., from artillery." Plate 320 is taken
from Barnard photographs made after the city's capture. At
center are *chevaux-de-frise* entanglements around the
Potter House, which was damaged by Yankee shells (inset).
The lower drawing pictures a fortified battery on
Peachtree Street. Taber's original illustration above is also
derived from a Barnard view of the Atlanta lines.

Generals
Sherman and
Thomas
at the Signal Tree.
June 27th 1864

PLATE 322   *Theodore R. Davis*   SHERMAN AND THOMAS AT KENNESAW MOUNTAIN

Hardee   Stewart.

Battle of Peach-Tree Creek July 20th 64   attack of Hardee & Stewarts Corps
General Jo. Hookers 20th corps   on the army of the Cumberland.
                                                  4 miles north of Atlanta.

PLATE 323   *Theodore R. Davis*   THE BATTLE OF PEACHTREE CREEK

On June 27 Sherman grew impatient and ordered a frontal attack on Johnston's
Kennesaw Mountain position; in Plate 322 slim Sherman and bulky Thomas observe
the battle from a telegrapher's station. Bloodily repulsed, Sherman resumed his
war of maneuver. When he forced a crossing of the Chattahoochee River, on Atlanta's
doorstep, Johnston was replaced by John Bell Hood, an aggressive but overly rash
fighter from Lee's army. On July 20, 22, and 28 Hood launched three major
offensives—the battles of Peachtree Creek, Atlanta, and Ezra Church—and was three
times beaten. Davis sketched Joe Hooker during the Peachtree Creek fight (above).
The Yankee train guard below drives off Rebel cavalry at Decatur on July 22.

Decatur July 22d 64
Spragues Brigade saves the
wagon trains of the army

PLATE 324   *Theodore R. Davis*   PROTECTING SHERMAN'S WAGON TRAINS

PLATE 325   *Walton Taber*   OCCUPIED ATLANTA

Hood withdrew his battered Army of Tennessee into the Atlanta fortifications, and Sherman put him under siege. Steadily the Yankees shelled the city, and steadily they snipped off its lifelines. On September 1 Hood had to pull out before he was hopelessly trapped. "So Atlanta is ours, and fairly won," Sherman wired the President. In Plate 325 is a Federal encampment in City Hall Square. Sherman then destroyed Atlanta's usefulness to the Confederacy, blowing up machine shops and factories, wrecking railroads, and ordering the civilian population to evacuate the city. "The unprecedented measure you propose transcends in studied and ingenious cruelty all acts . . . in the dark history of war. In the name of God and humanity, I protest," Hood wrote him. Sherman's reply was coldly blunt: "War is cruelty, and you cannot refine it. . . . You might as well appeal against the thunder-storm as against these terrible hardships of war."

PLATE 326   *Walton Taber*   DESTROYING RAILROADS, ATLANTA

XI The Last Campaigns

TOWARD THE END, when the Army of Northern Virginia was making its last march, Grant received a front-line report saying that "if the thing is pressed" there was a good chance that Lee would have to surrender. President Lincoln saw a copy of this, and he sent Grant a simple injunction: "Let the thing be pressed." The phrase can stand as the watchword of each of the war's closing campaigns examined here. The failing Confederacy was pressed everywhere by tough men who understood how to exert pressure. These men had risen to the top in the crucible of battle, and the process had annealed them to a hardness that would tolerate nothing short of total victory. So it proceeded: Grant relentlessly extending his siege lines at Petersburg until Lee was defending 37 miles of trenches with fewer than 50,000 men, something even he could not do successfully; Sheridan at long last driving the Rebels out of the Shenandoah Valley and so devastating that beautiful land that it was pointless for them to return; Thomas carefully and ponderously grinding Hood's army to pieces before Nashville; and Sherman driving into the hollow core of the Confederacy to make not only Georgia howl, as he had promised, but the Carolinas as well. The thing was pressed, and it was an ugly business, but it ended the war.

When the Petersburg siege sank into slow, grim routine after the failure of the Federal mining operation in July, 1864, Alf Waud made one of his rare trips out of sight of the Army of the Potomac to cover Sheridan's operations in the Shenandoah Valley. His view of the Battle of Cedar Creek (Plate 340) is a product of that journey. Writing to Alf from Petersburg in October, brother William assured him he was missing nothing by being off in the Valley: "I have made no sketches for the last month—for the simple reason of there being nothing to sketch although I have spent my time gyraling from left to right of the army in anticipation of the grand move always about to be made." That winter Alf returned to the Potomac army and William took a new *Harper's* assignment—covering Sherman's march north through the Carolinas.

Sherman's Westerners were tough enough fighters, but above all they were

PLATE 327   *Allen C. Redwood*   CONFEDERATE CASUALTY, PETERSBURG

marchers. Confederate Joe Johnston was amazed to find this host bridging flooded rivers and splashing through swamps at the rate of 13 miles a day; as he later wrote, "I made up my mind there had been no such army since the days of Julius Caesar." The *Century* artists effectively captured this campaign of movement in drawings such as James E. Taylor's Plate 351. Of particular interest in this connection is William Waud's spirited water color of Sherman's troops on the march, reproduced as Plate 354. This is his wartime original, sent to *Harper's* and published April 29, 1865. It ended up in the Century Collection after being used to illustrate one of the magazine's war papers in 1887 (the engravers had trouble rendering its freehand quality, and it did not appear in the *Battles and Leaders* volumes).

Three other scenes dealing with Sherman's campaign stem from William Waud's sketches: Plates 348, 350, and 352, all credited to brother Alf. When William died in 1878 his wartime *Harper's* sketches apparently went to his brother (the majority of those that survive are held today with the Alfred Waud drawings in the Library of Congress), who redrew selected ones in more finished form for *Battles and Leaders.*

There were no regular special artists with Thomas' Yankee army in Nashville, and that general's triumph over Hood, the most overwhelming victory in any major action of the war, went largely unrecognized pictorially. The Century Collection coverage of the Franklin-Nashville campaign is based entirely on photographs, most of them taken by George Barnard.

St. Nicholas, the Century Company's other magazine, commissioned two of the drawings that follow: Theodore Davis' water color of Sheridan's troopers firing a mill in the Shenandoah (Plate 341), and Redwood's drawing opposite, based on a photograph taken in the abandoned trenches at Petersburg in April, 1865. Redwood's Confederate compatriot William Sheppard tramped along with Lee's doomed army when it evacuated Petersburg, and his views of the Appomattox campaign reproduced here came out of that harrowing experience.

For four years the special artists had shared with Sheppard such "weary marches and dangerous voyages," as *Harper's* put it in a postwar tribute. "They have ridden and waded, and climbed and floundered, always trusting in lead pencils and keeping their paper dry." Thanks largely to them, the combat scenes in *Battles and Leaders* had a vitality and an honesty unprecedented for that era.

PLATE 328   *Alfred R. Waud*   ON PICKET DUTY

PLATE 329   *Walton Taber*   PICKET POST, FORT SEDGWICK

After the debacle of the Battle of the Crater, Grant abandoned the notion
of breaking Lee's Petersburg lines by frontal assault. "I now ordered the
troops to be put under cover," he recalled in his *Memoirs*. "They remained
quiet, except that there was more or less firing every day." Dozens of
strong points sprang up, few as elaborate as the one shown below by Waud,
but any of them posing a deadly barrier to an infantry attack. Between
the lines were the picket outposts. Waud explained on the back of Plate 328
how opposing pickets often worked out private cease-fire agreements
that included a pledge to sound a warning if orders came down to open fire.
Plate 329 is from a Brady photograph. A Rebel wrote that pickets "are
generally for *peace on any terms* toward the close of a cold wet night
but after the sun is up and they get warm they are in their usual spirits."

PLATE 330   *Alfred R. Waud*   FORTIFIED BATTERY, PETERSBURG

Finding he could not beat Lee, Grant tried to starve him. Three railroads
entered Petersburg from the south and west. The Norfolk & Petersburg
had been cut in the first Federal rush on the city; and in August
Gouverneur Warren's corps was assigned the job of cutting the second line,
the Welden & Petersburg. Warren was able to get astride the railroad—
Plate 331 pictures his headquarters on the line—but he could not destroy it
for any great distance. Lee detoured supplies around the break by
wagon, and held his grip on the third line, the South Side. In the fighting
a local church was wrecked, and during the winter the 50th New York
engineers built a replacement (Plate 332) of striking rustic design;
at the left are officers' quarters. In the winter of 1864-65 the barren,
makeshift military cemetery shown in Plate 333 (after a photograph)
at City Point, Grant's supply base on the James, grew ever more crowded.

PLATE 331   *Alfred R. Waud*   GENERAL WARREN'S HEADQUARTERS, GLOBE TAVERN

Plate 332   *Edwin J. Meeker*   Poplar Springs Church, Petersburg

Plate 333   *Edwin J. Meeker*   Military Cemetery, City Point

These scenes were photographed at war's end by Timothy O'Sullivan. Gracie's Salient formed part of the Rebel lines; the view is from inside the salient, showing the bomb-proofs cut into the reverse slope. Fort Sedgwick, a Yankee strong point, was better known as Fort Hell (opposite it was Rebel Fort Mahone, called Fort Damnation). The upper scene in Plate 335 shows the outer works, while the lower drawing pictures the bomb-proof quarters inside. One of Meade's staff officers described how such entrenchments were built: "The mass throw up earth; the engineer soldiers do the 'revetting,' that is the interior facing of logs. The engineer sergeants run about with tapes and stakes, measuring busily; and the engineer officers look as wise as possible and superintend." By the turn of the year the strain was beginning to tell on Lee's troops. "Our men need a good Victory badly," one of them wrote early in January, 1865. "It would do us a great deal of good for Grant to charge our lines."

PLATE 334   *Edwin J. Meeker*   GRACIE'S SALIENT, PETERSBURG

PLATE 335   *Walton Taber*   FORT SEDGWICK, PETERSBURG

As Stonewall Jackson had demonstrated back in 1862, the Shenandoah Valley was strategically very special. A major source of food and forage for Lee's army, it also offered the Rebels a "covered way" to get at Washington and points north. In May, 1864, Grant told General Franz Sigel to clear the Valley, but Sigel was not up to it. He was routed at New Market, where the young cadets of the Virginia Military Institute won everlasting glory for their part in the victory. Taber drew the cadets opposite for an 1889 *Century* article on VMI. Sheridan was put in charge, and at Winchester on September 19 he beat hard-fighting Jubal Early. The house below, after a Robert Sneden sketch, was used as a Federal hospital during the battle, as was Winchester's hotel (Plate 339). Sheridan now turned to carrying out Grant's orders that the Shenandoah Valley be reduced to "a barren waste."

PLATE 336 *Hughson Hawley* SPROUT'S SPRING MILL, OPEQUON CREEK, VIRGINIA

PLATE 337   *Walton Taber*
VMI CADET, 1861

PLATE 338   *Walton Taber*
VMI CADET, 1864

PLATE 339   *Walton Taber*   THE TAYLOR HOTEL, WINCHESTER, VIRGINIA

PLATE 340 *Alfred R. Waud* THE BATTLE OF CEDAR CREEK

Sheridan moved through the Valley like a scourge. On October 7
he reported to Grant: "I have destroyed over 2,000 barns
filled with wheat, hay, and farming implements; over seventy
mills filled with flour and wheat; have driven in front of the
army over 4,000 head of stock, and have killed . . . not less
than 3,000 sheep. . . . The Valley, from Winchester up to Staunton,
ninety-two miles, will have but little in it for man or
beast." Davis' water color opposite illustrated an article on
the campaign in *St. Nicholas*. Early made one last attempt
to save the Valley, catching the Yankees by surprise at
Cedar Creek on October 19, but Sheridan rallied his stunned troops
and they wrecked the little Rebel army for good. Waud
sketched Sheridan's men retaking guns lost early in the fight.

All the Mills were destroyed
and forage was burned but
dwellings were preserved.
—Sheridan

PLATE 341 *Theodore R. Davis* LAYING WASTE THE SHENANDOAH VALLEY

Before replacing Joe Johnston with Hood, President Davis had asked Lee for an
opinion of his one-time division commander. "Hood is a bold fighter,"
Lee replied; "I am doubtful as to other qualities necessary." Hood's bold
fighting had not saved Atlanta; now, after weeks of sparring along Sherman's line
of communications, he determined to strike out northward toward Nashville
to force Sherman to abandon Georgia and come after him. Sherman refused the
bait. Dispatching Thomas to manage the defense of the Tennessee capital
(Plate 343 is derived from a George Barnard photograph), he set out
on his famous March to the Sea. In the same week that Sherman marched east,
Hood marched north. On November 30 Hood hurled his army in a reckless frontal
assault on the Yankees holding Franklin, 18 miles south of Nashville.
Hand-to-hand fighting raged around a cotton-gin house at the center of the Union
position (Plate 342); then the Confederate attack faltered and collapsed.
The Federals pulled back to Nashville, and Hood followed with his broken army.

PLATE 342   *Walton Taber*   THE CARTER GIN HOUSE

PLATE 343   *Walton Taber*   THE STATE CAPITOL, NASHVILLE

PLATE 344 *Walton Taber* STEAMBOATS AT NASHVILLE

Nashville was as important logistically to the Federals in the West as Chattanooga had been to the Confederacy's operations, for military supplies were routed there by boat up the Cumberland as well as by rail. This phalanx of steamboats at the Nashville levee was drawn from a wartime photograph. Washington wanted Hood disposed of quickly; undue delay, Grant warned Thomas, could result "in a campaign back to the Ohio River." Patiently Thomas organized his disparate command and waited out a winter storm. Finally, on December 15, as Grant started west to take over the command himself, Thomas marched out to give battle.

PLATE 345 *Walton Taber* SOUTHWEST FRONT OF THE CAPITOL, NASHVILLE

These drawings, based on Barnard's photographs, suggest the
immense strength of the Nashville defenses. The marble
capitol (above) was turned into a citadel, and even the bridges
over the Cumberland were fortified (Plate 346). Redoubts
like Fort Negley (opposite), their guns emplaced in
armored casemates, studded the works. Hood was without
options—the Yankees were too strong to attack and too strong
to outflank; to retreat would only further demoralize
his army. He could only wait to be attacked. On December 15
Thomas drove the Rebels back with a massive blow, and
the next day he finished the job. Hood's army went streaming
from the field, in Thomas' words, "hopelessly broken."

PLATE 346   *Walton Taber*   FORTIFIED BRIDGE, NASHVILLE

Fort Negley.

Iron Clad casemates.
Fort Negley

PLATE 347   *Harry Fenn*   FORT NEGLEY, NASHVILLE

PLATE 348   *Alfred R. Waud*   THE THUNDERBOLT BATTERY, SAVANNAH

PLATE 349   *Walton Taber*   SHERMAN'S TROOPS DESTROYING A RAILROAD

PLATE 350 *Alfred R. Waud* FORCING A CROSSING OF THE LITTLE SALKEHATCHIE

While Hood made his doomed invasion of Tennessee, Sherman blazed a fiery trail through
the heart of Georgia, from Atlanta to the sea. His intention, wrote Henry Hitchcock,
one of his aides, was "to produce among the *people of Georgia* a thorough conviction of the
personal misery which attends war, and of the utter helplessness and inability of their
'rulers,' State or Confederate, to protect them." On December 20, four days after Thomas'
victory at Nashville, Sherman's army entered Savannah; the Yankees in Plate 348 inspect
one of the batteries that had protected the city from a waterborne attack. After resting and
refitting in Savannah for six weeks, Sherman put his 60,000 veterans on the roads leading
north into the Carolinas. Nothing, it seemed, could stop them; they paused only to
destroy every railroad they crossed and to burn anything of use to the Confederacy. Of the area
of South Carolina shown in the drawing above. Major Hitchcock wrote, "The streams in this
country might be pretty much all drawn by one picture . . . the same swampy approaches, the
same thick woods, of trees large and small, dense brush and dead and decaying logs . . . the
same infernal mud to wade through. . . ." Joe Johnston, called back into harness to command
the scratch force facing Sherman, confessed to Lee, "I can do no more than annoy him."

PLATE 351   *James E. Taylor*   Sherman's 17th Corps Crossing the Saluda

PLATE 352   *Alfred R. Waud*   Raising the Colors, Columbia, South Carolina

All three special artists who covered Sherman's
Carolinas campaign are represented here, directly or
indirectly. James Taylor had served two years in
the Union ranks before hiring on as an artist
for *Leslie's;* in his drawing above, a Federal column
makes a river crossing close to South Carolina's
capital, Columbia. On February 17, when the Yankees
entered Columbia, William Waud of *Harper's*
sketched them celebrating at the old State House,
and Alf Waud based Plate 352 on his brother's
sketch. That night Columbia was gutted by fire, the
responsibility for which became the subject of
hot debate. Davis of *Harper's* drew Yankees guarding
a local landmark (Plate 353) the next day.

PLATE 353   *Theodore R. Davis*   THE PALMETTO MONUMENT, COLUMBIA

PLATE 354   *William Waud*   SHERMAN'S 14TH CORPS CROSSING JUNIPER CREEK

William Waud's water-color sketch, published as
a woodcut in *Harper's*, was drawn on March 9, 1865,
at a crossing of a tributary of the Pee Dee River
near the North Carolina border. Smoke boils up from
barrels of rosin fired by the retreating Rebels.
In the group of horsemen at left, Henry Slocum, the
commander of Sherman's left wing, and Absalom Baird
watch Baird's division hurrying over the bridge, which
is beginning to take fire from the flaming rosin
floating down the creek. After Sherman's men crossed
into North Carolina, they were on reasonably
good behavior, but in South Carolina, where they
believed secession had originated, they acted
with a hard hand. "The army burned everything it came
near in the state of South Carolina, not under
orders but in spite of orders," wrote a Yankee major.
"Our track through the state is a desert waste."

PLATE 355 *Edwin J. Meeker* THE BENTONVILLE BATTLEFIELD

By mid-March Sherman had reached Fayetteville, North Carolina,
and opened communications with a column marching to his
support from the seacoast. As the drawing at right suggests,
the town was defended by only a rear guard; the inset
pictures the local arsenal, which Sherman destroyed, saying that
in the Carolinas there was no longer a need for arsenals.
A trickle of reinforcements was reaching Johnston, including
some 5,000 men from Hood's shattered Army of Tennessee,
and on March 19, near Bentonville, he lashed out at one of
Sherman's columns. It was the Rebel Western army's last
offensive, and it was unavailing. "As the sun went down that
night," wrote a Federal officer, "it undoubtedly carried
with it, in the mind of General Johnston, at least, the last
hopes of the Southern Confederacy." At battle's end
the field was thick with smoke from burning turpentine and
rosin stores (Plate 355). Both of these drawings are
derived from James Taylor's sketches engraved in *Leslie's*.

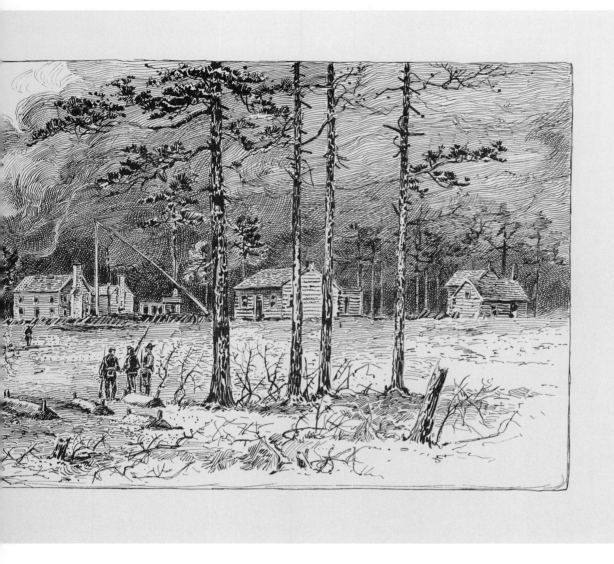

PLATE 356   *Edwin J. Meeker*   SKIRMISHING IN FAYETTEVILLE

PLATE 357 *Edwin J. Meeker* UNION WAGON TRAIN ENTERING PETERSBURG

In Virginia, too, the drama was fast coming to its close. Early in March one of Lee's men wrote: "It is useless to conceal the truth any longer. Many of our people at home have become so demoralized that they write to their husbands, sons and brothers that desertion *now* is not *dishonorable*." On March 25, to buy some time, Lee aimed a surprise strike at Grant's supply line. For a moment the way was open, but there was no weight behind the charge and the Yankees soon mended the break in their lines. On April 1 the inevitable happened and the Confederate right flank was turned. "The line has been stretched until it is broken," Lee said. Petersburg and Richmond were abandoned. The Army of Northern Virginia fled westward. Sheppard marched with it, and at right he shows Rebels making a meal of ground corn and flour paste. The incident below took place near Farmville. Plate 357 is from a photograph by John Reekie.

PLATE 358   *William L. Sheppard*
RETREAT FROM PETERSBURG: GRINDING CORN

PLATE 359   *William L. Sheppard*   RETREAT FROM PETERSBURG: HALT AT A WELL

Lee's last hope was to reach Appomattox Station, on the South Side line, where a trainload of rations waited; from there, perhaps, he could push on to join Johnston in North Carolina. But Sheridan's troopers reached the station first (Plate 360 derives from an O'Sullivan photograph), were joined by infantry, and the last hope evaporated. On April 9, Palm Sunday, Lee told his officers, "I have arranged to meet with General Grant with a view to surrender." The two generals rode into the pleasant little village of Appomattox Court House and met in the parlor of Wilmer McLean, who had brought his family there from his farm near Manassas Junction to get well away from war. The McLean House is at the right in Plate 361, after Robert Sneden's diary sketch. Plate 362 is from O'Sullivan's photograph taken a few days later. In this simple setting the nation's four-year agony was ended.

PLATE 360 *Walton Taber* APPOMATTOX STATION, VIRGINIA

PLATE 361   *Hughson Hawley*   APPOMATTOX COURT HOUSE, VIRGINIA

PLATE 362   *Walton Taber*   THE McLEAN HOUSE

Lee's men had few illusions about their army's fate in those final days as rations ran out, ammunition dwindled, and the battery horses grew too weak to pull the guns. Rebel gunner Sheppard described this scene: "Infantry destroying the railroad from Appomattox to Lynchburg. Artillerymen cutting down their guns at night fall on Saturday Apr. 8th 1865. From incidents observed by the artist." The formal surrender and stacking of arms was carried out with dignity, "honor answering honor," on April 12, four years exactly after that April morning when the first shells fell on Fort Sumter.

PLATE 363   *William L. Sheppard*
CONFEDERATES DISABLING GUNS, APPOMATTOX

XII   Battlefields of Yesterday

WHEN THE FIRST OF THE WAR PAPERS was published in *Century* for November, 1884, Appomattox had receded nearly 20 years into the past. What had happened in those two decades to the scenes of conflict was a question the magazine's editors asked themselves, and they believed that their readers, especially the ex-soldiers among them, were asking the same question. Consequently, one of the goals of the illustration program for *Battles and Leaders* was, as the editors stated it in their introduction to the war papers, "to picture the present look of battle-fields, to show how ramparts and rifle-pits have held their own against the leveling forces of nature." This proved to be one of the more popular features of the series, and on the following pages is a sampling of this art.

Attached to so many battlefields and the features on them were homespun, practical names like those in this chapter: Wilson's Creek, Crump's Landing, Frayser's Farm. In "Names from the War" Bruce Catton explains that in an earlier time

The names had no ring or shine to them, then. They were just names,
    put there so that a man could say where he was . . .
Then the armies came and the names
    became terrible. . . .

Twenty years later, when these pictures were drawn, it was different. This or that battlefield had a special meaning to a visitor who had once witnessed death there and been spared, and the names were no longer quite so terrible; now there was a ring or a shine to them. And the nation's scars were healing. Rebels and Yankees began holding joint reunions, such as one at Fredericksburg in May of 1884 that included tours of the several nearby Rappahannock battlefields, and the *Century* editors, launching their series, saw in this a healthy sign: "No time could be fitter, we think, for a publication of this kind than the present, when the passions and prejudices of the Civil War have nearly faded out of politics, and its

PLATE 364   *Walton Taber*   AFTER THE WAR

heroic events are passing into our common history where motives will be weighed without malice, and valor praised without distinction of uniform." The wide popularity of *Battles and Leaders* accelerated the healing. Renewed efforts were made to save the battle sites—the federal government took over the Gettysburg battlefield, for example, in 1894—and the reunions multiplied. The largest encampment took place at Gettysburg in 1913, on the fiftieth anniversary of the battle, when no fewer than 55,000 old soldiers camped out for a week to listen to fulsome oratory and renew acquaintances and wander again across the hot fields. (The last Gettysburg encampment was in 1938, on the seventy-fifth anniversary of the battle, and 1,845 veterans, average age 94, were on hand.)

The majority of the Civil War's battles took place off in the middle of nowhere, with the paradoxical result that the sites were either preserved reasonably intact or, like the old soldiers, just faded away. The face and features of a site like the Virginia Wilderness, where the battles of Chancellorsville and the Wilderness were fought, changed very little in 20 years (Plate 370); a tangle of second-growth timber and brambly undergrowth broken by occasional clearings, the Wilderness was no more exploited economically in the eighties than it had been in the sixties, and relics of the battles, including imperfectly buried human remains, were easily found. On the other hand, a battle that sprawled across a farmer's melon patch or wheatfield (overleaf) was soon likely to have all traces of rampart and rifle pit erased by the touch of the plow—a process exemplified in Taber's original illustration opposite, done as a decorated initial for the *Century* series.

In any event, a veteran returning two decades later to the average battle site was bound to be startled by the inevitable changes. Theodore Davis, writing in 1886, remarked on this from his own experience: "The visitor to those old battlefields . . . finds to-day only slight signs of conflict. Few of the old roads can be traced; towns have grown into cities; pleasant farms have overgrown the earthworks; and forests stand in the fields which, years ago, were marked with the smoke and strife of battle." Most of all, perhaps, it was the matter-of-fact calmness and peace of these fields, qualities that overlay the drawings and paintings on the following pages, which must have unnerved old soldiers who in their youth had seen there only a thunderous maelstrom of shot and shell that was, like the war itself, beyond comprehension.

PLATE 365   *Harry Fenn*   THE BATTLEFIELD OF MALVERN HILL

Many battlefields soon went under the plow again, leaving only the contours of the land to recall past struggles. Where farmers reap in Plate 365 Lee's men were cut down by Union artillery on the last of the Seven Days; the lower half of the drawing shows the house and outbuildings of Mr. Chew, site of McClellan's left flank. Missouri's major battle took place at Wilson's Creek near Springfield, on the low ridge christened Bloody Hill (below). The Rebels won the fight, in August, 1861, but lost the state.

PLATE 366   *Walton Taber*   BLOODY HILL, WILSON'S CREEK

Fenn's water color, like most of the pictures in this chapter,
was based on photographs taken in the 1880's. The Frayser farm
was the scene of another of the Seven Days' actions, a confusing
struggle on June 30, 1862, known as the Battle of Glendale
(or any of seven other names). The farmhouse was used as a field
hospital. The flag marks the site of a military cemetery.

National Cemetery, & Frasers' farm
house. from the Quaker Road
(looking South) —

PLATE 367   *Harry Fenn*   FRAYSER'S FARM

Widow Crump's House.

Crump's Landing.

PLATE 368   *George Gibson*   THE CRUMP HOUSE AND CRUMP'S LANDING

A large proportion of Civil War sites had a homey, backwoods flavor
to them. There was Crump's Landing, on the Tennessee River
in western Tennessee, named for a local family then headed by
the Widow Crump. In early April, 1862, General Lew Wallace
was posted here with his division, and it took him many hours to
march the half-dozen miles to the Shiloh battlefield, much
to the discomfiture of Grant and his hard-pressed men. Wallace's
success as an author *(Ben Hur)* outshone his reputation as a general.

Central Kentucky was gripped by a drought when the armies of Bragg and Buell collided at Perryville in October, 1862, and men by the score died in pitched battles for control of springs and creeks. Bragg's thirsty Rebels filled their canteens at the shaded spring sketched below by Fenn. In the smaller drawing is a century-old pear tree on the farm of one C. H. Bottom, which somehow survived shot and shell despite the fact that it was at the very center of the fierce Perryville battle.

Spring that watered Braggs army.

Pear tree 100 years old at the left of Rousseau's position

PLATE 369   *Harry Fenn*   THE PERRYVILLE BATTLEFIELD

PLATE 370 *Harry Fenn* WILDERNESS CHURCH

PLATE 371 *Walton Taber* BLOODY LANE, ANTIETAM

The old soldiers in Plate 370, obviously touched by
postwar prosperity, inspect a clearing along the
Wilderness turnpike in 1884, no doubt reliving the
crisis point of the Battle of Chancellorsville when
Stonewall Jackson's men came swarming past this little
whitewashed church and across the Hawkins farm (right)
in hot pursuit of the routed Yankee 11th Corps.
Nor could Antietam veterans visiting that battlefield
ever forget the September day when the humble,
dusty farm road above earned the name Bloody Lane.

PLATE 372   *William L. Lathrop*   FORT ST. PHILIP

PLATE 373   *Walton Taber*   ANDERSONVILLE AFTER THE WAR

Two decades after Farragut's big cruisers smashed past Fort St. Philip, on the lower Mississippi, the fort was weedy but intact (Plate 372); by the centennial of the battle the old works were engulfed by the delta jungle. By 1868, the date of the photographs on which Plate 373 was based, the Andersonville stockade was a ruin, but the cemetery with its 13,000 dead was testimony enough to the prison's existence. Monuments and heroic statues were raised on many fields as tangible evidence of past gallantry. The monument in Plate 374 commemorates Captain John Bigelow's 9th Massachusetts battery, which loaded its guns to the muzzles with canister and held off a Rebel breakthrough on the second day of Gettysburg. At Bull Run (below) a new Henry House had risen on the ashes of the old (Plate 126), and in the Henry backyard had been erected a stone tribute to 1861's battle of the amateurs.

PLATE 374   *Walton Taber*   GETTYSBURG MONUMENT

PLATE 375   *Walton Taber*   THE NEW HENRY HOUSE, BULL RUN

PLATE 376   *J. D. Woodward*   THE GRAVE OF COLONEL RODGERS

PLATE 377   *J. H. Cocks*   SOLDIERS' GRAVES, ARLINGTON NATIONAL CEMETERY

Decoration day - Chattanooga.
National Cemetery - 1883
The Resting Place of the Bridge Burners.

PLATE 378   *Theodore R. Davis*   DECORATION DAY IN CHATTANOOGA

Across the land, North and South, were graves of the honored dead, sometimes
arranged in serried ranks in Arlington or other national cemeteries,
sometimes standing alone in simple dignity (Plate 376). In the Battle of
Corinth in October, 1862, Colonel William Rogers of the 2nd Texas led
his charging men right to the parapet of a Federal redoubt, only to be shot
down as he planted the Confederate colors on the breastworks, and an
admiring Rosecrans ordered his body buried with military honors. Decoration
Day was initiated in 1868 to honor the war dead. Theodore Davis
sketched the ceremony above in Chattanooga's national cemetery in 1883.
In the foreground are the graves of six of the Andrews raiders (pages 254-55)
hanged as spies. Andrews was later interred here beside his comrades.

Catalogue

of the

American Heritage Century Collection

The catalogue arrangement is by artist. Plate-number references indicate works reproduced in the body of the book. The balance of the collection is illustrated within the catalogue, or the same page as the entry or on the page opposite, and identified by catalogue number; in these reproductions, overly generous margins have been cropped in the interest of visibility. The entries under each artist appear in a generally chronological order, with the entries for pictures in the body of the book positioned so that their plate-number references are in numerical sequence. The 29 Century Collection maps are listed at the end of the catalogue; problems of scale make it impractical to illustrate all of them.

Each catalogue entry includes dating and identification of the subject matter if necessary, followed by the "pedigree" of the drawing. Credit for source photographs is as it appears in *Century* or in *Battles and Leaders of the Civil War* unless another attribution can be confirmed. The term "original illustration" refers to a piece of art independently created rather than derived directly from such sources as a wartime sketch or photograph. Dimensions are in inches, with height preceding width. Sight size (picture area only) is given for pictures with excessive margins; otherwise the measurements are sheet size. Inscriptions are by the artist unless otherwise indicated, with spelling and punctuation (and facts) uncorrected; inscribed titles that are substantially the same as the assigned titles are not included, nor are inscriptions in other handwriting unless they are of special interest. The engraving references are to woodcut reproductions. Bound volumes of *Century* (six monthly issues per volume) are numbered in either of two ways; the references in this catalogue are "Old Series," i.e., volume numbers that date from 1870, when the magazine was founded under the name *Scribner's Monthly*. "New Series" numbering starts with 1881, when the *Century* name was adopted. (New Series converts to Old by adding 22.) *Battles and Leaders*, of course, stands for *Battles and Leaders of the Civil War*, four volumes, published by the Century Company in 1888.

Acknowledgments

Among the sources consulted for biographical material on the artists and for information on the Century Collection are the following: *American Art Annual* (1898-1945); *American Artists and their Works* (1899); the Archives of American Art, New York; William P. Campbell, *The Civil War: A Centennial Exhibition of Eyewitness Drawings* (1961); Mantle Fielding, *Dictionary of American Painters, Sculptors and Engravers* (1965); George C. Groce and David H. Wallace, *The New-York Historical Society's Dictionary of Artists in America, 1564-1860* (1957); Philip G. Hamerton, *Art of the American Wood-Engraver* (1894); Sinclair Hamilton, *Early American Book Illustrators and Wood Engravers, 1670-1870* (1958); Harold Lancour, *American Art Auction Catalogues, 1785-1942* (1944); Daniel Trowbridge Mallett, *Mallett's Index of Artists* (1948); Roy Meredith, *The American Wars: A Pictorial History from Quebec to Korea, 1755-1953* (1955); Henry P. Rossiter, M. & M. Karolik Collection of American Water Colors & Drawings, 1800-1875, Vol. II (1962); Philip Van Doren Stern, *They Were There: The Civil War in Action as Seen by its Combat Artists* (1959); Robert Taft, *Artists and Illustrators of the Old West, 1850-1900* (1953); W. Fletcher Thompson, Jr., *The Image of War: The Pictorial Reporting of the American Civil War* (1959); Frank Weitenkampf, *American Graphic Art* (1912); Hermann Warner Williams, Jr., *The Civil War: The Artists' Record* (1961).

Information regarding the Century Company and the *Battles and Leaders* project may be found in the Richard Watson Gilder Papers, the Robert Underwood Johnson Papers, and the Century Collection, all in the Manuscripts and Archives Division of the New York Public Library; and in Samuel C. Chew's *Fruit Among the Leaves: An Anniversary Anthology* (1950), a history of Appleton-Century-Crofts, Inc.

Special thanks are due the following individuals for their generous assistance and advice: Harold L. Peterson, Washington, D.C.; Milton Kaplan, of the Prints and Photographs Division, the Library of Congress; John L. Marion, president of Sotheby Parke Bernet, Inc., New York; E. B. Long, of the University of Wyoming; Louis D. Liskin, of the Salmagundi Club, New York; Terry Brown, of the Society of Illustrators, New York; Mrs. Elaine Evans Dee, of the Cooper-Hewitt Museum of Decorative Arts, New York; Jack Nead, Roselle, N.J.; and Kenneth W. Rapp, of the United States Military Academy.

OTTO H. BACHER

Illustrator, painter, etcher. Born Cleveland, Ohio, March 31, 1856; died Bronxville, N.Y., Aug. 16, 1909. Following some art training in Cincinnati, Bacher studied in Paris. He became a European acquaintance of Whistler's, and in 1908 published *With Whistler in Venice*. Best known for his etchings, he was a member of the Society of American Artists and the Society of Illustrators, and was elected to the National Academy of Design in 1906.

1.   CEDAR CREEK BATTLEFIELD
Cedar Creek, Va.; after a photograph, 1885.
Pen, 17 x 20-7/8, signed *Otto H. Bacher—88*. Inscribed *Cedar Creek Va. Hill occupied by Sheridan's left Oct. 19th/64 from Kershaw's Ford*.
Engraved: *Battles and Leaders* IV-516.

B. L. BLACKFORD

Confederate lieutenant of engineers, stationed at the Gosport Navy Yard in Norfolk, Va., in 1861.

2.   C.S.S. "VIRGINIA"
Facsimile of a sketch by the artist, March 7, 1862.
Pen, 6-1/2 x 13-5/8. Inscribed (unidentified) on verso *Copied from Sketch of the old Frigate Merrimac as she appeared after being converted into the Ironclad War Ship Virginia, made March 7—1862, Lt. B. L. Blackford, C.S. engrs. the day before the great naval engagement in Hampton Roads. Drawing is made to a scale & is perfectly accurate the measurements & details having been furnished by the Engineer Officers of the Ship*.
Engraved: *Century* 29:742, March, 1885; *Battles and Leaders* I-695.

H. E. BROWN

According to his letter of Sept. 8, 1887, to the *Century* editors, Brown was an enlisted man in John W. Geary's division of Hooker's 12th Corps during the Battle of Lookout Mountain, Nov. 24, 1863; he added that during the Chattanooga campaign he served as an "auxilliary" to a *Harper's Weekly* staff artist (probably Theodore R. Davis). After the war Brown lived in Bethlehem, Pa., where evidence indicates he was a portrait painter.

3.   BRIDGING LOOKOUT CREEK
Battle of Lookout Mountain, Nov. 24, 1863; after an eyewitness sketch by the artist.
Pen, 5-15/16 x 9-1/16, signed *H. E. Brown*. Inscribed *Bridging Lookout Creek preparitory to the assault*.
Engraved: *Battles and Leaders* III-699.
Collection of Robert B. Mayo.
PLATE 283

4.   THE BATTLE OF LOOKOUT MOUNTAIN
Nov. 24, 1863; after an eyewitness sketch by the artist.
Pen, 14 x 17, signed *H. E. Brown*. Inscribed *Battle of Lookout Mountain Nov. 24, 1863 / (3 P.M. At the first point that any marked resistence was shown, when our advance was 100 yds beyond the house the contest closed and at about 9 P.M.)*.
Engraved: *Battles and Leaders* III-702.
PLATE 284

MICHAEL J. BURNS

Illustrator and etcher, specializing in nautical scenes.
5.   THE "ALABAMA" TAKES A HIT
Alabama vs. *Kearsarge*, June 19, 1864; original illustration.
Oil, 14 x 18-3/8 on mount, signed *Burns*. Inscribed on verso *An Eleven inch Shell bursting on the Alabama*.
Engraved: *Century* 31:918, April, 1886.
PLATE 209

JOHN H. COCKS

Illustrator and sculptor. Born New York, 1850; died Plainfield, N.J., Jan. 23, 1938. Cocks' illustrations appeared regularly in *Scribner's*, *Century*, and *Harper's Weekly*. As a sculptor he specialized in portrait busts.

6.   SOLDIERS' GRAVES, ARLINGTON NATIONAL CEMETERY
Original illustration.
Water color, 4-3/4 x 8-7/8 on mount, signed *J. H. Cocks / 82*. Inscribed title.
Engraved: *Century* 27:659, March, 1884.
PLATE 377

J. O. DAVIDSON

Davidson was an illustrator for *Century* and *Harper's Weekly*, as well as for juvenile books and magazines, especially *St. Nicholas*. A member of the Salmagundi Club, he was best known for his scenes of maritime and naval history.

7.   CONFEDERATE RAM "STONEWALL JACKSON"
After a sketch by Beverley Kennon, 1862.
Pen, 3 x 8 (sight size), signed *J. O. Davidson*. Inscribed *Also of all the vessels comprising the "River Defense Fleet." Tonnage of each one about 150 tons. Drawn by J. O. Davidson* [from] *a sketch by the author*. On verso: consultant's critique.
Engraved: *Century* 32:451, July, 1886: *Battles and Leaders* II-54.
PLATE 77

8.   THE "GOVERNOR MOORE" RAMMING THE "VARUNA"
New Orleans, April 24, 1862; original illustration.
Tempera, 3-3/4 x 8-7/8, signed *J. O. Davidson*. Inscribed *The U.S. gunboat Varuna disabled by the Confederate rams Morgan* [sic] *and Stonewall Jackson*.
Engraved: *Century* 29:941, April, 1885, and 32:448, July, 1886 (detail); *Battles and Leaders* II-81 (detail).
PLATE 80

9.   FORT ST. PHILIP UNDER ATTACK
New Orleans, April 24, 1862; original illustration.
Tempera, 10-1/2 x 14-3/16, signed *J. O. Davidson*. Inscribed *The Assault on Fort St. Philip / the fight from the ramparts*; consultant's critique.
Engraved: *Century* 29:943, April, 1885; *Battles and Leaders* II-65.
PLATE 81

1

2

17

26

30

31

40

10. THE "GOVERNOR MOORE" IN FLAMES
New Orleans, April 24, 1862; original illustration.
Tempera, 8-1/2 x 12-1/2, signed *J. O. Davidson*.
Inscribed identifications.
Engraved: *Century* 32:454, July, 1886; *Battles and Leaders* II-87.
PLATE 82

11. FARRAGUT'S SQUADRON AT NEW ORLEANS
April 25, 1862; original illustration.
Tempera, 7 x 10, signed *J. O. Davidson*.
Engraved: *Century* 32:456, July, 1886; *Battles and Leaders* II-21.
PLATE 83

12. TAKING THE SURRENDER OF FORTS JACKSON AND ST. PHILIP
New Orleans, April 28, 1862; original illustration.
Tempera, 11-1/8 x 8-1/8, signed *J. O. Davidson*.
Inscribed *Porter accepting the commander of the forts.*
Engraved: *Century* 29:951, April, 1885; *Battles and Leaders* II-52.
PLATE 85

13. DESTRUCTION OF THE "ARKANSAS"
Baton Rouge, La., Aug. 6, 1862; original illustration.
Tempera, 11 x 13-3/4, signed *J. O. Davidson*.
Engraved: *Battles and Leaders* III-579.
PLATE 89

14. REMODELING THE "MERRIMACK"
Original illustration.
Pen, 6-7/8 x 10, signed *J. Davidson*. Inscribed title.
Engraved: *Century* 29:740, March, 1885; *Battles and Leaders* I-694.
PLATE 94

15. ARRIVAL OF THE "MONITOR" AT HAMPTON ROADS
March 8, 1862; original illustration.
Pen, 2-5/8 x 6 (sight size), signed *J. O. Davidson*.
Engraved: *Century* 29:757, March, 1885; *Battles and Leaders* I-719.
PLATE 95

16. HOSPITAL SHIP "RED ROVER"
After a wartime photograph.
Pen, 3 x 7-1/4 (sight size), signed *J. O. Davidson*.
Inscribed *U.S. Hospital Ship "Red Rover" Act. Vol. Lieut. W. R. Wells.*
Engraved: *Battles and Leaders* IV-361.
PLATE 170

17. THE "FLORIDA" CHASING THE "STAR OF PEACE"
Original illustration.
Tempera, 13 x 18, signed *J. O. Davidson*. Inscribed title.
Engraved: *Century* 56:420, July, 1898.

18. THE "WACHUSETT" RAMMING THE "FLORIDA"
Bahia, Brazil, Oct. 7, 1864; original illustration.
Tempera, 10-1/2 x 15, signed *J. O. Davidson*.
Inscribed title. Inscribed approval by consultant G. T. Sinclair.
Engraved: *Century* 56:424, July, 1898.
PLATE 201

19. THE "TALLAHASSEE" BURNING THE "ADRIATIC"
Aug. 14, 1864; original illustration.
Water color, 11-3/8 x 15, signed *J. O. Davidson*.
Inscribed title. Commentary by consultant G. T. Sinclair.
Engraved: *Century* 56:417, July, 1898.
PLATE 202

20. THE SCUTTLING OF THE "GLENARVON"
Aug., 1864; original illustration.
Pen, 9-1/2 x 12-5/8, signed *J. O. Davidson*.
Inscribed title.
Engraved: *Century* 56:414, July, 1898.
PLATE 203

21. "ALABAMA" VS. "KEARSARGE"
June 19, 1864; original illustration.
Tempera, 6-7/8 x 10-1/2 (sight size), signed *J. O. Davidson*. Inscribed title. On verso: commentary by consultant John McIntosh Kell.
Engraved: *Century* 31:909, April, 1886; *Battles and Leaders* IV-609.
PLATE 207

22. THE "ALABAMA" SINKING
June 19, 1864; original illustration.
Tempera, 9-7/8 x 13-5/8, signed *J. O. Davidson*.
PLATE 210

23. BOARDING THE "HARRIET LANE" AT GALVESTON
Jan. 1, 1863; original illustration.
Tempera, 10-3/8 x 15, signed *J. O. Davidson*. On verso: commentary by consultant H. D. Smith.
Engraved: *Battles and Leaders* III-587.
Collection of Robert B. Mayo.
PLATE 211

24. THE IRONCLAD RAM "DICTATOR"
Original illustration.
Tempera, 8-7/8 x 16, signed *J. O. Davidson*.
Engraved: *Century* 31:292, Dec., 1885.
PLATE 212

25. THE "MONTAUK" BEACHED FOR REPAIRS
Original illustration.
Pen, 7 x 9-3/4, signed *J. O. Davidson*. Inscribed title.
Engraved: *Battles and Leaders* IV-32.
PLATE 214

26. TRANSPORTING WHALEBOATS FOR THE ATTACK ON THE GUNBOAT "UNDERWRITER"
New Berne, N.C., Feb. 2, 1864; original illustration.
Pen, 7-3/4 x 11-3/8, signed *J. O. Davidson*.
Inscribed title.

27. CONFEDERATES BURNING THE GUNBOAT "UNDERWRITER"
New Berne, N.C., Feb. 2, 1864; original illustration.
Pen, 7-1/16 x 15, signed *J. O. Davidson*.
PLATE 219

28. PORTER PASSING THE VICKSBURG BATTERIES
April 16, 1863; after a sketch by eyewitness S. H. Lockett.
Water color, 10 x 11-1/2 on mount, signed *J. O. Davidson*. Inscribed on verso *Night passage of gun boats and steamboats past Vicksburg April 16, 1863 / J. O. Davidson / from Col. Lockett's painting.*
Engraved: *Battles and Leaders* III-485.
Collection of Robert B. Mayo.
PLATE 248

29. PORTER'S FLEET BELOW VICKSBURG
April 16, 1863; original illustration
Tempera, 13-1/2 x 17 on mount, signed *J. O. Davidson*. Inscribed *Com. Porter's gun boat fleet & transports passing the Vicksburg batteries by Night April 16th 1863* and identifications in margin.
Engraved: *Battles and Leaders* III-497.
PLATE 249

30. FEDERAL BATTERIES, CHARLESTON HARBOR
After photographs by Mathew B. Brady, c. 1863.
Pen, 5-1/4 x 6-5/8 (sight size), signed *J. O. Davidson*. Two drawings. Inscribed (top) *Interior Ft. Putnam Charleston Harbor South Carolina*; (bottom) *South east angle of Fort Marshall Sullivan Island Charleston Harbor.*
Engraved: *Battles and Leaders* IV-8.

31. THE BOAT ATTACK ON FORT SUMTER
Charleston Harbor, Sept. 9, 1863; original illustration.
Tempera, 11-3/4 x 15, signed *J. O. Davidson*. Inscribed title.
Engraved: *Battles and Leaders* IV-50.

ARTHUR B. DAVIES

Painter, graphic artist, tapestry designer. Born Utica, N.Y., Sept. 26, 1862; died Florence, Oct. 24, 1928. Davies studied at the Chicago Academy of Design and the Art Institute of Chicago and in New York at the Art Students' League, and in the late eighties and early nineties did illustrations for *Century* and *St. Nicholas*. Early in the new century he became one of The Eight, and in 1913 was the principal organizer of the Armory Show. Davies' best-known paintings are landscapes with themes of ethereal and romantic fantasy. He experimented in many artistic mediums, including the design of Gobelins tapestries.

32. JOHNSON'S ISLAND PRISONER OF WAR CAMP
Sandusky Bay, Ohio; after a wartime sketch by Edward Gould.
Pen, 11-3/4 x 18-1/4, signed *ABD–1890–*. Inscribed *From sketch by Edward Gould, Co B. 128 Regt O.V.I. / Depot Prisoners of War on Johnson's Island.*
Engraved: *Century* 41:707, March, 1891.
PLATE 175

THEODORE R. DAVIS

Newspaper artist-correspondent and illustrator. Born Boston, 1840; died Asbury Park, N.J., Nov. 10, 1894. Davis moved to Brooklyn at the age of 15, where he may have received art training. In 1861 he became a special artist for *Harper's Weekly*, and remained with *Harper's* for 23 years. He was the most traveled of all the Civil War "specials" and was twice wounded. Continuing his travels in the postwar years, Davis contributed extensive pictorial reporting from the South and Far West. In 1879 he designed a Haviland state dinner service for the White House, and in the mid-eighties he was a historical consultant for the Missionary Ridge and Atlanta cyclorama paintings. In 1884 Davis established a studio at Asbury Park and did freelance writing and illustrating.

33. VIEW OF MONTGOMERY, ALABAMA
After a sketch by the artist, May, 1861.
Pen and water color, 4-5/16 x 8-1/2 (sight size), signed *Theo. R. Davis*. Inscribed *Inauguration of Jefferson Davis. Montgomery Ala. Feby 18, 1861.*
Engraved: *Battles and Leaders* I-99.
PLATE 3

34. PENSACOLA HARBOR FROM THE BAR
After a sketch by the artist, May, 1861.
Pen, 6-13/16 x 11-1/4, signed *Theo. R. Davis / May 1861*. Inscribed title and identifications in margin.
Engraved: *Battles and Leaders* I-26.
PLATE 5

35. EVACUATION OF FORT MOULTRIE
Charleston Harbor, Dec. 26, 1860; after a sketch by the artist, 1861.
Pen, 7-3/8 x 12, signed *Theo. R. Davis*. Inscribed *Evacuation of Fort Moultrie—Evening Dec. 26th 1860* and identifications in margin.
Engraved: *Battles and Leaders* I-49.
PLATE 6

36. FIRING ON THE "STAR OF THE WEST"
Charleston Harbor, Jan. 9, 1861; after a sketch by the artist, 1861.
Pen, 7-3/8 x 10-3/8, signed *Theo. R. Davis*. Two drawings. Inscribed identifications in margin. Inset drawing of *Star of the West.*
Engraved: *Battles and Leaders* I-64.
PLATE 7

37. THE OPENING OF THE CIVIL WAR
Charleston Harbor, April 12, 1861; after a sketch by the artist, 1861.
Pen and water color, 4-3/4 x 15-1/4 on mount, signed *Theo. R. Davis*. Inscribed (not by Davis) *The signal to open fire was a shell from Fort Johnson which burst over Sumter at dawn, on the 12th of April, 1861. / Abner Doubleday / Bvt. Major General / U.S.A.*
Engraved: *Battles and Leaders* I-74.
PLATE 8

38. SERGEANT CARMODY MANS THE BARBETTE BATTERY
Fort Sumter, April 12, 1861; after a sketch by the artist, 1861.
Pen, 9-7/8 x 12-3/8. Inscribed title.
Engraved: *Battles and Leaders* I-69.
PLATE 9

39. ARRIVAL OF THE ORIGINAL CONTRABAND AT FORTRESS MONROE
Virginia peninsula, May, 1861; after a sketch by the artist, 1861.
Pen and water color, 7-1/8 x 12-5/8. Inscribed title.
Engraved: *Battles and Leaders* II-146.
PLATE 13

40. MARINES AND BARRACKS, WASHINGTON
After a sketch by the artist, 1861.
Pen, 9-1/4 x 10-3/4, signed *Theo. R. Davis / 1861*. Inscribed title.

41. ARRIVAL OF THE 7TH NEW YORK AT ANNAPOLIS
April 22, 1861; after a sketch by the artist, 1861.
Water color, 5-1/2 x 11-1/4. Inscribed title.
Engraved: *Battles and Leaders* I-150.
PLATE 15

42. BUILDING GUNBOATS AND MORTAR BOATS
Carondelet, Mo.; after a sketch by the artist, 1861.
Pen and wash, 6-9/16 x 11-5/16. Inscribed title and *Carondelet Mo—61 / The Turtles.*
Engraved: *Battles and Leaders* I-338.
PLATE 57

43. ARMY TRANSPORTS AT THE CAIRO LEVEE
Cairo, Ill.; after a sketch by the artist, 1861.
Water color, 7 x 12-1/2. Inscribed title.
Engraved: *Battles and Leaders* I-358.
PLATE 60

44. QUARTERMASTER'S DOCK, FORTRESS MONROE
Virginia peninsula; after a sketch by the artist, April, 1862.
Pen, 8-9/16 x 11-1/2. Inscribed title and *Supply depot for McClellan in front of Yorktown.*
Engraved: *Battles and Leaders* II-165.
PLATE 93

45. HOSPITAL SHIP "D. A. JANUARY"
After a sketch by the artist, 1863.
Pen, 7-3/8 x 12-1/2, signed *Theo. R. Davis*. Inscribed *On the Mississippi River Hospital boat D. A. January.*
Engraved: *Battles and Leaders* IV-366.
PLATE 171

46. MILITARY FUNERAL, VICKSBURG
After a sketch by the artist, April, 1863.
Pen, 7-1/4 x 11-7/16, signed *Theo. R. Davis*. Inscribed *Funeral on the Levee, the Duckport Canal April 1863.*
Engraved: *Battles and Leaders* III-495.
PLATE 174

47. VIEWS OF FORT PULASKI
Savannah River, Ga.; after wartime sketches by the artist.
Pen, 19-1/4 x 14, signed *Theo. R. Davis*. Three drawings. Inscribed (top) *Fort Pulaski / Mouth of Savannah river / May 61*; (center) *Mounting guns on the [barbette] of Fort Pulaski*; (bottom) *Bombardment and Breaching of Fort Pulaski / Lieut. Horace Porter directing the Mortar fire / April 11th 1862*. Center drawing inscribed *Not Pulaski* by consultant Col. Charles Olmstead.
Engraved: *Battles and Leaders* II-6 (top drawing only).
PLATE 198

48. CHARLESTON UNDER FIRE
Aug., 1863; after a wartime sketch by the artist.
Pen, 13-5/8 x 20-1/4, signed *Theo. R. Davis*. Inscribed *Charleston under fire—August 1863 / north from the Mills House* and identifications in margins.
Engraved: *Battles and Leaders* IV-17.
PLATE 218

49. WOODEN MORTAR, VICKSBURG
After a sketch by the artist, 1863.
Pen, 11-3/4 x 8, signed *Theo. R. Davis*. Inscribed title.
Engraved: *Battles and Leaders* III-522.
PLATE 227

50. THE BATTLE OF CHAMPION'S HILL
May 16, 1863; facsimile of an eyewitness sketch by the artist.
Pen, 5-3/4 x 14. Inscribed on verso *fac simile of note book sketch for one sketch made during battle of Champions Hill. May 16th 63.*
Engraved: *St. Nicholas* July, 1889.
PLATE 250

55

68

69

71

72

51.   AN INCIDENT IN THE VICKSBURG CAMPAIGN
May 16, 1863; an eyewitness sketch by the artist.
Pen, 5-7/8 x 9-1/8. Inscribed *It was the Enemy / Sketch made on the road side May 16th 63.*
Engraved: *St. Nicholas* July, 1889.
PLATE 251

52.   FEDERAL LINES, VICKSBURG
July 1, 1863; after an eyewitness sketch by the artist.
Pen, 8-5/16 x 13-7/8, signed *Theo. R. Davis.* Inscribed *The White House (Sherley I think) at entrance of McPhersons saps Vicksburg—July 1st 63.*
Engraved: *Battles and Leaders* III-539.
PLATE 253

53.   EFFECTS OF SHELLFIRE, VICKSBURG
July 4, 1863; after an eyewitness sketch by the artist.
Pen, 6-3/4 x 8-3/4. Inscribed *Effect of Shell Fire / McCutchean & Co. Vicksburg July 4th, 63.*
Engraved: *Battles and Leaders* III-488.
PLATE 254

54.   THE CONFEDERATE RIDGE BATTERY
Vicksburg, July 4, 1863; after an eyewitness sketch by the artist.
Pen, 6-7/8 x 12-3/4, signed *Theo. R. Davis.* Inscribed *The Ridge Batty. South of Vicksburg. Capt. Bond / July 4th 63.*
Engraved: *Battles and Leaders* III-546.
PLATE 255

55.   EXPLOSION OF THE VICKSBURG MINE
June 25, 1863; after an eyewitness sketch by the artist.
Pen, 10-7/8 x 14-7/8, signed *Theo. R. Davis.* Inscribed *Explosion of a ton and a half of powder in a mine under the Confederate works in front of 17th Corps—McPhersons* and identifications in margins.
Engraved: *Battles and Leaders* III-541.

56.   THE LAST DAY OF THE VICKSBURG SIEGE
July 2, 1863; after an eyewitness sketch by the artist.
Pen, 12-3/4 x 20, signed *Theo. R. Davis.* Inscribed identifications in margins.
Engraved: *Battles and Leaders* III-529.
PLATE 259

57.   GRANT AND PEMBERTON DISCUSS TERMS
Vicksburg, July 3, 1863; after an eyewitness sketch by the artist.
Pen, 9-7/16 x 8. Inscribed *Grant & Pemberton met near this tree & went at once to the point now occupied* and identifications in margin.
Engraved: *Battles and Leaders* III-531.
PLATE 260

58.   LOGAN'S DIVISION ENTERING VICKSBURG
July 4, 1863; after an eyewitness sketch by the artist.
Pen, 11-1/4 x 16-1/8, signed *Theo. R. Davis.* Inscribed *Logans Division Entering by the Jackson Road / Vicksburg July 4th 63.*
Engraved: *Battles and Leaders* III-490.
PLATE 261

59.   GRANT'S ARRIVAL IN VICKSBURG
July 4, 1863; after an eyewitness sketch by the artist.
Pen, 8 x 12, signed *Theo. R. Davis.* Inscribed *Vicksburg July 4th 63 / Arrival of Genl Grant at Genl Pemberton's Vicks House.*
Engraved: *Battles and Leaders* III-543.
PLATE 262

60.   HAZEN'S ASSAULT ON BROWN'S FERRY
Chattanooga campaign, Oct. 27, 1863; after a sketch by the artist, 1863.
Pen, 11 x 16-1/4, signed *Theo. R. Davis.* Inscribed *Hazens Lodgement Brown's Ferry / Oct. 27th 1863. Opening the Cracker line to Chattanooga.*
Engraved: *Battles and Leaders* III-688.
PLATE 277

61.   AN INCIDENT AT NEW HOPE CHURCH
Battle of New Hope Church, Ga.; *c.* May 25, 1864; after an eyewitness sketch by the artist.
Pen, 12-1/4 x 6-3/8, signed *D.* Inscribed *An Incident Battle of New Hope Church. Bad fix for a Confederate Sharpshooter.*
PLATE 319

62.   SHERMAN AND THOMAS AT KENNESAW MOUNTAIN
Battle of Kennesaw Mountain, Ga., June 27, 1864; after an eyewitness sketch by the artist.
Pen, 14 x 11. Inscribed *Generals Sherman and Thomas at the Signal tree. June 27th 1864.*
Engraved: *Battles and Leaders* IV-272.
PLATE 322

63.   THE BATTLE OF PEACHTREE CREEK
Peachtree Creek, Ga., July 20, 1864; after an eyewitness sketch by the artist.
Pen, 9 x 12-1/2, signed *Theo. R. Davis.* Inscribed *Battle of Peachtree Creek July 20th '64 / General Jo. Hookers 20th corps. / Attack of Hardee & Stewarts Corps on the Army of the Cumberland. 4 miles north of Atlanta* and identifications in margins.
Engraved: *Battles and Leaders* IV-336.
PLATE 323

64.   PROTECTING SHERMAN'S WAGON TRAINS
Decatur, Ga., July 22, 1864; after an eyewitness sketch by the artist.
Pen, 4-1/16 x 8-1/4. Inscribed *Decatur July 22d '64 / Spragues Brigade saves the wagon trains of the Army.*
Engraved: *Battles and Leaders* IV-314.
Collection of Robert B. Mayo.
PLATE 324

65.   LAYING WASTE THE SHENANDOAH VALLEY
Federal troops, 1864; original illustration.
Pen and wash, 9 x 11 (sight size), signed *Theo. R. Davis.* Inscribed *All the mills were destroyed and forage was burned but dwellings were preserved— / Sheridan.*
Engraved: *St. Nicholas* June, 1887.
Collection of Robert B. Mayo.
PLATE 341

66.   THE PALMETTO MONUMENT, COLUMBIA
Carolinas campaign, Feb. 18, 1865; after an eyewitness sketch by the artist.
Pen, 6-3/4 x 6-1/4, signed *D.* Inscribed *Gen'l Shermans Soldiers Guarding the Palmetto Monument / Columbia S.C. / Feby. 65.*
Engraved: *Century* 34:931, Oct., 1887; *Battles and Leaders* IV-687.
PLATE 353

67. DECORATION DAY IN CHATTANOOGA
Graves of the Andrews raiders, 1883; original illustration.
Pen, 7-3/8 x 7-7/8, signed *Theo. R. Davis.* Inscribed *Decoration day—Chattanooga / National Cemetery—1883 / the Resting Place of the Bridge Burners.*
Engraved: *Battles and Leaders* II-715.
PLATE 378

WILL H. DRAKE

Water colorist and illustrator. Born New York, 1856; died Los Angeles, 1926. Much of Drake's work appeared in *Century* and *St. Nicholas*, with children and animals his specialty. He was best known for illustrating Kipling's "Jungle Stories," first published in *St. Nicholas*, and Richard Blackmore's *Lorna Doone.* He was a member of the Salmagundi and New York Water Color clubs, and was elected to the National Academy of Design in 1902.

68. GRANT'S HEADQUARTERS, FORT DONELSON
Fort Donelson, Tenn.; after photographs, 1884.
Tempera, 10 x 12, signed *W. H. Drake.* Two drawings. Inscribed *Gen'l Grant's Headquarters. (House of Jared Crisp.)*
Engraved: *Century* 29:293, Dec., 1884; *Battles and Leaders* I-413.

69. SCENES ON THE SHILOH BATTLEFIELD
After photographs, 1884.
Tempera, 11-7/8 x 9-7/8, signed *W. H. Drake.* Two drawings. Inscribed *Site of Old Shiloh Church / Shiloh Spring.*
Engraved: *Century* 29:593, Feb., 1885; *Battles and Leaders* I-469.

70. QUARTERS OF THE 52ND ILLINOIS, CORINTH, MISSISSIPPI
After a photograph by George Armstead, 1862.
Pen, 14 x 18, signed *Drake.*
Engraved: *Century* 32:917, Oct., 1886; *Battles and Leaders* II-755.
PLATE 154

71. ROULETTE'S FARM, ANTIETAM BATTLEFIELD
After wartime photographs.
Pen, 14-7/8 x 13-7/16, signed *Drake.* Three drawings. Inscribed title.
Engraved: *Century* 32:301, June, 1886; *Battles and Leaders* II-670.

72. SALEM CHURCH
Chancellorsville battlefield; after a postwar photograph.
Pen, 8-1/4 x 9-15/16, signed *Drake.*

73. MONITOR "LEHIGH"
After a wartime photograph.
Pen, 16-7/16 x 12-1/2, signed *Drake.* Inscribed title.

HUGH M. EATON

Illustrator, muralist, print-maker. Born Brooklyn, 1865; died Brooklyn, Sept. 14, 1924. Eaton was for ten years art editor of *Frank Leslie's Illustrated Newspaper*, and contributed art criticism as well as illustrations to the magazines of the period.

74. GUNBOATS "TYLER" AND "LEXINGTON" AT THE BATTLE OF SHILOH
After a lithographed sketch by Alfred E. Mathews, 1862.
Pen, 18 x 20-1/4. signed *H. M. Eaton.* Inscribed *Shiloh / Gunboats Tyler & Lexington supporting National troops.*
Engraved: *Battles and Leaders* I-592.

HARRY C. EDWARDS

Painter and illustrator. Born Philadelphia, 1868; died Brooklyn, 1922. Edwards studied at Adelphi College in Brooklyn and the Art Students' League. A member of the Salmagundi Club and the Brooklyn Society of Artists, he was primarily a book illustrator.

75. SCENES AT FORTRESS MONROE
Virginia peninsula; after photographs by Alexander Gardner, 1862.
Pen, 20-1/4 x 18-3/16, signed *H. C. Edwards.* Three drawings. Inscribed *1. Fortress Monroe & Light House / 2. Chesapeake Hospital / 3. The Sallyport F. Monroe.*
Engraved: *Battles and Leaders* II-143.

76. FEDERAL OBSERVATION BALLOON
Peninsula campaign; after a sketch by Robert K. Sneden, c. May, 1862.
Pen, 12-7/16 x 15-15/16. Inscribed *View from Courtneys rear of Savage's Station Va. showing Genl McClellan's head quarters at Dr. Trent's &c. Rebels shelling balloon from across the Chickahominy River.*
PLATE 104

77. SAVAGE'S STATION, VIRGINIA
After a sketch by Robert K. Sneden, June, 1862.
Pen, 9-5/8 x 14-1/4 on mount, signed *Edwards.* Inscribed *View of rear of Savage's—Showing the Peach orchard—open graves—Savage's Barns, Hospitals etc.*
Engraved: *Battles and Leaders* II-372.

HARRY FENN

Water colorist and illustrator. Born Richmond, England, 1838; died Montclair, N.J., April 22, 1911. Fenn emigrated to the United States in 1857, and studied art in Italy during the Civil War. Among the deluxe editions he illustrated were Whittier's *Snow Bound* and *Ballads of New England*, Gray's "Elegy," and Tennyson's *In Memoriam*, but his reputation for landscape studies derived primarily from his work for *Picturesque America* (1872-74), edited by William Cullen Bryant; he went on to illustrate *Picturesque Europe* and *Picturesque Palestine, Sinai and Egypt*. Fenn's magazine work was extensive, and he was a member of the Salmagundi Club and a founder of the American Water Color Society.

73

74

75

77

92

96

97

98

99

78. CONFEDERATE FORTIFICATIONS AT MANASSAS
JUNCTION
After a photograph by George N. Barnard and
James F. Gibson, March, 1862.
Pen, 8-7/8 x 12-3/4, signed *HF*. Inscribed title.
Engraved: *Century* 29:101, Nov., 1884; *Battles and
Leaders* I-231.
PLATE 21

79. THE BATTLE OF BELMONT
Nov. 7, 1861; after a sketch by eyewitness Henry
N. Walke.
Water color, 10-5/16 x 16-9/16. Inscribed *Battle of
Belmont. U.S. Gunboats attacking the Batteries of
Columbus, Ky.*
Engraved: *Century* 29:426, Jan., 1885; *Battles and
Leaders* I-360.
PLATE 24

80. PROVOST-MARSHAL'S OFFICE, CORINTH,
MISSISSIPPI
After a photograph by George Armstead, 1862.
Water color, 6-1/2 x 13, signed *HF*.
Engraved: *Century* 32:910, Oct., 1886; *Battles and
Leaders* II-739.
PLATE 37

81. PONTOON BRIDGE OVER THE RAPPAHANNOCK
Fredericksburg, Va.; after a photograph by Tim-
othy H. O'Sullivan, Dec., 1862.
Pen, 10-1/4 x 12-3/8. Inscribed *Franklin's Crossing,
Pontoon bridge across the Rappahannock.*
Engraved: *Century* 32:639, Aug., 1886; *Battles and
Leaders* III-129.
PLATE 46

82. GUNBOATS AT FORT DONELSON
Feb. 14, 1862; after a sketch by eyewitness Henry
N. Walke.
Water color, 11 x 15-1/4. Inscribed title.
Engraved: *Century* 29:433, Jan., 1885; *Battles and
Leaders* I-435.
PLATE 59

83. THE "CARONDELET" PASSING ISLAND NUMBER TEN
Mississippi River, April 4, 1862; after a sketch by
eyewitness Henry N. Walke.
Water color, 10-1/2 x 13. Inscribed title.
Engraved: *Century* 29:440, Jan., 1885; *Battles and
Leaders* I-440.
PLATE 69

84. THE FAIR OAKS BATTLEFIELD
Peninsula campaign; after photographs by George
N. Barnard, *c.* May, 1862.
Water color, 14-3/4 x 12-3/8, signed *HF*. Two
drawings. Inscribed *Fair Oaks. Rear view of old
houses. Graves of 400 soldiers. / Front view of
same.*
Engraved: *Century* 30:123, May, 1885; *Battles and
Leaders* II-232.
PLATE 109

85. DEPOT AND HOTEL, CORINTH
Corinth, Miss.; after a photograph by George Arm-
stead, 1862.
Pen, 7-7/8 x 12-5/8 on mount. Inscribed title.
Engraved: *Century* 32:907, Oct., 1886: *Battles and
Leaders* II-742.
PLATE 146

86. FORT MITCHELL, CINCINNATI
Sept., 1862; after a lithographed sketch by Alfred
E. Mathews, 1862.
Pen, 10-1/4 x 13-5/16. Inscribed *The 103rd Regt.
O.V., in line of battle at Fort Mitchell, Cincinnati,
Sept. 11, 62.*
PLATE 148

87. DEFENSE OF CAGE'S FORD
Perryville campaign, Nov., 1862; after a litho-
graphed sketch by Alfred E. Mathews, 1862.
Water color, 10-1/2 x 14-7/8, signed *HF*. Inscribed
*Bragg's Campaign / The Camp of the 31st Ohio
Vols. shelled by the troops under Col Basil Duke.
Craig's [sic] Ford, Cumberland Riv.*
Engraved: *Battles and Leaders* III-25.
PLATE 150

88. CONFEDERATE LINES, VICKSBURG
After a photograph, 1863.
Pen, 7-1/8 x 11-1/2. Inscribed title.
Engraved: *Battles and Leaders* III-483.
PLATE 252

89. SCENES IN VICKSBURG
After photographs, *c.* 1885.
Pen, 12-3/8 x 9-1/2. Three Drawings. Inscribed
(top) *Double cave in the Rigby Hill;* (center) *Sky
Parlor Hill. A signal station during the siege. Taken
while telephone pole was being erected. Vicksburg;*
(bottom) *Cave near machine shop.*
Engraved: *Battles and Leaders* III-486.
PLATE 256

90. EXPLOSION OF THE VICKSBURG MINE
June 25, 1863; after a lithographed sketch by
Alfred E. Mathews, 1863.
Pen, 10-1/16 x 14-3/4.
Engraved: *Battles and Leaders* III-525.
PLATE 257

91. THE FIGHT IN THE CRATER
Vicksburg, June 25, 1863; after a lithographed
sketch by Alfred E. Mathews, 1863.
Pen, 11-1/8 x 14-3/8. Inscribed *[Siege] of Vicks-
burg / the fight in the Crater of Fort Hill, after the
explosion of June 25 63.*
Engraved: *Battles and Leaders* III-527.
PLATE 258

92. VICKSBURG MONUMENTS
Vicksburg battlefield; after postwar photographs.
Pen, 12-5/8 x 9-1/2. Two drawings. Inscribed (top)
*The Monument that first stood on the spot of inter-
view between Genls Grant & Pemberton now
standing in the National Cemetery / Vicksburg;*
(bottom) *Monument on the spot of interview between Grant & Pemberton, where the oak tree
stood.*
Engraved: *Battles and Leaders* III-489.

93. THE ROSS HOUSE
Rossville, Ga.; after a photograph by George N.
Barnard, 1863.
Pen, 9-11/16 x 15, signed *HF*. Inscribed *Ross House
War Time.*
Engraved: *Century* 33:960, April, 1887; *Battles and
Leaders* III-637.
PLATE 270

94. LOOKOUT MOUNTAIN
Chattanooga, Tenn.; after a wartime photograph.
Pen, 13 x 20-3/4, signed *HF*. Inscribed *Lookout Mt —from hill whence Hooker directed the battle* and identifications in margin.
Engraved: *Century* 33:940, April, 1887; *Battles and Leaders* III-694.
PLATE 281

95. FORT NEGLEY, NASHVILLE
After photographs by George N. Barnard, 1864.
Pen, 11-1/2 x 12-1/8 on mount. Two drawings. Inscribed title.
Engraved: *Century* 34:610, Aug., 1887; *Battles and Leaders* IV-458.
PLATE 347

96. JOHNSON'S ISLAND BATTERY
Prisoner of war camp, Sandusky Bay, Ohio; after a wartime photograph.
Pen, 7-1/2 x 14-5/8, signed *HF*. Inscribed *View looking east from Fort Hill / Johnsons Island.*
Engraved: *Century* 41:708, March, 1891.

97. CONFEDERATE RAIDER "GEORGIA"
After a wartime photograph.
Pen, 10-3/16 x 14, signed *HF*. Inscribed title.
Engraved: *Century* 56:594, Aug., 1898.

98. THE FORT DONELSON BATTLEFIELD
Fort Donelson, Tenn.; after photographs, 1884.
Water color, 9 x 13. Two drawings. Inscribed *View from position of gunboats on Cumberland R. Looking east—at Fort Donelson—Hickman's Creek, and Isaac Williams house on the hill.*
Engraved: *Century* 29:301, Dec., 1884; *Battles and Leaders* I-414.

99. THE CUMBERLAND RIVER FROM FORT DONELSON
Fort Donelson, Tenn.; after a photograph, 1884.
Water color, 13-5/8 x 10-7/8. Inscribed *A glimpse of the Cumberland R. looking west from Earth works of Fort Donelson. Point where gun boats first appeared.*
Engraved: *Century* 29:292, Dec., 1884; *Battles and Leaders* I-404.

100. PILLOW'S POSITION, FORT DONELSON
Fort Donelson, Tenn.; after a photograph, 1884.
Water color, 13 x 10-1/4, signed *HF*. Inscribed *Pillow's position, showing water in the ditches.*
Engraved: *Century* 29:298, Dec., 1884; *Battles and Leaders* I-421.

101. THE BATTLEFIELD OF MALVERN HILL
Virginia peninsula; after photographs, 1885.
Pen, 5-1/2 x 12-1/4 on mount. Two drawings. Inscribed (top) *View of main battle field on the Crew farm. From center of Union position*; (bottom) *Main battle field looking toward Union position.*
Engraved: *Century* 30:622, 623, Aug., 1885; *Battles and Leaders* II-418, 419.
PLATE 365

102. FRAYSER'S FARM
Virginia peninsula; after a photograph, 1885.
Water color, 10-3/4 x 11-1/8, signed *HF*. Inscribed *National Cemetery, & Frayer's Farm house. From the Quaker Road (looking south).*
Engraved: *Century* 30:473, July, 1885; *Battles and Leaders* II-398.
PLATE 367

103. PERRYVILLE, KENTUCKY
After a photograph, 1885.
Pen, 9-1/4 x 12-1/2. Inscribed *Perryville from the Macville pike.*
Engraved: *Battles and Leaders* III-52.

104. THE PERRYVILLE BATTLEFIELD
Perryville, Ky.; after photographs, 1885.
Pen, 9-5/16 x 12-13/16, signed *HF*. Two drawings. Inscribed (top) *Spring that watered Braggs Army*; (bottom) *Pear tree 100 years old at the left of Rousseau's position.*
Engraved: *Battles and Leaders* III-21.
PLATE 369

105. ROUSSEAU'S POSITION, PERRYVILLE
Perryville, Ky.; after a photograph, 1885.
Pen, 5 x 7-13/16 (sight size). Inscribed *Rousseau's position looking N.W.*
Engraved: *Battles and Leaders* III-54.

106. WILDERNESS CHURCH
Virginia Wilderness; after a photograph, 1884.
Water color, 8-7/8 x 11-1/8 on mount. Inscribed title.
Engraved: *Century* 32:765, Sept., 1886; *Battles and Leaders* III-193.
PLATE 370

107. WINSTEAD HILL, FRANKLIN BATTLEFIELD
Franklin, Tenn.; after a photograph, c. 1885.
Water color, 9-1/2 x 14-7/8, signed *HF*. Inscribed *View of Winstead Hill, Columbia Pike where Hood formed line of battle. Federals behind stone wall in foreground.*
Engraved: *Century* 34:603, Aug., 1887; *Battles and Leaders* IV-445.

108. GENERAL GRANT'S HEADQUARTERS
Chattanooga (numbers 1, 3, 4) and Germanna Ford, Va. (number 2); after postwar photographs.
Water color, 15 x 15-7/8, signed *HF*. Four drawings. Inscribed partial identifications.
Engraved: *Century* 53:24, Nov., 1896.

WALTER J. FENN

Artist and illustrator, the son of artist Harry Fenn.

109. CORINTH DWELLINGS
Corinth, Miss.; after photographs, c. 1885.
Pen, 18-3/4 x 13-3/16, signed *W. J. Fenn*. Five drawings. Inscribed identifications in margin.
Engraved: *Century* 32:905, Oct., 1886; *Battles and Leaders* I-580.
PLATE 75

EDWIN FORBES

Newspaper artist-correspondent, painter, etcher. Born New York, 1839; died Brooklyn, March 6, 1895. After some training in the fine arts Forbes became a war artist for *Frank Leslie's Illustrated Newspaper* in 1861. He covered the Army of the Potomac throughout the war, and subsequently made extensive use of those wartime sketches. He published *Life Studies of the Great Army* (1876) and *Thirty Years After: An Artist's Story of the Great War* (1890), both heavily illustrated with his etchings, and illustrated a number of juvenile works of biography and history.

100

103

105

107

108

121

123

125

128

110.   THE BATTLE OF CROSS KEYS
June 8, 1862; after an eyewitness sketch by the artist.
Water color, 6 x 9-1/2, signed *E. Forbes.* Inscribed *Battle of Cross Keys. Looking east Sunday morning. Shield's fight took place where the cross is at Port Republic.*
Engraved: *Battles and Leaders* II-292.
PLATE 96

111.   THE BATTLE OF GROVETON
Aug. 28, 1862; after an eyewitness sketch by the artist.
Water color, 7-5/16 x 12-1/2, signed *EF.* Inscribed *Battle of Gainesville. Augst 27 1862 / Sketched from the west side of the Warrenton turnpike looking towards Washington.*
Engraved: *Century* 31:454, Jan., 1886; *Battles and Leaders* II-468.
PLATE 121

112.   RETREAT OF THE ARMY OF VIRGINIA
Rappahannock Station, Va., Aug. 18, 1862; after an eyewitness sketch by the artist.
Water color, 4-5/8 x 7-11/16 (sight size), signed *E. Forbes.* Inscribed *The Army of the Rappahannock Gen. Pope retreating over the Rap. river at Rappahannock Station. View from below the bridge.*
Engraved: *Century* 31:602, Feb., 1886; *Battles and Leaders* II-455.
PLATE 122

113.   MARCH OF LONGSTREET'S CORPS THROUGH
         THOROUGHFARE GAP
Aug. 28, 1862; original illustration.
Pen and wash, 6 x 9-3/4, signed *E.F.* Inscribed title.
Engraved: *Century* 31:607, Feb., 1886; *Battles and Leaders* II-514.
PLATE 124

114.   THE SECOND BATTLE OF BULL RUN
Aug. 30, 1862; after an eyewitness sketch by the artist.
Water color, 6-5/8 x 15, signed *Ed. Forbes.* Inscribed *Battle of 2nd Bull Run. Sat. 30th. View from a point between the Robinson & Henry houses. Looking toward Groveton. Time about 4 o'clock. Last day. McDowell in foreground.*
Engraved: *Century* 31:471, Jan., 1886; *Battles and Leaders* II-522.
PLATE 127

115.   HOOKER'S CORPS CROSSING ANTIETAM CREEK
Sept. 16, 1862; after an eyewitness sketch by the artist.
Water color, 5 x 7-1/4 (sight size), signed *E. Forbes.* Inscribed *Genl. Hooker's Corps crossing Antietam Creek to attack the left flank of Confederates under command of [Jackson].*
Engraved: *Century* 32:291, June, 1886; *Battles and Leaders* II-632.
PLATE 133

116.   CHARGE OF HOOKER'S CORPS AT THE DUNKER
         CHURCH
Battle of Antietam, Sept. 17, 1862; after an eyewitness sketch by the artist.
Water color, 8-1/4 x 9, signed *E. Forbes.* Inscribed title.
Engraved: *Century* 32:298, June, 1886; *Battles and Leaders* II-646.
PLATE 135

117.   BURNSIDE'S BRIDGE
Battle of Antietam, Sept. 17, 1862; after an eyewitness sketch by the artist.
Water color, 5-1/8 x 7-1/4 (sight size), signed *Edwin Forbes.* Inscribed *The charge over the Burnside bridge. 3 PM.*
Engraved: *Century* 32:310, June, 1886; *Battles and Leaders* II-652.
PLATE 137

118.   BURNSIDE'S ATTACK TOWARD SHARPSBURG
Battle of Antietam, Sept. 17, 1862; after an eyewitness sketch by the artist.
Water color, 5 x 7-5/16 (sight size), signed *E. Forbes.* Inscribed *Fairchild's brigade, Genl. Burnside's Corps, carrying the hill on the right flank of the Confederate position. The village of Sharpsburg in the distance. Sept. 17th. 5 p.m.*
Engraved: *Century* 32:311, June, 1886; *Battles and Leaders* II-654.
PLATE 138

119.   ABANDONING WINTER CAMP, FALMOUTH
Falmouth, Va., April 27, 1863; after an eyewitness sketch by the artist.
Water color, 8-1/4 x 12-9/16, signed *E.F.* Inscribed on verso *Abandoning the Winter Camps near Falmouth, Va. The first day's March of the Chancellorsville Campaign.*
Engraved: *Century* 32:746, Sept., 1886; *Battles and Leaders* III-173.
PLATE 230

120.   CROSSING THE RAPPAHANNOCK
April 28, 1863; after an eyewitness sketch by the artist.
Water color 8-1/4 x 12-1/2, signed *E.F.* Inscribed on verso *The right wing of the Army of the Potomac. Crossing the Rappahannock river on pontoons at Kellys Ford. View looking up stream. / Chancellorsville.*
Engraved: *Century* 32:746, Sept., 1886; *Battles and Leaders* III-156.
PLATE 231

121.   CROSSING THE RAPIDAN
April 29, 1863; after an eyewitness sketch by the artist.
Water color, 8-3/16 x 12-1/2, signed *E.F.* Inscribed on verso *The right wing of the Army of the Potomac, fording the Rapidan river at Elys Ford. View from the south bank. Wed. / Chancellorsville.*
Engraved: *Century* 32:747, Sept., 1886; *Battles and Leaders* III-174.

122.   READING HOOKER'S ADDRESS TO THE ARMY
Chancellorsville, Va., April 30, 1863; after an eyewitness sketch by the artist.
Water color, 8-1/4 x 12-1/2, signed *E.F.* Inscribed title on verso.
PLATE 233

123.   THE CHANCELLORSVILLE HOUSE
Battle of Chancellorsville, May 2, 1863; after an eyewitness sketch by the artist.
Water color, 8-1/4 x 12-1/2, signed *E. Forbes.* Inscribed on verso *The Chancellorsville House. Genl. Hookers Headquarters. Sketch made Sat. morning, showing the line of breastworks between the old and new plank road / Chancellorsville.*
Engraved: *Century* 32:751, Sept., 1886; *Battles and Leaders* III-162.

124. MEETING JACKSON'S FLANK ATTACK, CHANCELLORSVILLE
May 2, 1863; after an eyewitness sketch by the artist.
Water color, 8-1/4 x 12-1/2, signed *E.F.* Inscribed on verso *The repulse of Stonewall Jackson's Corps by artillery massed across the Wilderness Road. Sat. eve. / Chancellorsville.*
Engraved: *Century* 32:768, Sept., 1886; *Battles and Leaders* III-166.
PLATE 234

125. THE SECOND LINE, CHANCELLORSVILLE
May 3, 1863; after an eyewitness sketch by the artist.
Water color, 8-1/4 x 12-1/2, signed *E.F.* Inscribed on verso *The second line at Chancellorsville at the junction of the Elys ford road and road to United States ford. Sunday morning. / Chancellorsville.*
Engraved: *Century* 32:759, Sept., 1886; *Battles and Leaders* III-169.

126. RESCUING WOUNDED FROM THE BURNING WOODS
Battle of Chancellorsville, May 3, 1863; after an eyewitness sketch by the artist.
Water color, 8-1/4 x 12-1/2, signed *E.F.* Inscribed on verso *Rescuing the wounded from the burning woods between the opposing lines. Sunday. Chancellorsville.*
Engraved: *Century* 32:758, Sept., 1886; *Battles and Leaders* III-202.
PLATE 238

127. CONFEDERATE ASSAULT ON CEMETERY HILL
Battle of Gettysburg, July 2, 1863; after a sketch by the artist, July, 1863.
Pencil, 11-1/4 x 15-1/8, signed *EF.* Inscribed on verso *Charge on Cemetery Hill / 2nd day / 8 PM.*
Engraved: *Century* 33:295, Dec., 1886; *Battles and Leaders* III-311.
PLATE 242

128. CEMETERY GATE, GETTYSBURG
July 2, 1863; after a sketch by the artist, July, 1863.
Pencil, 11 x 15-1/4, signed *EF.* Inscribed on verso *View of Cemetery gate from rear. Scene of heavy fighting on the second day.*
Engraved: *Century* 33:290, Dec., 1886; *Battles and Leaders* III-380.

129. CONFEDERATE ASSAULT ON CULP'S HILL
Battle of Gettysburg, July 3, 1863; after a sketch by the artist, July, 1863.
Pencil, 11-1/4 x 15-5/8, signed *EF.* Inscribed on verso *Culp's Hill. The morning of the 3rd day. The point of the hill occupied by the 12th Corps Geary's Brigade.*
Engraved: *Century* 33:293, Dec., 1886; *Battles and Leaders* III-312.
PLATE 243

130. GERMANNA FORD ON THE RAPIDAN
May 5, 1864; after an eyewitness sketch by the artist.
Pencil, 9-15/16 x 13-7/8, signed *E.F.* Inscribed *The Army of the Potomac Crossing the Rapidan at Germanna Ford. May 5th 1864. 10:30 A.M.*
Engraved: *Century* 34:278, June, 1887; *Battles and Leaders* IV-119.
PLATE 289

131. HANCOCK'S CORPS ON THE BROCK ROAD
Battle of the Wilderness, May 7, 1864; after an eyewitness sketch by the artist.
Pencil, 9-15/16 x 13-7/8, signed *E.F.* Inscribed *Sketch of 2nd Corps front on the Brock Road taken on the morning of Sat. the 7th May.*
Engraved: *Century* 34:285, June, 1887; *Battles and Leaders* IV-127.
PLATE 291

132. FEDERAL ARTILLERY AT SPOTSYLVANIA
Battle of Spotsylvania, May 10, 1864; after an eyewitness sketch by the artist.
Pen, 4-1/4 x 12, signed *E.F.* Inscribed *Battle of Spotsylvania C.H.: the centre of the position on the morning of May 10th 1864.*
Engraved: *Century* 34:290, June, 1887; *Battles and Leaders* IV-176.
PLATE 295

133. BUILDING BREASTWORKS, COLD HARBOR
Battle of Cold Harbor, June 1, 1864; after an eyewitness sketch by the artist.
Pen, 8-7/8 x 14, signed *EF.* Inscribed *Building breastworks at Cold Harbor / June 1st 1864 near Hawes store.*
Engraved: *Century* 34:297, June, 1887; *Battles and Leaders* IV-224.

MALCOLM FRASER

Painter and illustrator. Born Montreal, April 19, 1869; died Brookhaven, N.Y., June 12, 1949. Fraser studied art in New York and Paris, and his illustrations appeared primarily in *Century, St. Nicholas,* and the *Ladies Home Journal.* He was a member of the Salmagundi Club.

134. CAMP CHASE
Prisoner of war camp, Columbus, Ohio; after a photograph by M. Witt, *c.* 1890.
Pen, 8-7/8 x 28-1/2 on mount.

135. BLOCKHOUSE, JOHNSON'S ISLAND
Prisoner of war camp, Sandusky Bay, Ohio; after a photograph, 1890.
Pen, 9-1/2 x 16-1/2, signed *Malcolm Fraser.* Inscribed title.
Engraved: *Century* 41:706, March, 1891.

136. GUARD HOUSE, JOHNSON'S ISLAND
Prisoner of war camp, Sandusky Bay, Ohio; after a photograph, 1890.
Pen, 8-5/8 x 11-1/4. Inscribed title.
Engraved: *Century* 41:707, March, 1891.

137. POWDER MAGAZINE, JOHNSON'S ISLAND
Prisoner of war camp, Sandusky Bay, Ohio; after a photograph, 1890.
Pen, 7-1/4 x 7-1/4. Inscribed title. On verso: artist's portrait study.
Engraved: *Century* 41:712, March, 1891.

133

134

135

136

137

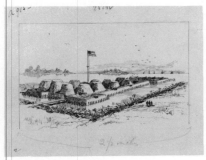
141

142

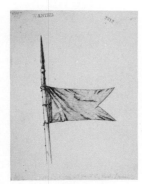
144

145

GEORGE GIBSON

138.   SCENES IN THE WILDERNESS
The Wilderness battlefield; after photographs by Mathew B. Brady, 1864.
Pen and wash, 17-3/8 x 10-7/8, signed *G. Gibson.* Two drawings. Inscribed on verso (top) *Union breastworks in woods between Dowdall's Tavern and Chancellorsville;* (bottom) *Relics of the dead in woods near Plank Road.*
Engraved: *Century* 32:767, Sept., 1886; *Battles and Leaders* III-199.
PLATE 292

139.   THE CRUMP HOUSE AND CRUMP'S LANDING
After photographs, 1884.
Water color, 11 x 12-3/16, signed *G. Gibson.* Two drawings. Inscribed titles.
Engraved: *Century* 29:597, Feb., 1885; *Battles and Leaders* I-467.
PLATE 368

WALTER H. GOATER

140.   WHARF BOAT, CAIRO, ILLINOIS
After a photograph, *c.* 1861.
Pen, 3-3/4 x 7 (sight size), signed *W.G.*
Engraved: *Battles and Leaders* I-359.
PLATE 25

141.   FORT MCALLISTER, SAVANNAH
After an unattributed wartime sketch.
Pen, 8-1/4 x 10-3/16, signed *W.G.* Inscribed *Rebel Fort McAllister.*
Engraved: *Century* 34:921, Oct., 1887; *Battles and Leaders* IV-683.

VALERIAN GRIBAYEDOFF

Illustrator and journalist. Born Kronstadt, Russia; died Paris, 1908. Emigrating to the United States as a youth, Gribayedoff settled in New York and wrote articles and reviews for local newspapers and magazines. He was a pioneer in newspaper illustration, and produced a popular series of humorous portraits for the New York *World.*

142.   COLONEL E. W. SERRELL
Siege of Charleston, 1863; after a wartime photograph.
Pen, 7-1/16 x 5-7/8, signed *V Gribayedoff Del.* Inscribed title.
Engraved: *Battles and Leaders* IV-70.

GEORGE R. HALM

Illustrator and decorative artist. Born Ogdensburg, N.Y., 1850; died 1899.

143.   15-INCH GUN
Defenses of Washington; after a wartime photograph by Alexander Gardner.
Pen, 5-3/4 x 8-3/16, signed *G. R. Halm.*
Engraved: *Battles and Leaders* IV-206.
PLATE 28

144.   CAVALRY LANCE PENNANT
After a wartime photograph.
Pen, 10-5/8 x 8-1/4, signed *G.R.H.* Inscribed *Lance used 1861-3 by the 6th Pa. V.C., Rush's Lancers.*
Engraved: *Battles and Leaders* III-215.

145.   OLD CAPITOL PRISON, WASHINGTON
After a wartime photograph by William R. Pywell.
Pen, 5-1/4 x 8-1/8, signed *G. R. Halm.* Inscribed title.

HUGHSON HAWLEY

Illustrator, water colorist, architectural artist. Born England, 1850; died Brighton, England, May 11, 1936. Most of Hawley's life was spent in the United States; he maintained a studio in New York for more than 50 years. His illustrations appeared in *Harper's Weekly, Century,* and *Scribner's.*

146.   SPROUT'S SPRING MILL, OPEQUON CREEK, VIRGINIA
After a sketch by Robert K. Sneden, 1864.
Pen, 6-1/8 x 10-1/2 (sight size), signed *Hughson Hawley.* Inscribed *Sprout's Spring Mill— Oppequon River—Virginia / Hospital of 6th army corps during the battle of Winchester. Sept. 18th 1864.*
Engraved: *Battles and Leaders* IV-505.
PLATE 336

147.   APPOMATTOX COURT HOUSE, VIRGINIA
After a sketch by Robert K. Sneden, April, 1865.
Pen, 9-1/2 x 13-1/2, signed *Hughson Hawley.* Inscribed title.
Engraved: *Century* 35:141, Nov., 1887; *Battles and Leaders* IV-731.
PLATE 361

THOMAS HOGAN

An Irish-born lithographer, Hogan was a long-time partner of artist Frank H. Schell in a lithographic firm in New York after the Civil War. He contributed illustrations to *Appleton's Journal.*

148.   CAMP OVEN
Federal camp; after a sketch by Frank H. Schell, 1861.
Pen, 6-3/4 x 11 (sight size), signed *Thos. Hogan.*
Engraved: *Battles and Leaders* II-157.
PLATE 40

149.   CAMP OF THE MILITARY TELEGRAPH CORPS, BRANDY STATION, VIRGINIA
Federal camp; after a photograph by Timothy H. O'Sullivan, April, 1864.
Pen, 8-5/16 x 10-1/16, signed *Tho. Hogan.*
Engraved: *Century* 38:785, Sept., 1889; *Battles and Leaders* IV-88,
PLATE 153

150.   BURNSIDE'S HEADQUARTERS, ROANOKE ISLAND, NORTH CAROLINA
After a sketch by Frank H. Schell, March, 1862.
Pen, 10-3/8 x 12, signed *Thos. Hogan / from Sketch by Frank H. Schell / March 1862.* Inscribed title.
Engraved: *Battles and Leaders* I-666.

151.   FORT MACON AFTER ITS SURRENDER
Morehead City, N.C.; after sketches by Frank H. Schell, April, 1862.
Pen, 12-1/4 x 15-1/2, signed *Thos. Hogan from Frank H. Schell's sketch, April, 1862.* Two drawings.
Engraved: *Battles and Leaders* I-653.
PLATE 191

152. CONFEDERATE BATTERY, GOSPORT NAVY YARD
Norfolk, Va.; after a sketch by Frank H. Schell, May, 1862.
Pen, 11 x 13-7/16, signed *Thos. Hogan.* Inscribed *Confederate battery on the terraced magazine in the Gosport Navy Yard commanding the land approach to the yard. Sketched by Frank H. Schell May 1862.*
Engraved: *Battles and Leaders* II-191.

M. H. HOKE

153. PLYMOUTH, NORTH CAROLINA
After a wartime sketch, possibly by the artist.
Pen, 7-9/16 x 14, signed *M. H. Hoke.* Inscribed on verso *View of Plymouth, N. Carolina, for "Albemarle" article. Copied from / (See letter from Miss Mattie H. Hoke, Mch. 21st/88).*

154. BUILDING C.S.S. "ALBEMARLE"
Roanoke River, N.C., 1864; after a wartime sketch, possibly by the artist.
Pen, 11 x 19-3/8, signed *M. H. Hoke.* Inscribed *[Build]ing of the Albemarle at Edward's Ferry.*
PLATE 220

CHARLES KENDRICK

Illustrator. Died Brooklyn, N.Y., June 16, 1914. Employed as a staff artist for *Frank Leslie's Illustrated Weekly.*

155. SENTRY ON DUTY
Probably after a wartime sketch by Alfred R. Waud.
Pen, 12-1/8 x 7-1/2, signed *Kendrick.* Inscribed *Sentry at Gen. Meades Tent. From life/114th Penn.*

156. A SAP ROLLER
Siege of Petersburg; after a drawing by Alfred R. Waud (Plate 304).
Pen, 12-1/2 x 15-1/4, signed *Kendrick.* Inscribed *Making approaches to the enemies Works under cover of the Sap Roller.*

157. CARRYING POWDER TO THE PETERSBURG MINE
Siege of Petersburg, July, 1864; after a sketch by Alfred R. Waud, 1864.
Pen, 12-1/8 x 15-1/16, signed *Kendrick.* Inscribed title.
Engraved: *Battles and Leaders* IV-550.

WILLIAM L. LATHROP

Landscape artist. Born Warren, Ill., 1859; died New Hope, Pa., 1938. Lathrop was a self-taught artist. His paintings went into the collections of, among others, the Metropolitan Museum of Art, the National Gallery, and the Minneapolis Art Museum.

158. THE SHILOH BATTLEFIELD
After photographs, 1885.
Pen, 12-3/4 x 12-1/2, signed *W. Lathrop.* Two drawings. Inscribed title.
Engraved: *Century* 29:768, March, 1886; *Battles and Leaders* I-561.

150

156

152

157

153

158

155

161

167

162

168

165 A

171

165 B

174

166

175

159.   FORT ST. PHILIP
New Orleans; after a photograph, 1886.
Pen, 4-3/8 x 8 (sight size), signed *W. Lathrop / 85.*
Inscribed *Entrance to Fort St. Philip.*
Engraved: *Century* 29:927, April, 1885; *Battles and Leaders* II-89.
PLATE 372

EDWIN J. MEEKER

A book and magazine illustrator, Meeker was commissioned most often by *Scribner's, Century,* and *Harper's Weekly.*

160.   SECESSION HALL, CHARLESTON
After a photograph by George S. Cook, *c.* 1861.
Pen, 11-1/8 x 7-3/4, on mount, signed *E.J.M.*
Engraved: *Battles and Leaders* I-78.
PLATE 2

161.   FORT SUMTER BARBETTE BATTERY AFTER THE
         SURRENDER
After a photograph, April, 1861.
Pen, 9-5/8 x 10-1/2 on mount, signed *E. J. Meeker.*
Inscribed *Barbette battery, right flank (Sea face) of Fort Sumpter—after Surrender—1861.*
Engraved: *Battles and Leaders* I-63.

162.   CONFEDERATE BATTLE FLAG
Drawn from a flag sewn in 1861 for General Earl Van Dorn.
Pen, 12-5/8 x 9-1/2. Inscribed title.
Engraved: *Century* 34:585, Aug., 1887; *Battles and Leaders* I-160.

163.   THE WASHINGTON ARSENAL
After a photograph by A. J. Russell, *c.* 1860.
Pen, 8-3/4 x 12-3/8 (sight size), signed *E. J. Meeker.* Inscribed *Arsenal—Washington / North Front / interior court.*
Engraved: *Battles and Leaders* I-12.
PLATE 14

164.   CAMP BURGESS, BOWLING GREEN, KENTUCKY
Federal camp; after a lithographed sketch by Alfred E. Mathews, 1861.
Pen, 9-3/4 x 13-1/8. Inscribed title and *Camp of the 70th Indiana Vols. Col. B. Harrison—Including a view of the Fortifications erected by the Rebel Genl. Buckner—the Regiment on dress parade. Sketched by A. E. Mathews, 31st O.V.I.*
Engraved: *Battles and Leaders* I-544.
PLATE 29

165.   THE WILSON'S CREEK BATTLEFIELD
Wilson's Creek, Mo.; after postwar photographs.
Pen, 12-1/2 x 31, signed *E.J.M.* Two sections. Inscribed title.
Engraved: *Battles and Leaders* I-294.

166.   MOUNT OLIVET CHURCH AND CLAREMONT
Fairfax Court House, Va.; after sketches by Robert K. Sneden, Sept., 1861.
Pen, 12-1/4 x 14-1/2. Two drawings. Inscribed (top) *Mount Olivet Church—Old Fairfax Road, Va. / Picket post of 40th N. Y. Sept 1861;* (bottom) *"Claremont" Residence of Comm. Forrest, Rebel Navy. Picket Post of 40th N.Y. Sept. 1861.*
Engraved: *Battles and Leaders* II-117.

167. CONFEDERATE WORKS, MUNSON'S HILL, VIRGINIA
After a sketch by Robert K. Sneden, Sept., 1861.
Pen, 9-3/8 x 15-3/4. Inscribed *Rebel works on Munson's Hill Va. / from Union advance posts, Bailey's Cross Roads, Sept 1861.*
Engraved: *Battles and Leaders* II-115.

168. BALL'S BLUFF, VIRGINIA
After a photograph, *c.* 1885.
Pen, 11-1/8 x 14, signed *E. J. Meeker.*
Engraved: *Battles and Leaders* II-128.

169. CAMP OF THE 40TH NEW YORK, ALEXANDRIA, VIRGINIA
After a sketch by Robert K. Sneden, Oct., 1861.
Pen, 10-3/8 x 13-3/8, signed *E.J.M.* Inscribed *Alexandria and Fort Lyon—Va. / from Camp of 40th N.Y. Vols. Oct. 1861.*
Engraved: *Battles and Leaders* II-162.
PLATE 30

170. HEADQUARTERS OF GENERAL SEDGWICK
Near Washington; after a sketch by Robert K. Sneden, Jan., 1862.
Pen, 11-1/2 x 15-1/4, signed *E.J.M.* Inscribed *Headquarters of Brig. Genl. John Sedgwick, U.S.A. / Leesburg Turnpike Va. Jany 1862.*
Engraved: *Battles and Leaders* II-163.
PLATE 32

171. CONFEDERATE BATTERY AT BUDD'S FERRY ON THE POTOMAC
After a sketch by Robert K. Sneden, Feb., 1862.
Pen, 9-5/16 x 15-1/2. Inscribed *Rebel Battery at Budd's Ferry Va. Potomac River / February 1862.*
Engraved: *Battles and Leaders* II-187.

172. COMMISSARY DEPOT AND HEADQUARTERS, PETERSBURG, VIRGINIA
Federal camp; after photographs by Timothy H. O'Sullivan, Nov., 1864.
Pen, 15-5/8 x 13-3/4, signed *E. J. Meeker.* Two drawings. Inscribed *1—Commissary Depot, Cedar Level—Petersburg / 2—50th N.Y. Engineers—Commissary Dept. Petersburg.*
PLATE 44

173. MILITARY RAILROAD BRIDGE OVER POTOMAC CREEK
After a photograph, 1864.
Pen, 6 x 13-1/2 (sight size), signed *E.J.M.* Inscribed *Military Rail Road bridge over Potomac Creek on the Richmond Fredericksburg and Potomac RR.*
PLATE 45

174. THE LOGAN'S CROSSROADS BATTLEFIELD
Logan's Crossroads, Ky.; after a photograph, 1887.
Pen, 12-1/16 x 12-1/8, signed *E. J. Meeker.*
Engraved: *Battles and Leaders* I-392.

175. PITTSBURG LANDING, TENNESSEE
After a photograph, 1885.
Pen, 9-5/16 x 12-7/8 on mount, signed *EJM.*
Engraved: *Century* 31:762, March, 1886; *Battles and Leaders* I-488.

176. WATERHOUSE'S BATTERY, SHILOH
Federal artillery; after a sketch by Dr. E. W. Andrews, April, 1862.
Pen, 9-13/16 x 13-1/8. Inscribed title.
Engraved: *Battles and Leaders* I-471.
PLATE 63

177. THE HORNET'S NEST, SHILOH
After a photograph, 1885.
Pen, 9-3/8 x 12-3/8, signed *E.J.M.* Inscribed title.
Engraved: *Battles and Leaders* I-588.

177

178. MORTAR BOATS SHELLING ISLAND NUMBER TEN
Mississippi River, March, 1862; after a sketch by eyewitness Henry N. Walke.
Pen, 13-3/4 x 16-3/4, signed *E.J.M.*
Engraved: *Century* 29:438, Jan., 1885; *Battles and Leaders* I-438.
PLATE 68

179. INTERIOR OF FORT ST. PHILIP
New Orleans; after a postwar photograph.
Pen, 9-5/8 x 14, signed *E. J. Meeker.*
Engraved: *Century* 32:444, July, 1886; *Battles and Leaders* II-76.

179

180. THE UNITED STATES MINT, NEW ORLEANS
After a photograph.
Pen, 9-3/16 x 13-3/4, signed *E. J. Meeker.* Inscribed title.
Engraved: *Century* 32:456, July, 1886.

181. QUARTERS OF IMPRISONED CONFEDERATE OFFICERS, NEW ORLEANS
After photographs.
Pen, 9-11/16 x 10-1/2, signed *E.J.M.* Two drawings. Inscribed *Houses on Rampart St. used as prison for C.S. Officers.*
Engraved: *Century* 32:485, July, 1886; *Battles and Leaders* III-583.

180

182. HALLECK'S ARMY ON THE MARCH TO CORINTH
Corinth, Miss., May, 1862; after a lithographed sketch by Alfred E. Mathews, 1862.
Pen, 11-3/8 x 18-7/8, signed *E.J.M.* Inscribed *On the March from Hamburg to Camp before Corinth.*
Engraved: *Battles and Leaders* II-717.
PLATE 74

183. BUILDING BREASTWORKS BEFORE CORINTH
Corinth, Miss., May, 1862; after a lithographed sketch by Alfred E. Mathews, 1862.
Pen, 8 x 13 (sight size), signed *E.J.M.* Inscribed *The 31st Ohio Vols. building breastworks before Corinth.*
Engraved: *Battles and Leaders* II-719.
PLATE 76

181

184. ENCAMPMENT OF POPE'S ARMY, CORINTH
Corinth, Miss., May, 1862; after a lithographed sketch by Alfred E. Mathews, 1862.
Pen, 8-7/8 x 19, signed *E.J.M.* Inscribed title.
Engraved: *Battles and Leaders* II-721.

185. THE KERNSTOWN BATTLEFIELD
Kernstown, Va.; after a photograph, 1885.
Pen, 10-1/8 x 16, signed *EJM.* Inscribed *Kernstown Battlefield Va. Sept. 1885. Stone wall, on this side Jackson formed his line of battle. / Mar. 1862.*
Engraved: *Battles and Leaders* II-309.

184

186. THE RUINS OF HAMPTON, VIRGINIA
After a sketch by Robert K. Sneden, *c.* March, 1862.
Pen, 11-1/2 x 12-5/16. Inscribed *Ruins of Hampton Va. Burnt by order of Gen. Magruder C.S.A. Aug. 7, 1861.*
Engraved: *Battles and Leaders* II-152.
PLATE 91

185

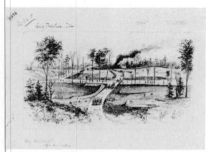

187

190

193

196

187. CONFEDERATE WORKS, BIG BETHEL, VIRGINIA
After a sketch by Robert K. Sneden, April, 1862.
Pen, 9-1/2 x 14-1/4. Inscribed title.
Engraved: *Battles and Leaders* II-150.

188. BATTERY NUMBER 4, YORKTOWN
Federal siege guns, Peninsula campaign; after a sketch by Robert K. Sneden, April, 1862.
Pen, 9-1/4 x 14-1/4, signed *E.J.M.* Inscribed *View from Battery no. 4 / The 13 inch mortars—looking towards Yorktown, 16 Apr. 1862.*
Engraved: *Battles and Leaders* II-171.
PLATE 98

189. HEINTZELMAN'S HEADQUARTERS BEFORE YORKTOWN
Federal camp, Peninsula campaign; after a sketch by Robert K. Sneden, c. April, 1862.
Pen, 8-15/16 x 14-1/4 on mount, signed *E.J.M.* Inscribed title and *3rd Army Corps at Howe's Sawmill. Before Yorktown.*
Engraved: *Battles and Leaders* II-169.
PLATE 99

190. THE CLARK HOUSE, YORKTOWN
Peninsula campaign; after a sketch by Robert K. Sneden, April, 1862.
Pen, 9-5/8 x 12-15/16. Inscribed *Clark's House / near the Sawmill front of Yorktown / Hospital of 3rd Army Corps—Apl 11, 1862.*
Engraved: *Battles and Leaders* II-172.

191. UNION TROOPS ENTERING YORKTOWN
Peninsula campaign, May 4, 1862; after a sketch by Robert K. Sneden, May, 1862.
Pen, 11-7/16 x 16-1/2, signed *E.J.M.* Inscribed *View on Main St. Yorktown May 4, 1862. Union troops marching in.*
Engraved: *Battles and Leaders* II-173.
PLATE 100

192. RUINS OF THE HENRY HOUSE
Bull Run battlefield; after a photograph by Alexander Gardner, March, 1862.
Pen, 9 x 10-3/16, signed *E.J.M.*
Engraved: *Century* 30:92, May, 1885; *Battles and Leaders* II-511.
PLATE 126

193. HARPER'S FERRY, VIRGINIA
After a photograph by James Gardner, July, 1865.
Pen, 13-1/4 x 14-3/4, signed *E.J.M.*
Engraved: *Century* 29:283, Dec., 1884, and 32:286, June, 1886; *Battles and Leaders* II-155.

194. LEE'S HEADQUARTERS, SHARPSBURG
Sharpsburg, Md.; after a photograph, 1885.
Pen, 11-1/2 x 11-5/8, signed *E.J.M.*
Engraved: *Century* 32:287, June, 1886; *Battles and Leaders* II-666.
PLATE 131

195. CUMBERLAND GAP
Federal encampment, 1862; after a wartime lithograph.
Pen, 12-5/8 x 16-1/8. Inscribed identifications.
Engraved: *Battles and Leaders* III-67.
PLATE 147

196. FEDERAL FORT, MUNFORDVILLE, KENTUCKY
After a photograph, 1886.
Pen, 12-3/4 x 16-1/4, signed *E. J. Meeker.* Inscribed *South Bank of Green River . . . Hardon Co. Ky. Wilder surrendered here to Bragg . . . bridge in distance—Hart Co. Ky.*
Engraved: *Battles and Leaders* III-9.

197. HEADQUARTERS, ARMY OF THE POTOMAC, BRANDY STATION, VIRGINIA
After a photograph by Timothy H. O'Sullivan, Feb., 1864.
Pen, 4-3/4 x 10-1/4 (sight size), signed *E.J.M.* Inscribed title.
Engraved: *Battles and Leaders* IV-97.

198. CAMP OF THE ONEIDA CAVALRY, PETERSBURG, VIRGINIA
Federal camp; after a photograph, Feb., 1865.
Pen, 12-1/2 x 15-1/4, signed *E. J. Meeker.* Inscribed title.
PLATE 152

199. CAMP ORDERLIES
Federal camp; after a photograph, 1862.
Pen, 13-1/4 x 16-3/4, signed *E. J. Meeker—85.* Inscribed *Orderlies & Servants.*
Engraved: *Century* 30:633, Aug., 1885.

200. PREACHING AT CAMP DICK ROBINSON, KENTUCKY
Federal camp; after a lithographed sketch by Alfred E. Mathews, 1861.
Pen, 9-7/8 x 13-1/8. Inscribed *Rev. L. F. Drake, Chap. 31st Ohio Vols Preaching at Camp Dick Robinson, Ky. Nov 10th 1861.*
Engraved: *Battles and Leaders* I-569.
PLATE 163

201. THE FARM HOUSE, CAMP DICK ROBINSON, KENTUCKY
Federal camp; after an unattributed wartime sketch.
Pen, 10-7/8 x 11-13/16. Inscribed *Residence of Rich'd M. Robinson / On the Danville & Lexington turnpike—Kentucky.*
Engraved: *Battles and Leaders* I-381.

202. CROSSING FISHING CREEK
Federal troops, Kentucky; after a lithographed sketch by Alfred E. Mathews, 1862.
Pen, 8-7/16 x 13-9/16 (sight size).
Engraved: *Battles and Leaders* I-547.
PLATE 166

203. TUG "PLATO" SEARCHING FOR TORPEDOES
Stono River, S.C.; after a sketch by Horatio L. Wait, 1863.
Pen, 4-1/8 x 9-1/4 (sight size), signed *E J Meeker.* Inscribed title.
Engraved: *Battles and Leaders* IV-27.
PLATE 186

204. CONFEDERATE TORPEDOES AND TORPEDO BOATS
After wartime sketches by Horatio L. Wait.
Pen, 18-1/2 x 13-3/4, signed *E J Meeker.* Inscribed identifications in margin.
Engraved: *Century* 56:926, Oct., 1898.
PLATE 187

205. DISMAL SWAMP CANAL
N.C.; after a wartime sketch by Horatio L. Wait.
Pen, 10-1/8 x 13-1/8, signed *E. J. Meeker.* Inscribed
title.
Engraved: *Battles and Leaders* I-658.

206. FREDERICKSBURG, VIRGINIA
After a wartime photograph by Mathew B. Brady.
Pen, 11-3/8 x 18-3/8, signed *E. J. Meeker.* Inscribed
on verso *Fredericksburg—from Willis' Hill. /
Present site of Federal Cemetery.*
Engraved: *Century* 32:632, Aug., 1886; *Battles and
Leaders* III-89.

207. FEDERAL REINFORCEMENTS AT MURFREESBORO
Battle of Murfreesboro, Dec. 31, 1862; after a litho-
graphed sketch by Alfred E. Mathews, 1863.
Pen, 12-3/8 x 19, signed *E. J. Meeker.* Inscribed *The
Battle of Stone River or Murfreesboro. (Position of
Sam. Beatty's Brigade) Dec 31st 1862—from Sketch
by A. E. Matthews.*
Engraved: *Battles and Leaders* III-622.
PLATE 267

208. POSITION OF HOVEY'S DIVISION, SIEGE OF
        VICKSBURG
After a lithographed sketch by Alfred E. Mathews,
1863.
Pen, 12-3/8 x 18-3/4, signed *E.J.M.* Inscribed title.
Engraved: *Battles and Leaders* III-523.

209. POSITION OF QUINBY'S DIVISION, SIEGE OF
        VICKSBURG
After a lithographed sketch by Alfred E. Mathews,
1863.
Pen, 12-3/8 x 18-3/4, signed *E.J.M.* Inscribed *The
Siege of Vicksburg. / Representing position of 7th
Division / Genl. McPherson's Corps.*
Engraved: *Battles and Leaders* III-524.

210. THE MARSH BATTERY, MORRIS ISLAND
Charleston Harbor; after a sketch by Horatio L.
Wait, 1863.
Pen, 6 x 12-1/4. Inscribed *"Swamp Angel" Battery
/ Charleston, S.C.*
Engraved: *Battles and Leaders* IV-71.

211. CAPTAIN HUGUENIN, HEADQUARTERS ROOM,
        FORT SUMTER
Captain Thomas A. Huguenin, C.S.A., Dec. 7,
1864; after an unattributed wartime sketch.
Pen, 12-5/16 x 18-5/8, signed *E.J.M.* Inscribed title.
Engraved: *Battles and Leaders* IV-24.

212. PANORAMA OF THE CHATTANOOGA AREA
After a wartime lithograph.
Pen, 9 x 17-7/8. Inscribed title and identifications.
Engraved: *Century* 33:941, April, 1887; *Battles and
Leaders* III-690.
PLATE 274

213. ARMY OF THE CUMBERLAND, CHATTANOOGA
After a lithographed sketch by Alfred E. Mathews,
1863.
Pen, 9-3/4 x 14-7/16 on mount. Inscribed title.
Engraved: *Battles and Leaders* III-682.
PLATE 276

214. KNOXVILLE, TENNESSEE
After a wartime lithograph.
Pen, 4-3/16 x 15-1/2 on mount. Inscribed *Knoxville
Tenn— / from Fort Stanley.*

197

208

199

209

201

210

205

211

206

214

216

218

219

223

215. FORT STANLEY, KNOXVILLE
After a photograph, *c.* Dec., 1863.
Pen, 6 x 8 (sight size). Inscribed *A part of Fort Stanley—Knoxville Tenn.*
Engraved: *Battles and Leaders* III-749.
PLATE 279

216. BULLETIN BOARD ANNOUNCEMENT OF BATTLE
BETWEEN "ALABAMA" AND "KEARSARGE"
London, June, 1864; original illustration.
Pen, 11-3/4 x 9, signed *E.J.M.*

217. CONFEDERATE LINES BEFORE PETERSBURG
Siege of Petersburg; after a photograph by Alexander Gardner, 1865.
Pen, 7-5/8 x 10-3/4 (sight size), signed *E.J.M.* Inscribed *Mahone's Front looking toward Fort Steadman.*
Engraved: *Battles and Leaders* IV-714.
PLATE 309

218. AFTER THE BATTLE OF THE CRATER
Siege of Petersburg, *c.* Aug., 1864; after a sketch by Lieutenant Henderson, C.S.A.
Pen, 12-1/4 x 17, signed *E.J.M.* Inscribed *Drawn after Battle of Crater by Lieut Henderson, on Staff of Gen. Walter H. Stevens, Chief Engineer, Army Northern Va. C.S.A.*
Engraved: *Century* 34:769, Sept., 1887; *Battles and Leaders* IV-557.

219. THE RESACA BATTLEFIELD
Resaca, Ga.; after a photograph by George N. Barnard, 1864.
Pen, 12-1/2 x 16-1/2, signed *E. J. Meeker.*
Engraved: *Battles and Leaders* IV-298.

220. CONFEDERATE DEFENSES AT ETOWAH BRIDGE
Etowah River, Ga.; after a photograph by George N. Barnard, 1864.
Pen, 12-1/2 x 16-1/2, signed *E. J. Meeker.* Inscribed title.
Engraved: *Battles and Leaders* IV-283.
PLATE 317

221. CONFEDERATE ENTRENCHMENTS AT NEW HOPE CHURCH
New Hope Church, Ga.; after a photograph by George N. Barnard, 1864.
Pen, 11-3/16 x 14-7/8, signed *E. J. Meeker.*
Engraved: *Century* 34:593, Aug., 1887; *Battles and Leaders* IV-307.
PLATE 318

222. THE DEFENSES OF ATLANTA
After photographs by George N. Barnard, 1864.
Pen, 17-1/4 x 14-1/4, signed *E. J. Meeker.* Three drawings. Inscribed (top) *The Potter House, Atlanta;* (center) *View of Conf. lines from first fort east of W & A RR looking eastward;* (bottom) *View from Conf. fort on Peach Tree Street north of Atlanta—looking north-west.*
Engraved: *Century* 34:459, July, 1887; *Battles and Leaders* IV-340.
PLATE 320

223. THE SITE OF GENERAL MCPHERSON'S DEATH
Atlanta, Ga.; after photographs by George N. Barnard, 1864.
Pen, 16-3/8 x 13-5/8, signed *E. J. Meeker.* Two drawings. Inscribed title.
Engraved: *Century* 34:455, July, 1887; *Battles and Leaders* IV-315.

224. STRASBURG, VIRGINIA
After a photograph, 1885.
Pen, 6 x 10-5/8, signed *EJM.* Inscribed *Fishers Hill Va. Sept. 1885. / From Bank's Ford, across Strasburg, to Fisher's Hill.*
Engraved: *Battles and Leaders* II-289.

225. POPLAR SPRINGS CHURCH, PETERSBURG
Siege of Petersburg; after a photograph by Timothy H. O'Sullivan, 1864.
Pen, 9-3/16 x 15-3/4, signed *E.J.M.* Inscribed *50th N.Y. Engineers / Officers Quarters & church—Petersburg.*
PLATE 332

226. MILITARY CEMETERY, CITY POINT
Siege of Petersburg; after a photograph, 1865.
Pen, 4-1/2 x 8 (sight size). Inscribed *Soldiers graves at City Point.*
Engraved: *Century* 35:152, Nov., 1887; *Battles and Leaders* IV-753.
PLATE 333

227. GRACIE'S SALIENT, PETERSBURG
Siege of Petersburg; after a photograph by Timothy H. O'Sullivan, May, 1865.
Pen, 11-3/4 x 15-1/2, signed *E. J. Meeker.* Inscribed *Interior view of Confederate Line at Gracie's Salient, May, 1865.*
Engraved: *Battles and Leaders* IV-543.
PLATE 334

228. THE BENTONVILLE BATTLEFIELD
Bentonville, N.C., March 20, 1865; after a sketch by James E. Taylor engraved in *Frank Leslie's Illustrated Newspaper,* April 22, 1865, p. 76.
Pen, 5-3/8 x 16-1/2 (sight size), signed *E.J.M.* Inscribed *Bentonville N.C. / The morning after the battle—great quantities of Rosin fired by the Rebels.*
Engraved: *Century* 34:939, Oct., 1887; *Battles and Leaders* IV-695.
PLATE 355

229. SKIRMISHING IN FAYETTEVILLE
Fayetteville, N.C., March 11, 1865; after sketches by James E. Taylor engraved in *Frank Leslie's Illustrated Newspaper,* April 8, 1865, p. 45.
Pen, 12-1/2 x 18-3/4, signed *E.J.M.* Two drawings. Inscribed *1—Arsenal at Fayetteville / 2—Sherman's men driving Rebels out of Fayetteville / Mch 11—1865.*
Engraved: *Century* 34:935, Oct., 1887; *Battles and Leaders* IV-690.
PLATE 356

230. GOLDSBOROUGH, NORTH CAROLINA
March, 1865; after a sketch by James E. Taylor engraved in *Frank Leslie's Illustrated Newspaper,* April 22, 1865, p. 76.
Pen, 4-7/8 x 15-7/8 (sight size), signed *E.J.M.* Inscribed title.
Engraved: *Battles and Leaders* IV-754.

231. UNION WAGON TRAIN ENTERING PETERSBURG
April 3, 1865; after a photograph by John Reekie, April, 1865.
Pen, 12-1/2 x 15-1/8, signed *E.J.M.* Inscribed title.
PLATE 357

232. PREPARING FOR THE GRAND REVIEW,
     WASHINGTON
After a photograph by Alexander Gardner, May,
1865.
Pen, 7-1/2 x 11-1/8, signed *E.J.M.* Inscribed *Reviewing Stand.*
Engraved: *Battles and Leaders* IV-758.

233. NATIONAL CEMETERY, LOGAN'S CROSSROADS,
     KENTUCKY
After a photograph, 1887.
Pen, 7-5/8 x 12-1/2, signed *E.J.M.*
Engraved: *Battles and Leaders* I-391.

234. NATIONAL CEMETERY, PITTSBURG LANDING,
     TENNESSEE
After a photograph, 1884.
Pen, 8-1/8 x 12-3/4 on mount, signed *E. J. Meeker.*
Inscribed title.
Engraved: *Century* 31:763, March, 1886; *Battles
and Leaders* I-486.

235. TWO VIEWS OF STONE'S RIVER NATIONAL
     CEMETERY
Murfreesboro, Tenn.; after photographs, 1884.
Pen, 11 x 14-1/8. Two drawings. Inscribed (top)
View from S.R. Cemetery—looking S.E. Murfreesboro in extreme distance; (bottom) *Hazen's Monument. Front of Federal Cemetery.*
Engraved: *Battles and Leaders* III-617.

236. THREE VIEWS OF STONE'S RIVER NATIONAL
     CEMETERY
Murfreesboro, Tenn.; after photographs, 1884.
Pen, 13-5/8 x 14-1/4, signed *E.J.M.* Three drawings. Inscribed (top) *Cannon giving number buried
in Stone's River Cemetery;* (center) *Soldiers Monument, Stone River Cemetery;* (bottom) *Stone's
River Cemetery / Nashville R.R. in foreground.*
Engraved: *Battles and Leaders* III-615.

237. CONFEDERATE MONUMENT
Shepherdstown, W.Va.; after a photograph, 1885.
Pen, 9 x 11-3/4, signed *E.J.M.* Inscribed *First Conf.
Monument errected in the South (Shepherdstown,
W. Va.).*
Engraved: *Century* 32:443, July, 1886; *Battles and
Leaders* II-694.

T. F. MOESSNER

238. FEDERAL HEADQUARTERS, BEAUFORT, SOUTH
     CAROLINA
After photographs by Alexander Gardner, 1862.
Pen, 9-9/16 x 14, signed *T. F. Moessner.* Two drawings. Inscribed *Burnside Expedition—Signal station.
Fuller House.*
Engraved: *Battles and Leaders* I-690.
PLATE 193

HENRY A. OGDEN

Illustrator. Born Philadelphia, July 17, 1856; died
Englewood, N.J., June 14, 1936. At the age of 17
Ogden became a staff artist for *Frank Leslie's Illustrated Newspaper.* After eight years he left *Leslie's*
and from 1881 to 1923 was the New York artist for
the Strobridge Lithograph Co. of Cincinnati. A specialist in military art, he is best known for his
plates in *Uniform of the Army of the United States,
1774-1907* and *Pageant of America* (1925-29).

224

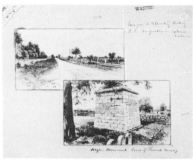

235

230

236

232

237

233

234

239

240

241

242

243

244

245

246

247

248

239.   UNIFORM OF THE 83RD PENNSYLVANIA INFANTRY
After a wartime photograph.
Pen, 8-1/4 x 6-1/4, signed *Ogden*. Inscribed title.
Engraved: *Battles and Leaders* II-336.

240.   UNIFORM OF THE POTOMAC LIGHT INFANTRY
After a wartime photograph.
Pen, 8-1/4 x 6-3/8, signed *H.A.O.* Inscribed title.
Engraved: *Battles and Leaders* I-9.

241.   UNIFORM OF THE 55TH NEW YORK VOLUNTEERS
After a museum exhibit.
Pen, 8-1/4 x 6-1/4, signed *H.A.O.* Inscribed title.

242.   UNIFORM OF THE 5TH NEW YORK ENGINEER
        BATTALION
Probably after a wartime photograph.
Pen, 8-1/4 x 6-1/4, signed *H.A.O.* Inscribed title.

243.   UNIFORM OF THE 33RD PENNSYLVANIA INFANTRY
Probably after a wartime photograph.
Pen, 8-1/4 x 6-1/4, signed *H.A.O.* Inscribed title.

244.   UNIFORM OF SCHENCK'S 2ND OHIO INFANTRY
After an unattributed sketch, 1861.
Pen, 8-1/4 x 6-1/4, signed *H.A.O.* Inscribed title.
On verso: artist's comments.
Engraved: *Battles and Leaders* I-171.

245.   UNIFORM OF THE 1ST NEW YORK VOLUNTEERS
Probably after a wartime photograph.
Pen, 8-1/4 x 6-1/4, signed *H.A.O.* Inscribed title.
On verso: artist's comments.

246.   UNIFORM OF ELLSWORTH'S FIRE ZOUAVES
From a wartime photograph and illustrations in
Harper's and *Leslie's*.
Pen, 8-1/4 x 6-1/4, signed *Ogden*. Inscribed title.
On verso: artist's comments.
Engraved: *Battles and Leaders* I-179.

247.   UNIFORM OF THE NEW YORK NATIONAL ZOUAVES
After a museum exhibit.
Pen, 8-1/4 x 6-1/4, signed *H.A.O.* Inscribed title.

248.   UNIFORM OF DURYEA'S NEW YORK ZOUAVES
After a wartime photograph and a museum exhibit.
Pen, 8-1/4 x 6-1/4, signed *Ogden*. Inscribed title.
On verso: artist's comments.
Engraved: *Battles and Leaders* II-148.

249.   UNIFORM OF THE 1ST MASSACHUSETTS
        VOLUNTEERS
After a wartime photograph.
Pen, 8-1/4 x 6-1/4, signed *Ogden*. Inscribed title.
Engraved: *Battles and Leaders* I-169.

250.   A LOUISIANA PRIVATE
After a wartime photograph.
Pen, 8-3/8 x 6-3/8. Inscribed *Southern Private—
No. 5. (Mansfield, La.)*.
Engraved: *Battles and Leaders* I-393.
PLATE 313

251.   AN ALABAMA PRIVATE
After a wartime photograph.
Pen, 8-3/8 x 6-3/8. Inscribed *Southern Private IV /
Huntsville, Ala.*
Engraved: *Battles and Leaders* I-349.

252. A Tennessee Private
After a wartime photograph.
Pen, 8-3/8 x 6-3/8. Inscribed *Southern Private No. 10. (Memphis, Tenn.)*.
Engraved: *Battles and Leaders* I-349 (reversed).

253. Confederate Private
After a wartime photograph.
Pen, 8-3/8 x 6-3/8. Inscribed *Southern Private #I*.
Engraved: *Battles and Leaders* I-348.

254. Confederate Private
After a wartime photograph.
Pen, 8-3/8 x 6-3/8. Inscribed *Southern Private III*.
Engraved: *Battles and Leaders* I-349.

255. The Jug
Military prison; original illustration.
Pen, 6-13/16 x 6-1/16.

256. A Federal Medical Headquarters
Siege of Petersburg; after a photograph, 1864.
Pen, 11-1/8 x 15-3/4, signed *Ogden / After Photo*.

257. The Hornet's Nest
Battle of Shiloh, April 6, 1862; after a cyclorama painting of the battle.
Pen and crayon, 13 x 18-3/8, signed *Ogden*. Inscribed *Union left from the "Hornet's Nest" (Shiloh)*.
Engraved: *Battles and Leaders* I-504.
Plate 65

258. Infantry Device, U.S. Army
Original illustration.
Pen, 6-1/4 x 8-1/4. Inscribed *Device of Infantry Arm of U.S. Army Service (Civil War)*.

259. Artillery Device, U.S. Army
Original illustration.
Pen, 6-1/4 x 8-1/4. Inscribed *Device of Artillery Arm of U.S. Army Service (Civil War)*.

260. Cavalry Device, U.S. Army
Original illustration.
Pen, 6-1/4 x 8-1/4. Inscribed *Device of Cavalry Arm of U.S. Army Service*.

261. Officers' Swords
Original illustration.
Pen, 6-1/4 x 8-1/4. Inscribed *A. Cavalry Officer's Sabre. B. Foot Officer's Sword Inf'try*.

262. Confederate Naval Button
Facsimile drawing.
Pen, 8-1/4 x 6-1/4.

HARPER PENNINGTON

Painter and illustrator. Born Newport, R.I., 1854; died Baltimore, Md., March 15, 1920. Pennington studied in Paris at the Ecole des Beaux-Arts and with Whistler. Most of his illustration work appeared in *Century* magazine.

249

251

252

253

254

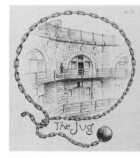

255

256

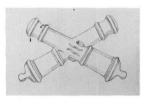

258

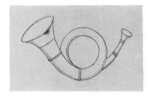

259

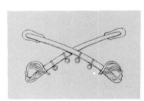

260

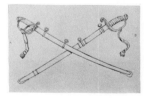

261

262

263

264

275

276

277

263. DEFIANCE
Battle of Fredericksburg, Dec. 13, 1862; original illustration for a work of fiction.
Pen, 15-1/4 x 12-1/2, signed *Harper Pennington*.
Engraved: *Century* 40:528, Aug., 1890.

VICTOR S. PERARD

Painter and illustrator. Born Paris, 1870; died Bellport, N.Y., July 9, 1957. Perard was a student at the National Academy of Design and the Art Students' League in New York and at the Ecole des Beaux-Arts in Paris, and taught at New York's Cooper Union and Traphagen School of Fashion. *Century*, *Scribner's*, and *Harper's* commissioned many of his illustrations.

264. FORT MARION
St. Augustine, Fla.; probably after a photograph.
Water color, 10-5/8 x 15-15/16, signed *V. Perard*.
Inscribed *Fort Marion. View from the water battery.*

ALLEN CARTER REDWOOD

Illustrator. 1834-1922. Redwood enlisted in the 55th Virginia regiment in 1861 and served throughout the war in the Army of Northern Virginia. He was captured at Second Bull Run and subsequently exchanged, and rose to the rank of major on the staffs of Generals Lunsford Lomax and Henry Heth. His extensive body of book and magazine illustration included cartoons and Civil War scenes.

265. CONFEDERATE TYPES
Original illustration.
Pen, 15-3/4 x 12.
Engraved: *Battles and Leaders* I-548.
PLATE 55

266. THE BATTLE OF SHILOH
April 6, 1862; original illustration.
Pen, 12-1/2 x 16, signed *A. C. Redwood—84.*
Engraved: *Century* 29:600, Feb., 1885; *Battles and Leaders* I-472.
PLATE 64

267. AN INCIDENT IN THE DEFENSE OF NEW ORLEANS
April, 1862; original illustration.
Pen, 16-1/4 x 12-1/2, signed *A.C.R. / E.J.M.* Inscribed *Confederate sharp shooters & swamp hunters attacking the mortar boats.*
Engraved: *Century* 29:935, April, 1885; *Battles and Leaders* II-28.
PLATE 79

268. CAPTURED BY STONEWALL JACKSON
Peninsula campaign, June 27, 1862; original illustration.
Pen, 17-7/16 x 12-3/8, signed *A. C. Redwood.*
Engraved: *Century* 30:308, June, 1885; *Battles and Leaders* II-360.
PLATE 113

269. CONFEDERATE SHARPSHOOTERS, FREDERICKSBURG
Battle of Fredericksburg, Dec. 13, 1862; original illustration.
Pen, 16 x 12-1/2, signed *A. C. Redwood / 1886.*
Engraved: *Century* 32:614, Aug., 1886; *Battles and Leaders* III-87.
PLATE 229

270. CONFEDERATES ON THE MARCH TO GETTYSBURG
May, 1863; original illustration.
Chalk and tempera, 11-1/4 x 13-1/8, signed *A.C.R.*
Engraved: *Battles and Leaders* III-250.
PLATE 239

271. STEUART'S BRIGADE AT CULP'S HILL
Battle of Gettysburg, July 3, 1863; original illustration.
Water color, 11-7/8 x 16-1/2, signed *A.C.R. 86.*
Engraved: *Century* 33:452, Jan., 1887; *Battles and Leaders* III-370.
PLATE 244

272. CONFEDERATE WORKS, CHESTERFIELD BRIDGE
North Anna River, Va.; after a photograph by Alexander Gardner, May, 1864.
Pen, 7-7/8 x 8-1/8 (sight size).
Engraved: *Century* 34:293, June, 1887; *Battles and Leaders* IV-135.
PLATE 297

273. IN THE TRENCHES
Siege of Petersburg; original illustration.
Water color, 14-3/4 x 11-1/2 on mount, signed *A.C.R.* Inscribed title.
Engraved: *St. Nicholas*, March, 1882.
PLATE 310

274. CONFEDERATE CASUALTY, PETERSBURG
Siege of Petersburg; after a photograph attributed to Thomas C. Roche, April, 1865.
Pen, 13-1/2 x 12-1/2, signed *A.C.R.*
Engraved: *St. Nicholas* March, 1882.
PLATE 327

275. FEDERAL TROOPS DESTROYING THE WELDEN RAILROAD
Siege of Petersburg; original illustration.
Pen, 4-7/8 x 8-3/8. Inscribed title.
Engraved: *St. Nicholas* April, 1882.

276. ILLUSTRATIONS OF ARMY LIFE
Original illustrations.
Pen, 16-1/2 x 12-1/2, signed *A.C.R.* Two drawings. Inscribed captions.
Engraved: *St. Nicholas* Feb., 1882.

277. INSTRUCTIONS TO THE ORDERLY
Federal camp; original illustration.
Water color, 13-1/4 x 10-1/8 on mount, signed *A.C.R.*
Engraved: *St. Nicholas* Oct., 1883.

CHARLES W. REED

Reed enlisted in 1862, serving as a bugler in the 9th Massachusetts Light Artillery and later as an engineering officer in the 5th Corps of the Army of the Potomac. Some of his wartime pencil sketches, redrawn in pen and ink, illustrated J. D. Billings' *Hardtack and Coffee* (1887).

278. GENERAL GRANT IN THE WILDERNESS
Battle of the Wilderness, May 5, 1864; after an eyewitness sketch by the artist.
Pen, 11-1/8 x 8-3/4, signed *C. W. Reed.*
Engraved: *Century* 31:582, Feb., 1886; *Battles and Leaders* IV-145.

279. A TERRIBLE DECISION
Original illustration.
Water color, 10-1/8 x 14-1/8 on mount, signed *C. W. Reed.* Inscribed title.

308.　THE QUARTERMASTER'S BATTERY
Original illustration.
Water color, 13-3/8 x 16-1/2.

309.　MORGAN'S RAIDERS AT A WELL
John Hunt Morgan's Confederate cavalry, July,
1863; original illustration.
Oil, 18-1/2 x 21-1/2, signed *W. H. Shelton.*
Engraved: *Century* 41:407, Jan., 1891.

310.　A MORGAN RECRUIT
John Hunt Morgan's Confederate cavalry; original
illustration.
Oil, 18-1/2 x 17, signed *W. H. Shelton.*
Engraved: *Century* 41:405, Jan., 1891.

311.　GENERAL DUKE TRACKING THE VAN
John Hunt Morgan's Confederate cavalry, July,
1863; original illustration.
Oil, 18-1/2 x 24-1/2, signed *W. H. Shelton.*
Engraved: *Century* 41:408, Jan., 1891.

312.　JOHN HUNT MORGAN'S ESCAPE
Ohio State Penitentiary, Columbus, Nov. 26, 1863;
original illustration.
Oil, 18-1/2 x 24-1/2, signed *W. H. Shelton.*
Engraved: *Century* 41:422, Jan., 1891.

313.　TRANSPORTING PRISONERS OF WAR
Original illustration.
Oil, 18-1/2 x 24-1/2, signed *W. H. Shelton.*

314.　DISPOSING OF DIRT FROM AN ESCAPE TUNNEL
Prisoners of war; original illustration.
Pen, 9-7/8 x 14-1/4.

315.　THE ARRIVAL AT HEADEN'S
Haven for escaped Federal prisoners of war; origi-
nal illustration.
Tempera, 15-1/2 x 19-1/2, signed *W. H. Shelton.*
Engraved: *Century* 40:938, Oct., 1890.

316.　THE ESCAPE OF HEADEN
Guide for escaped Federal prisoners of war; original
illustration.
Tempera, 21 x 16-1/2.
Engraved: *Century* 40:939, Oct., 1890

317.　ESCAPED PRISONERS AT A STILL
Federal prisoners of war; original illustration.
Water color, 14 x 12-1/4, signed *W. H. Shelton.*
Engraved: *Century* 40:945, Oct., 1890.

318.　CAMPFIRE PAROLE
Confederate prisoners of war; original illustration.
Oil, 18-1/2 x 24-1/2, signed *W. H. Shelton.*
Engraved: *Century* 41:845, April, 1891.

319.　SELLING BREAD AT CAMP MORTON
Prisoner of war camp, Indianapolis, Ind.; original
illustration.
Oil, 18-1/2 x 24-1/2, signed *W. H. Shelton.*
Engraved: *Century* 41:847, April, 1891.

320.　ESCAPE FROM CAMP MORTON
Prisoner of war camp, Indianapolis, Ind.; original
illustration.
Oil, 24-1/2 x 18-1/2, signed *W. H. Shelton.*
Engraved: *Century* 41:848, April, 1891.

310

316

311

317

312

318

313

319

314

320

315

321

322

323

327

331

332

321. SOLDIERS AROUND A FIREPLACE
Original illustration.
Oil, 18-3/8 x 24-1/2.

322. INITIAL LETTER
Original illustration.
Pen, 5-1/2 x 3-3/4 (sight size).
Engraved: *Century* 40:931, Oct., 1890.

323. INITIAL LETTER
Original illustration.
Pen, 12-3/4 x 7-1/2.

WILLIAM LUDWELL SHEPPARD

Illustrator, painter, sculptor. Born Richmond, Va., 1833; died Richmond, March 27, 1912. Sheppard studied art in New York and Paris before joining the Richmond Howitzers at the outbreak of the war. He remained in the army four years, attaining the rank of engineering officer. Resuming his studies after the war, Sheppard became a painter and book illustrator. His series of water colors on life in the Southern ranks is in the Confederate Museum in Richmond; also in Richmond are his best-known works of sculpture, the Soldiers and Sailors Monument and a statue of General A. P. Hill.

324. FLOYD'S COMMAND, GAULEY BRIDGE, VIRGINIA
Confederate unit, Oct., 1861; after a sketch by eyewitness W. D. Washington.
Pen, 12-3/8 x 10-7/8, signed *W.L.S.* after *W. D. Washington*. Inscribed *Detachment from Floyd's Command preparing to shell Genl. Rosecrans' Camp at Gauley Bridge (then) Va. From a picture by W. D. Washington (present with the detachment) in the possession of J. F. Gibson, Esq. Richmond Va.*
Engraved: *Battles and Leaders* I-147.
PLATE 17

325. SLAVES CONSTRUCTING EARTHWORKS, CORINTH, MISSISSIPPI
April, 1862; original illustration.
Wash and charcoal, 14-1/8 x 18-3/16, signed *W. L. Sheppard.*
Engraved: *Battles and Leaders* I-577.
PLATE 61

326. CONFEDERATE SKIRMISHERS
Peninsula campaign, May, 1862; after a painting by the artist.
Pen, 16-1/4 x 20-5/8, signed *W. L. Sheppard.* Inscribed *An Incident in the Peninsula Campaign / Confederate skirmish line driven in by Federal line of battle. / From the picture owned by R. A. Wootridge Esq. Baltimore.*
Engraved: *Century* 30:297, June, 1885; *Battles and Leaders* II-349.
PLATE 102

327. ALLEN'S FARM
Virginia peninsula; an eyewitness drawing, 1885.
Pen, 9-9/16 x 14-1/8, signed *W.L.S.* Inscribed title and *On Williamsburg Turnpike 1-1/2 miles (estimated) from Savage's Station. Unoccupied and going to decay. The pines in the background, except the late ones, have all grown up since the battles in 1862.*
Engraved: *Battles and Leaders* II-239.

328. RICHMOND DEFENSE LINES
After a sketch by the artist.
Water color, 14-5/8 x 10-1/8, signed *W. L. Sheppard.* Inscribed *The Exterior Line, Richmond Defences, on the Mechanicsville Pike, looking S.E.* and detailed description.
Engraved: *Century* 30:296, June, 1885; *Battles and Leaders* II-350.
PLATE 106

329. A RABBIT IN CAMP
Confederate camp; after a painting by the artist.
Pen, 8-7/16 x 12-13/16 on mount, signed *W.L.S.* Inscribed title and *An incident in Confederate Camp Life from a picture by W. L. Sheppard in the possession of Maj. F. M. Colston, Balto.*
Engraved: *Battles and Leaders* IV-144.
PLATE 164

330. UNDER FIRE AT CHANCELLORSVILLE
Federal troops, May 3, 1863; after a painting by the artist.
Water color, 12-3/16 x 16-9/16, signed *W. L. Sheppard.* Inscribed *Shelling in the Wilderness Chancellorsville May 3 1863. Foreground 29th Penn. Vols 2d Brigade 2d Division 12 Corps Army Potomac. From original picture in the possession of Capt. W. L. Stork.*
Engraved: *Century* 32:768, Sept., 1886; *Battles and Leaders* III-168.
PLATE 235

331. REINFORCING CULP'S HILL, GETTYSBURG
Federal troops, July 3, 1863; after a painting by the artist.
Pen, 10-5/16 x 16-13/16 on mount, signed *W. L. Sheppard.* Inscribed *Reinforcing Culps Hill an Incident at Gettysburg. From a picture by W. L. Sheppard owned by Capt W. L. Stork 29th Penn Regt. Baltimore from descriptions and diagrams furnished by him. The troops represented are two companies of the 29th Penn Regt. Genl Kanes Brigade, Gearys Div. Slocums Corps (12th)—Time about 10 A.M. 3d July.*
Engraved: *Battles and Leaders* III-371.

332. TAVERN AT NEW COLD HARBOR, VIRGINIA
After a wartime sketch by the artist.
Pen, 5-1/2 x 7-3/4, signed *W.L.S.* Inscribed *The Tavern at "New Cold Harbor" Hanover Co. Va. as it appeared 1864 not long after Genl Grant's change of position.*
Engraved: *Battles and Leaders* IV-141.

333. THE CRATER AFTER THE EXPLOSION
Siege of Petersburg, July 30, 1864; after an unattributed eyewitness sketch.
Pen, 6-5/8 x 19-3/16 on mount, signed *W.L.S.* Inscribed *The Crater on the Confederate lines around Petersburg. The drawing is from a sketch by an artillery officer on the morning (July 30th 1864) at the explosion of the mine & before the assault by Mahone's brigade; the Confederate dead remaining as they fell.*
Engraved: *Century* 34:768, Sept., 1887; *Battles and Leaders* IV-555.
PLATE 307

334. UNDER FIRE, PETERSBURG
Siege of Petersburg; original illustration.
Water color, 8-13/16 x 11-5/8 (sight size), signed *W. L. Sheppard / 86.* Inscribed *The siege of Petersburg Shell behind the Confederate works.*
PLATE 311

335. RETREAT FROM PETERSBURG: GRINDING CORN
Confederate troops, April, 1865; original illustration.
Pen, 11-7/8 x 10-7/8, signed *W.L.S.* Inscribed *Confederate Soldiers in the Retreat from Petersburg grinding corn between stones & grating in old tins with holes driven through them & cooking flour paste on ramrods, from incident witnessed by the artist.*
Engraved: *Century* 35:139, Nov., 1887.
PLATE 358

336. RETREAT FROM PETERSBURG: HALT AT A WELL
Confederate troops, April, 1865; original illustration.
Pen, 8-5/16 x 11-5/8 (sight size), signed *W.L.S.* Inscribed *The Retreat from Petersburg / Confederate Soldiers at a well near Farmville Va. observed by artist.*
Engraved: *Century* 35:138, Nov., 1887.
PLATE 359

337. CONFEDERATES DISABLING GUNS, APPOMATTOX
April 8, 1865; original illustration.
Water color, 11-3/16 x 13-1/4, signed *W. L. Sheppard.* Inscribed *Infantry destroying the railroad from Appomattox to Lynchburg. Artillerymen cutting down their guns at night fall on Saturday Apr. 8th 1865. From incidents observed by the artist.*
Engraved: *Century* 35:143, Nov., 1887; *Battles and Leaders* IV-722.
PLATE 363.

338. THE DAY AFTER THEIR FIRST FIGHT
Confederate troops; original illustration.
Pen, 10-1/8 x 7-7/8, signed *W.L.S.* Inscribed title.
Engraved: *Century* 31:467, Jan., 1886; *Battles and Leaders* III-284.

339. THE CLIFTON HOUSE, RICHMOND
Original illustration.
Pen, 14 x 10, signed *W.L.S.* Inscribed title.
Engraved: *Battles and Leaders* II-439.

SIDNEY L. SMITH

Engraver and painter. Born Foxboro, Mass., 1845; died Boston, 1929. Smith saw brief service in the Union army near the end of the war, then resumed his engraving career. He was a prolific designer of book plates.

340. COLONEL JAMES A. MULLIGAN
Federal commander, siege of Lexington, Mo., Sept., 1861; after a wartime photograph.
Pen, 11-1/2 x 8-1/2, signed *S.L.S.* Inscribed title and *Sidney L. Smith/Feb. 1887.*
Engraved: *Battles and Leaders* I-312.

XANTHUS SMITH

Painter. Born Philadelphia, Feb. 26, 1839; died Edgehill, Pa., Dec. 2, 1929. Smith trained in medicine before turning to art studies at the Pennsylvania Academy of the Fine Arts and the Royal Academy in London. He enlisted in the Union navy and saw extensive war service. In his later career he painted many Civil War battle scenes as well as nautical subjects and portrait studies.

341. A BATTERY AT FORT BEAUREGARD
Port Royal, S.C.; after a sketch by the artist, 1861.
Pen, 7-5/8 x 11, signed *Xanthus Smith.* Inscribed *Rifle Gun—Fort Beauregard—Bay Point—Port Royal.*
Engraved: *Battles and Leaders* I-683.
PLATE 192.

342. U.S.S. "WABASH"
After a wartime sketch by the artist.
Pen, 5 x 10-3/4 (sight size), signed *X.S.* Inscribed *U.S. Steam Frigate Wabash / Flag Ship of the South Atlantic Squadron.*
PLATE 194

343. HILTON HEAD, SOUTH CAROLINA
After a sketch by the artist, 1863.
Pen, 5 x 14-3/4 (sight size), signed *X.S.* Inscribed title and identifications in margin.
Engraved: *Battles and Leaders* I-671.
PLATE 195.

344. U.S.S. "VANDALIA"
After a wartime sketch by the artist.
Pen, 4-1/2 x 4 (sight size), signed *X.S.* Inscribed *U.S. Sloop of War Vandalia. Rear ship of the line at the bombardment of Port Royal, S.C.*
Engraved: *Battles and Leaders* I-677
PLATE 196

345. GUNBOAT U.S.S. "SENECA"
After a wartime sketch by the artist.
Pen, 8-3/4 x 11-1/4, signed *X.S.* Inscribed *U.S. Gunboat Seneca / Admiral Ammen's vessel at the bombardment of Port Royal, S.C.*
Engraved: *Battles and Leaders* I-676.

346. FORT PULASKI AFTER ITS SURRENDER
Savannah River, Ga.; after sketch by the artist, April, 1862.
Pen, 10-5/16 x 14-1/2, signed *Xanthus Smith.* Inscribed title.
Engraved: *Battles and Leaders* II-1.
PLATE 197

347. TOWER AND LIGHT HOUSE NEAR FORT PULASKI
Savannah River, Ga.; after a sketch by the artist, April, 1862.
Pen, 8-3/4 x 11-3/8, signed *X.S.* Inscribed *Tybee / Martello Tower & Light House. Mouth of the Savannah River near Fort Pulaski.*
Engraved: *Battles and Leaders* II-4.

348. DAMAGE TO THE "WEEHAWKEN"
Charleston Harbor; after photographs, 1863.
Pen, 7 x 7 (sight size), signed *X.S.* Two drawings. Inscribed *effect of Blakeley shot from Fort Sumter on plating of Monitor Weehawken;* approval by consultant Thornton Jenkins.
Engraved: *Battles and Leaders* IV-15.
PLATE 217

349. U.S.S. "MERCEDITA"
After a wartime sketch by the artist.
Pen, 9 x 14-1/2, signed *X.S.* Inscribed *Mercedita captured by Rebel ram off Charleston.*
Engraved: *Century* 56:916, Oct., 1898.

338

339

340

345

347

349

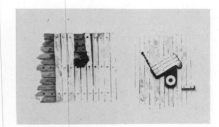

350

351

353

354

355

356

350. EXTERIOR DAMAGE TO C.S.S. "ATLANTA"
Wilmington River, Ga.; after sketches by the artist, June, 1863.
Pen, 9-1/16 x 14-1/2, signed *X.S.* Two drawings. Inscribed *Effect of 400 pound shot on plating of "Atlanta"—outside*; approval by consultant Thornton Jenkins.

351. INTERIOR DAMAGE TO C.S.S. "ATLANTA"
Wilmington River, Ga.; after a sketch by the artist, June, 1863.
Pen, 9 x 14-1/2, signed *X.S.* Inscribed *Effect on 18 inch teak lining—inside*; approval by consultant Thornton Jenkins.

352. "RICHMOND" AND "LACKAWANNA"
After a sketch by the artist, 1864.
Pen, 9 x 14-1/2, signed *X.S.* Inscribed *"Richmond" & "Lackawanna" stripped for the fight* and Smith's commentary on the critique of consultant Thornton Jenkins.
Engraved: *Battles and Leaders* IV-381.
PLATE 222

353. U.S.S. "GALENA" OFF MOBILE
After a sketch by the artist, 1864.
Pen, 9 x 14-1/2, signed *X.S.* Inscribed title; approval by consultant Thornton Jenkins.
Engraved: *Battles and Leaders* IV-389.

354. U.S.S. "BROOKLYN" AFTER THE BATTLE OF MOBILE BAY
After a sketch by the artist, Aug., 1864.
Pen, 9 x 14-1/2, signed *Xanthus Smith.* Inscribed identifications and *Sketched after the battle of Mobile. Struck 23 times in the hull—(Brooklyn)*; critique by consultant Thornton Jenkins.
Engraved: *Battles and Leaders* IV-379.

355. U.S.S. "MONONGAHELA" AFTER THE BATTLE OF MOBILE BAY
After a sketch by the artist, Aug., 1864.
Pen, 9 x 14-1/2, signed *Xanthus Smith.* Inscribed *Sketched after the Battle of Mobile. Shows damage done in attempting to ram the "Tennessee," and shot holes made by the latter*; critique by consultant Thornton Jenkins.
Engraved: *Battles and Leaders* IV-392.

356. PLYMOUTH, NORTH CAROLINA
After a wartime sketch by the artist.
Pen, 5-1/8 x 9-1/4.

C. H. STEPHENS

Illustrator. Born Philadelphia; died Pittsburgh, 1831. A specialist on the American Indian.

357. SUDLEY SPRINGS FORD
Bull Run battlefield; after a photograph by George N. Barnard, 1862.
Pen, 12 x 8-1/2 on mount, signed *Stephens.* Inscribed *Sudley Spring showing old church.*
Engraved: *Century* 30:99, May, 1885; *Battles and Leaders* I-183.

ALBERT E. STERNER

Illustrator and portrait painter. Born London, March 8, 1863; died New York, Dec. 16, 1946. Coming to the United States in 1879, Sterner settled first in Chicago, then in New York, where he became a book and magazine illustrator and a teacher. He was a member of the National Academy, the Society of Illustrators, and the Salmagundi Club.

358. METHOD OF REMOVING WOUNDED FROM THE FIELD
After a photograph of an ambulance drill, 1862.
Pen, 15-5/8 x 20-3/4, signed *Albert E. Sterner / after photograph / 87.* Inscribed title.

WALTON TABER

Nearly 250 illustrations in the *Battles and Leaders* volumes are credited to Taber, and he did additional hundreds of drawings for *Century*, the original *Scribner's* (*Century's* forebear), and *St. Nicholas.* Considering this volume of work, it seems probable that he was a long-time Century Company staff artist; only in the late nineties did his work begin to appear in other publications. Taber was active in the Salmagundi Club from 1871 until about 1900, and was active as an artist as late as 1931, the date of a drawing in the collection of the Society of Illustrators.

359. CONFEDERATE CANTEEN
After a museum exhibit.
Pen, 4 x 2-3/4 (sight size), signed *Taber / 85.* Inscribed title.
Engraved: *Century* 32:315, June, 1886; *Battles and Leaders* I–xi.
PLATE I (p. 1)

360. NATIONAL CEMETERY, CORINTH, MISSISSIPPI
After a photograph, 1884.
Pen, 3-3/4 x 6-1/2 (sight size), signed *Taber.* Inscribed title.
Engraved: *Century* 32:918, Oct., 1886; *Battles and Leaders* II-760.
PLATE III (p. 4)

361. CONFEDERATE QUAKER GUN
Centreville, Va.; after a photograph by George N. Barnard and James F. Gibson, March, 1862.
Pen, 2-3/4 x 3-1/4 (sight size), signed *Taber / After Photo.*
Engraved: *Battles and Leaders* I-240.
PLATE 1

362. THE OLD NAVY DEPARTMENT BUILDING, WASHINGTON
After a photograph by Mathew B. Brady, 1861.
Pen, 5 x 8 (sight size), signed *Taber.* Inscribed title.
Engraved: *Battles and Leaders* I-618.
PLATE 4

363. FORT SUMTER CASEMATES IN RUINS
After a photograph, April, 1861.
Pen, 6-7/8 x 6-3/8 (sight size), signed *Taber.* Inscribed *Sumter 1861 / Interior of Gorge Showing Sally Port and flag staff, with ruins of Officers quarters.*
PLATE 10

364. SOUTHWEST FACE OF FORT SUMTER
After photographs, April, 1861.
Pen, 4 x 16-1/4 (sight size). Inscribed title and *Fort Sumter / Showing Shot-holes / April 8* [sic] *61.*
Engraved: *Battles and Leaders* I-50.
PLATE 11

365. EXTERIOR VIEW OF FORT SUMTER
After photographs, April, 1861.
Pen, 2 x 9 (sight size). Rejected as inaccurate; inscribed commentary (unattributed) on corrections needed.

366. INTERIOR OF FORT SUMTER AFTER THE
SURRENDER
After a photograph, April, 1861.
Pen, 7 x 9-1/8 (sight size), signed *Taber / After
Photo.* Inscribed *The Interior of Fort Sumter, April
15th 1861—the day following the Surrender of
Major Anderson.*
Engraved: *Battles and Leaders* I-57.
PLATE 12

367. HARPER'S FERRY, LOOKING DOWN THE POTOMAC
Harper's Ferry, Va.; after a photograph by James
Gardner, July, 1865.
Pen, 5 x 9-1/2 (sight size), signed *Taber.* Inscribed
title.
Engraved: *Battles and Leaders* I-119.
PLATE 16

368. THE McLEAN HOUSE
Bull Run battlefield; after a photograph by Alex-
ander Gardner, March, 1862.
Pen, 3-1/2 x 4-3/4 (sight size), signed *Taber.* In-
scribed *Gen. Beauregard's headquarters, Manassas.*
Engraved: *Battles and Leaders* I-201.
PLATE 18

369. SIEGE OF LEXINGTON, MISSOURI
Confederate troops; Sept., 1861; original illustration.
Pen and crayon, 9-1/2 x 16, signed *Taber.*
Engraved: *Battles and Leaders* I-307.
PLATE 22

370. OFF TO THE WAR
Federal troop train; original illustration.
Pen, 7 x 13 (sight size), signed *Taber.*
Engraved: *Battles and Leaders* I-278.
PLATE 23

371. TROOP TRAINS AT HARPER'S FERRY
Harper's Ferry, Va.; original illustration.
Pen, 12-5/8 x 15-7/8, signed *Taber.* Inscribed
*Soldiers to the front, through Harper's Ferry five
minutes for refreshments—trains both ways—some
coming from the slaughter pen, others going to it.*

372. THE BATTLE OF LOGAN'S CROSSROADS
Jan. 19, 1862; after a lithographed sketch by Alfred
E. Mathews, 1862.
Pen and crayon, 13-1/4 x 18, signed *Taber.*
Engraved: *Battles and Leaders* I-546.
Collection of Robert B. Mayo.
PLATE 27

373. CAMP DENNISON, CINCINNATI
After a photograph, c. 1861.
Pen, 9-7/16 x 13-1/8. Inscribed identifications.
Engraved: *Battles and Leaders* I-98.
PLATE 31

374. THE AWKWARD SQUAD
Federal recruits; original illustration.
Pen, 7 x 13 (sight size), signed *Taber.*
Engraved: *Battles and Leaders* I-84.
PLATE 33

375. PARADE OF THE 110TH PENNSYLVANIA INFANTRY
Falmouth, Va.; after a photograph by Alexander
Gardner, April, 1863.
Pen, 7 x 14-1/2 (sight size), signed *Taber / After
Photo.*
Engraved: *Century* 32:749, Sept., 1886; *Battles and
Leaders* III-172.
PLATE 34

376. PARADE OF THE 3RD PENNSYLVANIA ARTILLERY
Fortress Monroe, Va.; after a photograph by Alex-
ander Gardner, Dec., 1862.
Pen and crayon, 3-3/4 x 15-1/2 (sight size), signed
Taber. Inscribed title.
Engraved: *Battles and Leaders*, II-160.
PLATE 35

377. THE HOFFMAN BATTALION, JOHNSON'S ISLAND
Prisoner of war camp, Sandusky Bay, Ohio; after a
wartime photograph.
Pen, 5-3/4 x 10 (sight size), signed *Taber.* Inscribed
title.
Engraved: *Century* 41:709, March, 1891.
PLATE 36

378. FUGITIVE SLAVES FORDING THE RAPPAHANNOCK
After a photograph by Alexander Gardner, Aug.,
1862.
Pen, 4-1/4 x 4-1/2 (sight size), signed *Taber.* In-
scribed title.
Engraved: *Century* 34:129, May, 1887; *Battles and
Leaders* IV-94.
PLATE 38

379. UNION ARMY COOK
After a photograph by Mathew B. Brady or assist-
ant, 1864.
Pen, 3 x 3 (sight size), signed *Taber / 85.*
Engraved: *Century* 32:770, Sept., 1886.
PLATE 39

380. CAMP OF THE 153RD NEW YORK INFANTRY
After a wartime photograph by Alexander Gardner.
Pen, 5 x 7-3/4 (sight size). Inscribed title.
PLATE 41

381. COMMISSARY TENT
Federal camp; after a wartime photograph by Alex-
ander Gardner.
Pen, 4-1/4 x 7-1/2 (sight size), signed *Taber / After
Photo.* Inscribed title.
PLATE 42

382. PONTOON BRIDGE OVER BULL RUN
Centreville, Va.; after a photograph, 1862.
Pen, 12-5/8 x 16-1/2, signed *Taber / 84.* Inscribed
[Black]*burn's Ford, Bull Run.*
Engraved: *Century* 29:84, Nov., 1884.
PLATE 47

383. FEDERAL TELEGRAPH CONSTRUCTION CORPS
After a photograph by Timothy H. O'Sullivan,
April, 1864.
Pen, 5-1/2 x 9-1/4, signed *Taber / 85.* Inscribed
title.
Engraved: *Century* 38:790, Sept., 1889.

384. TELEGRAPHING IN THE FIELD
Federal telegraphers; original illustration.
Pen and crayon, 19-5/8 x 12-1/4, signed *Taber.*
Engraved: *Century* 38:786, Sept., 1889.
PLATE 48

385. LINEMAN, MILITARY TELEGRAPH
Federal telegrapher; original illustration.
Pen, 8 x 4 (sight size).
Engraved: *Century* 38:782, Sept., 1889.
PLATE 49

386. LINEMEN UNDER FIRE
Federal telegraphers; original illustration.
Pen, 21-1/2 x 13-3/8, signed *Taber.*
Engraved: *Century* 38:787, Sept., 1889.

357

358

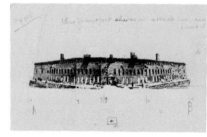

365

371

383

386

387

395

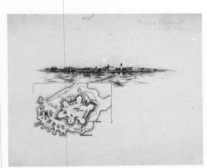
400

401

404

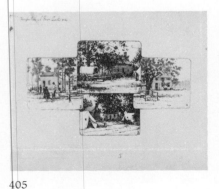
405

387.   TAPPING A WIRE
Federal telegrapher; original illustration.
Pen, 13-3/4 x 21-1/2, signed *Taber*.
Engraved: *Century* 38:788, Sept., 1889.

388.   ARMY FORGE, BRANDY STATION, VIRGINIA
Federal camp; after a photograph by Alexander
Gardner, Aug., 1863.
Pen, 4-3/4 x 9-1/2 (sight size), signed *Taber*.
Engraved: *Battles and Leaders* IV-87.
PLATE 50

389.   UNION CAVALRYMAN
After a photograph by Alexander Gardner, Oct.,
1862.
Pen, 3 x 3 (sight size), signed *Taber*. Inscribed *A
Cavalry Orderly*.
Engraved: *Century* 35:481, Jan., 1888; *Battles and
Leaders* II-103.
PLATE 51

390.   CAMP OF THE 18TH PENNSYLVANIA CAVALRY
Brandy Station, Va.; after a photograph by Tim-
othy H. O'Sullivan, March, 1864.
Pen and crayon, 7 x 10-3/8 (sight size), signed
Taber.
Engraved: *Battles and Leaders* IV-96.
PLATE 52

391.   FALL OF THE LEADERS
Federal artillery, Battle of Fredericksburg, Dec. 13,
1862; original illustration.
Pen and crayon, 12-3/4 x 18, signed *Taber / 86*.
Engraved: *Century* 32:626, Aug., 1886; *Battles and
Leaders* III-105.
Collection of Robert B. Mayo.
PLATE 53

392.   A UNION VOLUNTEER
After a photograph, 1861.
Pen, 10-1/4 x 5 (sight size), signed *Taber / 84*.
Inscribed *14th New York Volunteer*.
Engraved: *Century* 29:107, Nov., 1884; *Battles and
Leaders* I-167.
PLATE 54

393.   MAINTOP OF THE "HARTFORD"
Farragut's flagship; original illustration.
Pen, 10-11/16 x 7-13/16 on mount, signed *Taber / 86*.
Engraved: *Century* 32:455, July, 1886; *Battles and
Leaders* II-91.
PLATE 56

394.   SIEGE BATTERY, PITTSBURG LANDING
Federal artillery, Shiloh battlefield; after a photo-
graph, April, 1862.
Pen, 5-1/4 x 9-5/16 (sight size), signed *Taber / 85*.
Engraved: *Century* 31:766, March, 1886; *Battles
and Leaders* I-514.
PLATE 62

395.   SITE OF GENERAL ALBERT SIDNEY JOHNSTON'S
       DEATH
Shiloh battlefield; after a photograph, 1884.
Pen, 11-3/4 x 15-3/4, signed *Taber / 84*. Inscribed
*Stump of tree under which Albert S. Johnson died
near Hamburg & Savannah road*.
Engraved: *Century* 29:625, Feb., 1885; *Battles and
Leaders* I-563.

396.   BYPASS CHANNEL ABOVE ISLAND NUMBER TEN
Mississippi River, March, 1862; original illustration.
Pen, 4-1/8 x 8-3/4 (sight size). Inscribed title.
Engraved: *Century* 30:326, June, 1885; *Battles and
Leaders* I-460.
PLATE 67

397.   CONFEDERATE IRONCLAD "LOUISIANA"
New Orleans, 1862; original illustration.
Pen, 2-3/4 x 10 (sight size), signed *Taber*. Inscribed
title.
Engraved: *Century* 29:938, April, 1885; *Battles and
Leaders* II-48.
PLATE 78

398.   UNION WARSHIPS "MISSISSIPPI" AND
       "WINONA"
Baton Rouge, La.; after wartime photographs.
Pen, 5 x 6-1/4 (sight size), signed *Taber / After
Photos*. Two drawings. Inscribed identifications.
Engraved: *Battles and Leaders* III-565.
PLATE 87

399.   FORTRESS MONROE
Virginia peninsula; after a lithograph, 1860.
Pen, 3-3/4 x 8-1/2 (sight size).
Engraved: *Battles and Leaders* II-144.
PLATE 92

400.   FORTRESS MONROE AND PLAN
Virginia peninsula; after sketches by Robert K.
Sneden, c. 1862.
Pen, 13-1/4 x 18-1/4. Two drawings.

401.   UNION MORTAR BATTERY BEFORE YORKTOWN
Peninsula campaign; after a photograph by James
F. Gibson, May, 1862.
Pen, 4-1/4 x 5-5/8 (sight size), signed *Taber / 84*.
Inscribed *Battery 4. Yorktown*.
Engraved: *Century* 29:770, March, 1885; *Battles
and Leaders* II-194.

402.   FORTIFICATIONS AT YORKTOWN
Peninsula campaign; after photographs by Alex-
ander Gardner, c. May, 1862.
Pen, 7-1/2 x 7-5/8 (sight size), signed *Taber / 84*.
Four drawings. Inscribed identifications.
Engraved: *Century* 29:771, March, 1885; *Battles
and Leaders* II-174.
PLATE 97

403.   FORWARD TO RICHMOND
Peninsula campaign; original illustration.
Pen, 3-3/4 x 5-1/4 (sight size), signed *Taber*.
Engraved: *Century* 30:136, May, 1885; *Battles and
Leaders* II-189.
PLATE 101

404.   THE SEVEN PINES
Virginia peninsula; after a wartime sketch by G. L.
Frankenstein.
Pen, 9-7/8 x 10-1/8.
Engraved: *Century* 30:122, May, 1885; *Battles and
Leaders* II-220.

405.   UNION FIELD HOSPITALS, FAIR OAKS
Peninsula campaign; after photographs by Alex-
ander Gardner, June, 1862.
Pen, 11-1/2 x 15-1/18, signed *Taber*. Four draw-
ings. Inscribed identifications in margin.
Engraved: *Century* 30:125, May, 1885; *Battles and
Leaders* II-251.

406.   CUMBERLAND LANDING ON THE PAMUNKEY
Peninsula campaign; after a photograph by James
F. Gibson, May, 1862.
Pen, 8-3/4 x 13-1/2, signed *Taber / 84*.
Engraved: *Century* 29:773, March, 1885; *Battles
and Leaders* II-199.

407. UNION CAMP AT CUMBERLAND LANDING
Peninsula campaign; after a photograph by James F. Gibson, May, 1862.
Pen, 9-1/4 x 15-5/8, signed *Taber / 84*.
Engraved: *Century* 29:772; March, 1885; *Battles and Leaders* II-198.

408. OLD COLD HARBOR TAVERN
Virginia peninsula; after a photograph, 1885.
Pen, 5-1/4 x 9-1/2 (sight size), signed *Taber / 85*.
Inscribed *Old Cold Harbor Tavern from the south*.
Engraved: *Century* 30:307, June, 1885; *Battles and Leaders* II-354.
PLATE 111

409. RUINS OF GAINES' MILL
Virginia peninsula; after a photograph by John Reekie, April, 1865.
Pen, 7-1/8 x 9 (sight size), signed *Taber / 85*. Inscribed title.
PLATE 112

410. WOODBURY'S BRIDGE, CHICKAHOMINY RIVER
Peninsula campaign; after a photograph by James F. Gibson, June, 1862.
Pen, 11-1/4 x 10-3/8, signed *Taber / 85*.
Engraved: *Century* 30:454, July, 1885; *Battles and Leaders* II-383.

411. SOLDIERS' MONUMENT, BULL RUN
After a photograph by Alexander Gardner, 1865.
Pen, 5-3/4 x 7 (sight size), signed *Taber / 85*.
Engraved: *Century* 31:461, Jan., 1886; *Battles and Leaders* II-485.
PLATE 120

412. CULPEPPER, VIRGINIA
After a photograph by Timothy H. O'Sullivan, Aug., 1862.
Pen, 8-3/8 x 9-11/16, signed *Taber / 85*. Inscribed title.
Engraved: *Century* 31:601, Feb., 1886; *Battles and Leaders* II-451.

413. A DISORGANIZED PRIVATE
Federal soldier, Manassas Junction, Va.; after a photograph by Timothy H. O'Sullivan, *c.* Aug., 1862.
Pen, 4-5/8 x 3-1/2 (sight size), signed *Taber / After Photo*.
Engraved: *Century* 32:131, May, 1886; *Battles and Leaders* II-556.
Collection of Robert B. Mayo.
PLATE 123

414. RUINS OF THE HENRY HOUSE
Bull Run battlefield; after a photograph by George N. Barnard, March, 1862.
Pen, 3-1/4 x 3-7/8 (sight size), signed *Taber / 85*.
Inscribed title.
Engraved: *Century* 31:467, Jan., 1886.

415. JACKSON'S POSITION AT SECOND BULL RUN
After a photograph, 1885.
Pen, 4 x 8 (sight size), signed *Taber / 85*.
Engraved: *Century* 31:460, Jan., 1886; *Battles and Leaders* II-518.
PLATE 125

416. HARPER'S FERRY, FROM THE MARYLAND SIDE
Harper's Ferry, Va.; after a photograph by Mathew B. Brady, *c.* 1861.
Pen 6 x 9 (sight size), signed *Taber*. Inscribed title.
Engraved: *Battles and Leaders* I-120.
PLATE 128

417. CONFEDERATE DEAD AT FOX'S GAP
Antietam campaign, Sept. 15, 1862; after an eyewitness sketch by James E. Tayler.
Pen, 9-5/16 x 13-1/2. Inscribed *On the Mountain Top Cross Roads Day after Reno's fight*.
Engraved: *Battles and Leaders* II-583.

418. LUTHERAN CHURCH, SHARPSBURG, MARYLAND
After a photograph by Alexander Gardner, Sept., 1862.
Pen, 6-1/4 x 9-3/8 (sight size), signed *Taber / 85*.
Inscribed title.
Engraved: *Century* 32:288, June, 1886; *Battles and Leaders* II-665.
PLATE 129

419. UNION SIGNAL STATION, ELK MOUNTAIN
Antietam campaign; after a photograph by Alexander Gardner, Sept., 1862.
Pen, 8-1/2 x 5-3/4 (sight size), signed *Taber / 85*.
Engraved: *Century* 32:289, June, 1886; *Battles and Leaders* II-631.
PLATE 130

420. WASHINGTON MONUMENT, SOUTH MOUNTAIN
Federal signal station, Antietam campaign; after photographs.
Pen, 4-3/4 x 5-3/4 (sight size), signed *Taber / After Photo*. Two drawings.
Engraved: *Century* 32:139, May, 1886; *Battles and Leaders* II-588.

421. UNION CHARGE THROUGH THE CORNFIELD
Battle of Antietam, Sept. 17, 1862; original illustration.
Pen, 14 x 19.
Engraved: *Century* 32:296, June, 1886; *Battles and Leaders* II-630.
PLATE 134

422. BLOODY LANE
Antietam battlefield; after a photograph by Alexander Gardner, Sept., 1862.
Pen 12 x 16, signed *Taber / 85*. Inscribed *Ditch on Right Wing where a large number of Confederates were killed / Antietam*.
Engraved: *Century* 32:302, June, 1886; *Battles and Leaders* II-669.
PLATE 139

423. THE HAGERSTOWN TURNPIKE
Antietam battlefield; after a photograph by Alexander Gardner, Sept., 1862.
Pen, 5-3/4 x 9 (sight size), signed *Taber / 85*. Inscribed title.
Engraved: *Century* 32:296, June, 1886; *Battles and Leaders* II-679.
PLATE 140

424. THE DUNKER CHURCH
Antietam battlefield; after a photograph by James Gardner, Sept., 1862.
Pen, 9-1/4 x 4-3/8, signed *Taber / After Photo*.
Inscribed *Completely Silenced*.
Engraved: *Century* 32:299, June, 1886; *Battles and Leaders* II-671.
PLATE 141

425. BURYING THE DEAD
Antietam battlefield; after a photograph by Alexander Gardner, Sept., 1862.
Pen, 11-3/8 x 15-5/8, signed *Taber / 85*. Inscribed title.
Engraved: *Battles and Leaders* II-682.
PLATE 142

406

407

410

412

414

417

420

427

435

429

436

431

443

426. CONFEDERATE WOUNDED AFTER ANTIETAM
Sept., 1862; original illustration.
Pen and crayon, 12-3/4 x 18, signed *Taber / 86.*
Inscribed *Antietam / on the road to Shepherds-town.* On verso: artist's preliminary sketch.
Engraved: *Century* 32:435, July, 1886; *Battles and Leaders* II-686.
PLATE 143

427. DWELLINGS IN IUKA, MISSISSIPPI
After photographs, 1884.
Pen, 17-3/4 x 13-3/4, signed *Taber / 85.* Seven drawings. Inscribed identifications in margin.
Engraved: *Battles and Leaders* II-729.

428. UNION SOLDIERS, CORINTH, MISSISSIPPI
After a photograph by George Armstead, 1862.
Pen, 10 x 13. Inscribed title.
Engraved: *Battles and Leaders* II-754.
PLATE 144

429. CORONA COLLEGE, CORINTH
Corinth, Miss.; after a wartime photograph by George Armstead.
Pen, 5 x 7-1/2 (sight size), signed *Taber / 85.* Inscribed title.
Engraved: *Century* 32:909, Oct., 1886; *Battles and Leaders* II-740.

430. BATTERY ROBINETTE, CORINTH
Corinth, Miss.; after a photograph attributed to George Armstead, Oct., 1862.
Pen, 5 x 7-1/2 (sight size), signed *Taber.* Inscribed title.
Engraved: *Battles and Leaders* II-751.
PLATE 145

431. BATTERIES WILLIAMS AND ROBINETTE, CORINTH
Corinth, Miss.; after a photograph by George Armstead, Oct., 1862.
Pen, 9-1/4 x 12-1/2, signed *Taber / 85.*
Engraved: *Century* 32:914, Oct., 1886; *Battles and Leaders* II-745.

432. CONFEDERATE CAVALRY
Original illustration.
Pen and crayon, 15 x 21-1/2, signed *Taber.*
Engraved: *Battles and Leaders* III-1.
Collection of Robert B. Mayo.
PLATE 149

433. SENTRY DUTY
Federal soldier; original illustration.
Pen, 7 x 4-1/2 (sight size).
Engraved: *Century* 53:19, Nov., 1896.
PLATE 151

434. CAMP GOSSIP
Federal officers; after a wartime photograph by Alexander Gardner.
Pen, 6-1/4 x 11-1/4 (sight size), signed *Taber.* Inscribed title.
Engraved: *Battles and Leaders* I-ix.
PLATE 156

435. FEDERAL WINTER QUARTERS, FALMOUTH, VIRGINIA
After a photograph, *c.* May, 1863.
Pen, 10 x 12-1/2, signed *Taber / After Photo.*
Engraved: *Century* 33:107, Nov., 1886; *Battles and Leaders* III-239.

436. PROVOST GUARD, ARMY OF THE POTOMAC
Siege of Petersburg; after a photograph, Aug.,
1864.
Pen, 5 x 9-5/8 (sight size), signed *Taber*. Inscribed
*114th Penn. Infy—Provost Guard at Hdqtrs A. of P.
Aug. 1864 / Petersburg.*
Engraved: *Battles and Leaders* IV-81.

437. HEADQUARTERS OF GENERALS WARREN AND
        CRAWFORD, PETERSBURG, VIRGINIA
After a photograph, 1864.
Pen, 7-1/2 x 9-1/4 (sight size), signed *Taber*. Inscribed title.
PLATE 157.

438. DRUMMER BOYS
Federal camp; original illustration, based in part on
a photograph by Timothy H. O'Sullivan, Aug.,
1863.
Pen and crayon, 5-3/4 x 14-1/2 (sight size), signed
Taber / 87.
Engraved: *Battles and Leaders* I-1.
PLATE 158

439. REVEILLE
Federal cavalry camp; original illustration.
Pen and crayon, 7-1/4 x 14 (sight size), signed
Taber.
Engraved: *Battles and Leaders* IV-475.
PLATE 159

440. SICK CALL
Federal camp; original illustration.
Pen and crayon, 11-7/8 x 16-3/4, signed *Taber*.
Inscribed title.
PLATE 161

441. RIDING THE WOODEN HORSE
Federal soldiers; after a photograph, *c*. 1863.
Pen, 5-1/2 x 4-3/4 (sight size), signed *Taber*. Inscribed *U.S. Provost Marshal's Guard House /
Vicksburg.*
PLATE 162

442. A GAME OF CARDS
Federal soldiers; after a wartime photograph by
Alexander Gardner.
Pen, 5 x 7-1/4 (sight size), signed *Taber / After
Photo.*
PLATE 165

443. FEDERAL MEDICAL CORPS IN THE FIELD
After a wartime sketch by Charles W. Reed.
Pen, 5 x 6-1/2 (sight size), signed *Taber.*

444. FIELD HOSPITALS, ANTIETAM
After photographs by Alexander Gardner, Sept.,
1862.
Pen, 4-1/4 x 6-7/8 (sight size), signed *Taber / 85.*
Two drawings. Inscribed *Conf. wounded at Smith
Barn, Antietam.*
Engraved: *Century* 32:305, June, 1886; *Battles and
Leaders* II-672.
PLATE 169

445. UNION HOSPITAL, FREDERICKSBURG
After a photograph by Alexander Gardner, May,
1864.
Pen, 5 x 13-1/2 (sight size), signed *Taber / 84.*
Inscribed *Factory Hospital / Fredericksburg May
11th 1864.*
Engraved: *Century* 32:633, Aug., 1886; *Battles and
Leaders* III-117.
PLATE 172

446. BURIAL SQUAD, SPOTSYLVANIA COURT HOUSE
After a photograph by Alexander Gardner, 1864.
Pen, 6-1/4 x 8-1/4 (sight size), signed *Taber / 85.*
Inscribed *Allsops House / Campaign of 1864.*
Engraved: *Century* 34:290, June, 1887; *Battles and
Leaders* IV-174.
PLATE 173

447. PRISONER OF WAR CAMP, FLORENCE, SOUTH
        CAROLINA
After a sketch by Robert K. Sneden, 1864.
Pen, 3-1/2 x 7 (sight size). Inscribed title.
Engraved: *Century* 40:620, Aug., 1890.
PLATE 176

448. LIBBY PRISON, RICHMOND
After a photograph by Alexander Gardner, 1865.
Pen, 5 x 10 (sight size), signed *Taber / After Photo.*
Inscribed title.
Engraved: *Century* 35:771, March, 1888.
PLATE 177

449. MAIN GATE, CAMP MORTON
Prisoner of war camp, Indianapolis, Ind.; after a
wartime photograph.
Pen, 3-1/2 x 6-7/8 (sight size), signed *Taber*. Inscribed title.
Engraved: *Century* 42:759, Sept., 1891.

450. ISSUING RATIONS, ANDERSONVILLE
Prisoner of war camp, Andersonville, Ga.; after a
photograph by A. J. Riddle, Aug., 1864.
Pen, 11-5/16 x 16-1/8, signed *Taber*. Inscribed title.
Engraved: *Century* 40:457, July, 1890.
PLATE 178

451. ALLOTMENT OF RATIONS, ANDERSONVILLE
Prisoner of war camp, Andersonville, Ga.; original
illustration.
Pen, 13-3/8 x 20, signed *Taber*. Inscribed *Andersonville / Serving rations by squad.*
Engraved: *Century* 40:458, July, 1890.

452. WEARY HOURS, ANDERSONVILLE
Prisoner of war camp, Andersonville, Ga.; original
illustration.
Pen, 4-1/2 x 11-3/8 (sight size), signed *Taber*. Inscribed title.
Engraved: *Century* 40:447, July, 1890.
PLATE 179

453. SENTRY, JOHNSON'S ISLAND
Prisoner of war camp, Sandusky Bay, Ohio; original illustration.
Pen, 13-1/2 x 9-1/2. Inscribed *Johnson's Island /
The Limit.*
Engraved: *Century* 41:711, March, 1891.

454. THE DEADLINE, JOHNSON'S ISLAND
Prisoner of war camp, Sandusky Bay, Ohio; original illustration.
Pen, 8-1/2 x 7-1/2 (sight size), signed *Taber*. Inscribed title. On verso: two artist's preliminary
sketches.
Engraved: *Century* 41:711, March, 1891.
PLATE 180

455. COLD QUARTERS, JOHNSON'S ISLAND
Prisoner of war camp, Sandusky Bay, Ohio; original illustration.
Pen, 4-1/2 x 10 (sight size), signed *Taber / 90.*
Inscribed title. On verso: artist's preliminary
sketches.
Engraved: *Century* 41:705, March, 1891.
PLATE 181

449

451

453

458

459

460

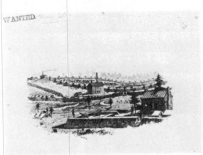

461

462

463

464

467

468

469

470

474

456. VISITORS AT ANDERSONVILLE
Prisoner of war camp, Andersonville, Ga.; original illustration.
Pen, 9-1/2 x 5-1/4 (sight size).
Engraved: *Century* 40:606, Aug., 1890.
PLATE 182

457. ANDERSONVILLE STOCKADE
Prisoner of war camp, Andersonville, Ga.; after a photograph by A. J. Riddle, Aug., 1864.
Pen, 7 x 18 (sight size), signed *Taber*. Inscribed *Looking N.E. from SW corner.*
Engraved: *Century* 40:608, Aug., 1890.
PLATE 183

458. TENT LODGINGS, ANDERSONVILLE
Prisoner of war camp, Andersonville, Ga.; after a photograph by A. J. Riddle, Aug., 1864.
Pen and wash, 12 x 7 (sight size), signed *Taber*. Inscribed *The Cells of Andersonville.*
Engraved: *Century* 40:606, Aug., 1890.

459. NORTH END, ANDERSONVILLE STOCKADE
Prisoner of war camp, Andersonville, Ga.; after a photograph by A. J. Riddle, Aug., 1864.
Pen, 13-1/2 x 21-1/2, signed *Taber*. Inscribed *Birds Eye view of North End of Andersonville Prison. Prisoners digging roots etc.*
Engraved: *Century* 40:460, July, 1890.

460. SOUTH END, ANDERSONVILLE STOCKADE
Prisoner of war camp, Andersonville, Ga.; after a photograph by A. J. Riddle, Aug., 1864.
Pen, 10 x 16-1/2, signed *Taber*. Inscribed title.
Engraved: *Century* 40:459, July, 1890.

461. ANDERSONVILLE STOCKADE, FROM CAPTAIN WIRZ' HEADQUARTERS
Prisoner of war camp, Andersonville, Ga.; after a sketch by Robert K. Sneden, *c.* 1864.
Pen, 8 x 10-3/4. Inscribed title.
Engraved: *Century* 40:612, Aug., 1890

462. SOUTH GATE, ANDERSONVILLE
Prisoner of war camp, Andersonville, Ga.; after a sketch by Robert K. Sneden, *c.* 1864.
Pen, 7-5/8 x 13-1/2. Inscribed title.
Engraved: *Century* 40:454, July, 1890.

463. GRAVES OF THE "RAIDERS," ANDERSONVILLE
Executed by fellow prisoners for murder, prisoner of war camp, Andersonville, Ga.; after a postwar photograph.
Pen, 3-1/8 x 2-15/16 (sight size). Inscribed *Graves of six Raiders / Hung July 11 1864 / Andersonville Prison.*
Engraved: *Century* 40:609, Aug., 1890.

464. ESCAPE FROM ANDERSONVILLE
Prisoner of war camp, Andersonville, Ga.; original illustration.
Pen and wash, 16-1/2 x 13-3/8 on mount.

465. CONFEDERATE RAIDERS, HATTERAS ISLAND
Oct., 1861; original illustration.
Pen and crayon, 5 x 14-1/2 (sight size), signed *Taber*. Inscribed *Retreat to the Boats.*
Engraved: *Battles and Leaders* I-638.
PLATE 188

466. CONFEDERATE WATER BATTERY, PENSACOLA
After a photograph by J. D. Edwards, Feb., 1861.
Pen, 7-1/4 x 10-1/2, signed *Taber*.
Engraved: *Battles and Leaders* I-30.
PLATE 189

467.   32-POUNDER, GUNBOAT C.S.S. "TEASER"
James River, Va.; after a photograph, July, 1862.
Pen, 4-1/2 x 5 (sight size), signed *Taber*. Inscribed
*Vicksburg / 100 pdr gun on Confederate blockade
runner Teaser* [sic].

468.   NAVAL AMMUNITION
After a wartime photograph.
Pen, 3 x 3 (sight size), signed *Taber / 86*. Inscribed
Initial / Alabama.
Engraved: *Century* 31:923, April, 1886; *Battles and
Leaders* IV-615.

469.   C.S.S. "SHENANDOAH"
After a wartime sketch by one of the ship's officers,
Dabney M. Scales.
Pen, 3-1/2 x 6-1/2 (sight size). On verso: critique
by one of the ship's officers, John T. Mason.
Engraved: *Century* 56:602, Aug., 1898.

470.   C.S.S. "ALABAMA"
After an unattributed wartime sketch.
Pen, 4-3/4 x 9-1/4 (sight size). Inscribed *Alabama
or "290."*
Engraved: *Century* 31:901, April, 1886; *Battles and
Leaders* IV-601.

471.   DIVERSION ON DECK
Alabama crewmen; original illustration.
Pen, 12-7/8 x 17-1/2, signed *Taber / 85*. Inscribed
title.
Engraved: *Century* 31:903, April, 1886.
PLATE 204

472.   LOOTING ABOARD A PRIZE
Alabama crewmen; original illustration.
Pen, 12-1/2 x 16-1/4, signed *Taber / 85*. Inscribed
Looting an American.
Engraved: *Century* 31:903, April, 1886.
PLATE 205

473.   CHRISTMAS ON ARACAS KEYS
Alabama crewmen; original illustration.
Pen, 12 x 17-1/2, signed *Taber / 85*. Inscribed
Skylarking Ashore.
Engraved: *Century* 31:904, April, 1886.
PLATE 206

474.   AN "ALABAMA" SAILOR IN PORT
Original illustration.
Pen, 7 x 5-1/4 (sight size). Inscribed *An object of
Curiosity*.
Engraved: *Century* 31:905, April, 1886.

475.   U.S.S. "KEARSARGE"
After a sketch by Edward E. Preble, 1864.
Pen, 3 x 6 (sight size).
Engraved: *Century* 31:922, April, 1886; *Battles and
Leaders* IV-614.

476.   CREW OF U.S.S. "KEARSARGE"
After a wartime photograph.
Pen, 11-3/8 x 13-3/16, signed *Taber / After Photo*.
Inscribed *The Crew at Quarters / The Kearsarge*.
Engraved: *Century* 31:925, April, 1886; *Battles and
Leaders* IV-616.

477.   "KEARSARGE" GUN CREW
Original illustration.
Pen and crayon, 8-1/2 x 13-3/4 (sight size), signed
Taber / 86.
Engraved: *Century* 31:929, April, 1886.
Collection of Robert B. Mayo.
PLATE 208

478.   CREW OF THE MONITOR "LEHIGH"
After a photograph, c. 1863.
Pen, 5-1/2 x 9-1/8 (sight size), signed *Taber / 85*.
Inscribed title.
Engraved: *Century* 31:290, Dec., 1895.
PLATE 213

479.   THE MARSH BATTERY, MORRIS ISLAND
Charleston Harbor; after a photograph, 1863.
Pen, 4-3/16 x 7-15/16 (sight size), signed *Taber*.
Inscribed title.
Engraved: *Battles and Leaders* IV-66.
PLATE 215

480.   BATTERY HAYS, MORRIS ISLAND
Charleston Harbor; after a photograph, 1863.
Pen, 4-1/2 x 7-1/4 (sight size), signed *Taber*. In-
scribed *Battery Hays. / 30 pounder Parrott Rifles—
against Wagner— / Charleston / 1863*.
Engraved: *Battles and Leaders* IV-52.
PLATE 216

481.   THE FATE OF THE "ALBEMARLE"
Plymouth, N.C.; after eyewitness sketches by Alexander C. Stuart, 1864.
Pen, 12-1/2 x 12, signed (by proxy) *A. C. Stuart /
U.S.N. 1864*. Two drawings. Inscribed (top) *Confederate Ram Albermarle as she lay sunk at Plymouth N.C.*; (bottom) *Attack of Ram Albermarle
on Fleet in Albermarle Sound—"Sassacus" ramming the Ram*.
PLATE 221

482.   RUINS OF FORT FISHER
Wilmington, N.C.; after a photograph by Timothy
H. O'Sullivan, Jan., 1865.
Pen, 5-1/2 x 9-1/4, signed *Taber*. Inscribed *Land
front Ft. Fisher*.
Engraved: *Battles and Leaders* IV-647.
PLATE 225

483.   LAND FACE, FORT FISHER
Wilmington, N.C.; after a photograph by Timothy
H. O'Sullivan, Jan., 1865.
Pen, 3 x 10-1/4 (sight size), signed *Taber*. Inscribed
Land face of Northeast Salient / Ft. Fisher.
Engraved: *Battles and Leaders* IV-659.

484.   INTERIOR OF SEA FACE, FORT FISHER
Wilmington, N.C.; after a photograph by Timothy
H. O'Sullivan, Jan., 1865.
Pen, 9 x 12-1/2, signed *Taber*. Inscribed *Interior
view of first six traverses on sea-face / Ft. Fisher*.
Engraved: *Battles and Leaders* IV-655.

485.   MAIN MAGAZINE, FORT FISHER
Wilmington, N.C.; after a photograph by Timothy
H. O'Sullivan, Jan., 1865.
Pen, 4-1/2 x 9-3/4 (sight size).
Engraved: *Battles and Leaders* IV-649.

486.   DISMOUNTED GUNS, FORT FISHER
Wilmington, N.C.; after photographs by Timothy
H. O'Sullivan, Jan., 1865.
Pen, 8-1/2 x 8-1/2 (sight size), signed *Taber*. Four
drawings. Inscribed title.
PLATE 226

487.   THE LACY HOUSE
Falmouth, Va.; after a photograph by Alexander
Gardner, Dec., 1862.
Pen, 5 x 10 (sight size), signed *Taber / After Photo*.
Inscribed title.
Engraved: *Century* 32:605, Aug., 1886; *Battles and
Leaders* III-107.

475

476

483

484

485

487

64

489

490

494

495

496

488. THE PHILLIPS HOUSE
Falmouth, Va ; after a photograph by Alexander
Gardner, Feb., 1863.
Pen and crayon, 7-5/16 x 9-1/2 on mount, signed
Taber / After Photo.
Engraved: *Century* 32:627, Aug., 1886; *Battles and
Leaders* III-108.
PLATE 228

489. THE MARYE HOUSE
Fredericksburg, Va.; after a wartime photograph by
Alexander Gardner.
Pen, 4-1/2 x 3-7/8 (sight size), signed *Taber / After
Photo*.
Engraved: *Century* 32:618, Aug., 1886; *Battles and
Leaders* III-76.

490. HOUSE BY THE STONE WALL, FREDERICKSBURG
After a wartime photograph.
Pen, 11-1/2 x 8-3/4, signed *Taber / After Photo*.
Inscribed *House where* [Confederate] *Gen'l Cobb
died*.
Engraved: *Century* 32:618, Aug., 1886; *Battles and
Leaders* III-78.

491. THE STONE WALL, FREDERICKSBURG
Battle of Chancellorsville, May 3, 1863; after a pho-
tograph by Mathew B. Brady, May, 1863.
Pen, 8-1/2 x 14-3/4 (sight size), signed *Taber /
After Photo*.
Engraved: *Century* 32:624, Aug., 1886; *Battles and
Leaders* III-226.
PLATE 236

492. SALEM CHURCH
Chancellorsville battlefield; after a photograph,
1884.
Pen, 12-1/2 x 15-3/4, signed *Taber / After Photo*.
Inscribed title.
Engraved: *Century* 32:774, Sept., 1886; *Battles and
Leaders* III-230.
PLATE 237

493. GOING INTO ACTION UNDER FIRE
Federal artillery; after a wartime sketch by Charles
W. Reed.
Pen and crayon, 5-3/4 x 12-1/2 (sight size).
Engraved: *Century* 40:150, May, 1890.
PLATE 241

494. DEDICATION OF THE GETTYSBURG CEMETERY
Nov. 19, 1863; after a photograph.
Pen, 4-3/4 x 9-1/2 (sight size), signed *Taber / After
Photo*.
Engraved: *Century* 33:463, Jan., 1887; *Battles and
Leaders* III-440.

495. VICKSBURG, MISSISSIPPI
After a photograph, c. 1877.
Pen, 2-1/2 x 7-3/4 (sight size), signed *Taber*. In-
scribed title and commentary on dating of source
photograph.
Engraved: *Battles and Leaders* III-542.

496. UNION SIGNAL CORPS HEADQUARTERS,
     VICKSBURG
After a wartime photograph.
Pen, 4 x 7 (sight size), signed *Taber*. Inscribed title.
Engraved: *Battles and Leaders* III-520.

497. UMBRELLA ROCK, LOOKOUT MOUNTAIN
Chattanooga, Tenn.; after a wartime photograph.
Pen, 3 x 2-1/2 (sight size). Inscribed title.
Engraved: *Battles and Leaders* III-714.
PLATE 263

498. THE ANDREWS RAID: BEGINNING OF THE
     PURSUIT
April 12, 1862; original illustration.
Pen, 4-1/2 x 4-1/2 (sight size), signed *Taber*.
Engraved: *Battles and Leaders* II-709.

499. THE ANDREWS RAID: CLEARING THE TRACK
April 12, 1862; original illustration.
Pen, 6-1/2 x 6 (sight size), signed *Taber*. Inscribed
*Andrews Railroad Raid / Pushing the burning car
from under the bridge*.
Engraved: *Battles and Leaders* II-714.
PLATE 264.

500. THE ANDREWS RAID: CONFEDERATES IN PURSUIT
April 12, 1862; original illustration.
Pen and crayon, 12-5/8 x 20-1/2, signed *Taber*.
Engraved: *Century* 35:141, May, 1888; *Battles and
Leaders* II-709.
PLATE 265

501. THE ANDREWS RAID: ABANDONING THE
     "GENERAL"
April 12, 1862; original illustration.
Pen and crayon, 12-1/2 x 19-1/2, signed *Taber*.
Inscribed title.
Engraved: *Battles and Leaders* II-715.
PLATE 266

502. THE FEDERAL RIGHT, MURFREESBORO
Battle of Murfreesboro, Dec. 31, 1862; after a lith-
ographed sketch by Alfred E. Mathews, 1863.
Pen, 5-7/8 x 13 (sight size), signed *Taber*. Inscribed
*The Battle of Stone River or Murfreesboro / Pal-
mer's Scribner's & Beatty's Brigades / From
Guenther's and Loomis' Batteries*.
Engraved: *Battles and Leaders* III-624.
PLATE 269

503. THE LEE HOUSE
Chickamauga battlefield; after a photograph, 1884.
Pen, 4-7/8 x 7-1/2 (sight size), signed *Taber / After
Photo*. Inscribed *J. M. Lee's house—Crawfish
Spring Ga. near battlefield—Rosecrans' hdqtrs—
Site of field hospital*.
Engraved: *Century* 33:951, April, 1887; *Battles and
Leaders* III-668.
PLATE 271

504. LEE AND GORDON'S MILLS
Chickamauga battlefield; after a photograph, 1884.
Pen, 4 x 8-1/2 (sight size), signed *Taber / After
Photo*. Inscribed *Lee & Gordon's Mill (new) Site of
old mill / Chickamauga*.
PLATE 272

505. CONFEDERATE BATTLE LINE AT CHICKAMAUGA
Battle of Chickamauga, Sept. 20, 1863; original il-
lustration.
Pen and crayon, 7-1/2 x 13-1/4, signed *Taber*.
Engraved: *Century* 33:937, April, 1887; *Battles and
Leaders* III-638.
Collection of Robert B. Mayo.
PLATE 273

506. ARMY WAGON
After a wartime photograph.
Pen, 2 x 2-5/8 (sight size), signed *Taber*. Inscribed
title.
Engraved: *Century* 33:133, Nov., 1886.
PLATE 275

507.   THE STEAMBOAT "CHATTANOOGA"
Chattanooga campaign; after a photograph, Nov., 1863.
Pen, 5-1/2 x 9 (sight size), signed *Taber*. Inscribed *Steamer Chattanooga unloading forage at Kellys Landing—Nov. 1863.*
Engraved: *Battles and Leaders* III-677.
PLATE 278

508.   FORT SANDERS, KNOXVILLE
After a photograph, c. Nov., 1863.
Pen, 12-1/2 x 16-1/2, signed *Taber*. Inscribed *Ft. Sanders—Knoxville / Scene of the assault / Northwestern bastion.*
Engraved: *Battles and Leaders* III-738.
PLATE 280

509.   FORT SANDERS BASTION, KNOXVILLE
After a photograph, c. Nov., 1863.
Pen, 2-3/4 x 3-3/16 (sight size). Inscribed *Ft. Sanders / Knoxville / A view of the western face and adjacent ditch of the north western bastion from the south western bastion—showing ground passed over by the enemy in assaulting.*
Engraved: *Battles and Leaders* III-742.

510.   GENERAL HOOKER AND HIS STAFF
Chattanooga campaign; after a photograph, Nov., 1863.
Pen, 12-1/2 x 16-1/2, signed *Taber*. Inscribed title.
Engraved: *Battles and Leaders* III-722.
PLATE 282

511.   U.S. MILITARY BRIDGE AT CHATTANOOGA
After a photograph by R. M. Cressey, March, 1864.
Pen, 13-5/8 x 24-1/4, signed *Taber / After Photo*. Inscribed *U.S. Military Bridge over Tennessee River, Chattanooga, Tenn. Built in Oct. 1863 [sic] by the army engineer force after Battle of Chickamauga.*
Engraved: *Century* 33:939, April, 1887; *Battles and Leaders* III-719.
PLATE 285

512.   LOOKING FOR A FRIEND
Original illustration.
Pen, 5 x 7-1/4 (sight size), signed *Taber*. Inscribed title.
Engraved: *Battles and Leaders* IV-195.
PLATE 286

513.   THE WILDERNESS TAVERN
Virginia Wilderness; after a photograph, 1884.
Pen, 8 x 8-1/2 (sight size), signed *Taber / 85*. Inscribed *Wilderness Tavern—(1884) / Gen. Grant's Headquarters 1864.*
Engraved: *Century* 34:277, June, 1887; *Battles and Leaders* IV-147.
PLATE 290

514.   DOWDALL'S TAVERN
Virginia Wilderness; after a wartime photograph.
Pen, 3 x 3-1/4 (sight size), signed *Taber / After Photo*. Inscribed *Dowdall's Tavern / Hdqtrs—Howard.*
Engraved: *Century* 32:762, Sept., 1886; *Battles and Leaders* III-192.

515.   SPOTSYLVANIA COURT HOUSE AND TAVERN
Spotsylvania Court House, Va.; after photographs, 1864.
Pen, 5 x 5-7/8 (sight size), signed *Taber*. Two drawings. Inscribed title.
Engraved: *Century* 34:287, June, 1887; *Battles and Leaders* IV-132.
PLATE 294

516.   FEDERAL WOUNDED ON THE GROUNDS OF THE MARYE HOUSE
Fredericksburg, Va.; after a photograph by Mathew B. Brady or assistant, May, 1864.
Pen, 8-3/4 x 13 (sight size), signed *Taber / After Photo.*
Engraved: *Century* 32:617, Aug., 1886; *Battles and Leaders* IV-149.
PLATE 296

517.   AN INCIDENT AT COLD HARBOR
Cold Harbor, Va.; after a sketch by Charles W. Reed, June, 1864.
Pen and crayon, 12-1/4 x 17-15/16, signed *Taber*. Inscribed *Incident in 5th Battery Cold Harbor / Reed's Sketch Book.*
Engraved: *Battles and Leaders* IV-221.

518.   UNION BATTERY, PETERSBURG
Siege of Petersburg; after a photograph by Timothy H. O'Sullivan, June, 1864.
Pen and crayon, 11 x 19-3/4, signed *Taber*.
Engraved: *Century* 35:582, Feb., 1888; *Battles and Leaders* IV-533.
PLATE 301

519.   BATTERY WAGON
Federal telegraph corps, siege of Petersburg; after a photograph by David Knox, Sept., 1864.
Pen, 5-3/8 x 8-7/8, signed *Taber / After Photo*. Inscribed *Field Telegraph / Battery Wagon.*
Engraved: *Century* 38:791, Sept., 1889.
PLATE 303

520.   ALLATOONA PASS, GEORGIA
After a photograph by George N. Barnard, 1864.
Pen, 7 x 14-1/2 (sight size), signed *Taber*. Inscribed *Allatoona Pass / Looking north / Corse's Ft. on the left.*
Engraved: *Battles and Leaders* IV-323.
PLATE 315

521.   THE RESACA BATTLEFIELD
Resaca, Ga.; after a photograph by George N. Barnard, 1864.
Pen, 6-3/4 x 12-1/2, signed *Taber*.
Engraved: *Battles and Leaders* IV-299.
PLATE 316

522.   CONFEDERATE GUNNERS
Original illustration, based on a photograph by George N. Barnard, Atlanta, 1864.
Pen and crayon, 6-1/2 x 13.
Engraved: *Battles and Leaders* IV-440.
Collection of Robert B. Mayo.
PLATE 321

523.   OCCUPIED ATLANTA
After a photograph, 1864.
Pen, 5 x 8-3/4 (sight size), signed *Taber*.
Engraved: *Century* 34:464, July, 1887; *Battles and Leaders* IV-671.
PLATE 325

524.   THE CALICO HOUSE
Atlanta, Ga.; after a wartime photograph.
Pen, 10-11/16 x 12-1/2, signed *Taber*. Inscribed title.
Engraved: *Century* 34:462, July, 1887; *Battles and Leaders* IV-259.

498

509

514

517

524

528

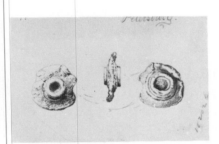

529

530

531

535

536

525.   DESTROYING RAILROADS, ATLANTA
After a photograph by George N. Barnard, 1864.
Pen, 6 x 9-1/4 (sight size), signed *Taber*. Inscribed *Sherman's Soldiers tearing up the Railroad before leaving Atlanta.*
Engraved: *Century* 34:917, Oct., 1887; *Battles and Leaders* IV-664.
PLATE 326

526.   PICKET POST, FORT SEDGWICK
Siege of Petersburg; after a photograph by Mathew B. Brady, 1864.
Pen, 4 x 8-1/4 (sight size), signed *Taber*. Inscribed *Union Picket line in front of Fort Mahone / Petersburg.*
Engraved: *Century* 34:760, Sept., 1887; *Battles and Leaders* IV-568.
PLATE 329

527.   FORT SEDGWICK, PETERSBURG
Siege of Petersburg; after photographs by Timothy H. O'Sullivan, April, 1865.
Pen, 9-1/4 x 9 (sight size), signed *Taber*. Three drawings. Inscribed *Fort Sedgwick—generally known as "Fort Hell" / Looking north from its center April 1865 / Bomb-proof quarters of men in Fort Sedgwick.*
Engraved: *Century* 34:772, Sept., 1887; *Battles and Leaders* IV-715.
PLATE 335

528.   FORT MAHONE, PETERSBURG
Siege of Petersburg; after a photograph attributed to Thomas C. Roche, April, 1865.
Pen, 5-3/8 x 10-1/8 (sight size), signed *Taber*. Inscribed *Fort Mahone (or Fort Damnation) Petersburg / April 1865.*
Engraved: *Century* 34:782, Sept., 1887; *Battles and Leaders* IV-716.

529.   BULLETS THAT MET IN MIDAIR
Siege of Petersburg; after a museum exhibit.
Pen, 2-1/2 x 5-3/4 (sight size).
Engraved: *Century* 34:773, Sept., 1887; *Battles and Leaders* IV-560.

530.   CONFEDERATE BATTERY, JAMES RIVER
Virginia peninsula; after a photograph, 1865.
Pen, 3 x 3-3/4 (sight size), signed *Taber*. Inscribed title.

531.   CONFEDERATE FORT DARLING
Virginia peninsula; after a photograph.
Pen, 3 x 4-1/8 (sight size), signed *Taber / 85*. Inscribed title.
Engraved: *Century* 30:615, Aug., 1885; *Battles and Leaders* II-267.

532.   VMI CADET, 1861
Virginia Military Institute cadet; original illustration.
Pen, 5-5/8 x 2 (sight size), signed *Taber*.
Engraved: *Century* 37:461, Jan., 1889.
PLATE 337

533.   VMI CADET, 1864
Virginia Military Institute cadet; original illustration.
Pen, 5 x 2 (sight size).
Engraved: *Century* 37:465, Jan., 1889; *Battles and Leaders* IV-480.
PLATE 338

534.   THE TAYLOR HOTEL, WINCHESTER, VIRGINIA
After a postwar photograph.
Pen, 6-1/2 x 6-3/4 (sight size), signed *Taber*. Inscribed *Taylor House—Winchester Va. / Army Hospital during the war.*
PLATE 339

535.   THE CARTER HOUSE
Franklin, Tenn., battlefield; after a photograph, 1884.
Pen, 6-7/8 x 12-1/2, signed *Taber*. Inscribed *Corner view of Col. Carter's house from lane.*
Engraved: *Century* 34:605, Aug., 1887; *Battles and Leaders* IV-449.

536.   THE COLUMBIA TURNPIKE AND THE CARTER HOUSE
Franklin, Tenn., battlefield; after photographs, 1884.
Pen, 7-3/16 x 16-5/8. Two drawings. Inscribed (left) *Carter House from Columbia Turnpike looking north—Gen. Cox's headquarters. Centre of Federal position;* (right) *Col. Carter's House / from Columbia pike.*
Engraved: *Century* 34:605, Aug., 1887; *Battles and Leaders* IV-449.

537.   THE CARTER GIN HOUSE
Franklin, Tenn., battlefield; after photographs, 1886.
Pen, 8 x 12 (sight size), signed *Taber*. Two drawings. Inscribed (top) *Carter's gin house, with view of Rofiers Knob—house and spot where Gen. Adams fell;* (bottom) *Carter's Gin house from Columbia pike (20 feet inside Federal lines).*
Engraved: *Century* 34:606, Aug., 1887; *Battles and Leaders* IV-451.
PLATE 342

538.   HARPETH RIVER BRIDGE, FRANKLIN, TENNESSEE
After a wartime photograph.
Pen, 3-1/4 x 7-1/2 (sight size), signed *Taber*. Inscribed *Big Harpeth River / Murfreesboro bridge / Within Federal lines—Rofiers Knob to the right.*
Engraved: *Century* 34:606, Aug., 1887; *Battles and Leaders* IV-452.

539.   THE STATE CAPITOL, NASHVILLE
After a photograph by George N. Barnard, 1864.
Pen, 11-7/16 x 16-7/8, signed *Taber*. Inscribed title.
Engraved: *Century* 34:614, Aug., 1887; *Battles and Leaders* IV-456.
PLATE 343

540.   STEAMBOATS AT NASHVILLE
After a wartime photograph by R. Poole.
Pen, 9-1/8 x 16-1/2 on mount, signed *Taber*. Inscribed title.
Engraved: *Century* 34:597, Aug., 1887; *Battles and Leaders* IV-413.
PLATE 344

541.   SOUTHWEST FRONT OF THE CAPITOL, NASHVILLE
After a photograph by George N. Barnard, 1864.
Pen, 13-7/8 x 18, signed *Taber*. Inscribed title.
Engraved: *Century* 34:612, Aug., 1887; *Battles and Leaders* IV-461.
PLATE 345

542.   FORTIFIED BRIDGE, NASHVILLE
Cumberland River; after a photograph by George
N. Barnard, 1864.
Pen, 3-1/2 x 3-1/2 (sight size), signed *Taber*.
Engraved: *Century* 34:597, Aug., 1887; *Battles and
Leaders* IV-465.
PLATE 346

543.   UNION DEFENSE LINES, NASHVILLE
After a photograph by George N. Barnard, Dec.,
1864.
Pen, 7 x 8-5/8 on mount, signed *Taber*. Inscribed
View looking over battle field of Nashville.
Engraved: *Century* 34:615, Aug., 1887; *Battles and
Leaders* IV-460.

544.   SHERMAN'S TROOPS DESTROYING A RAILROAD
Carolinas campaign; original illustration.
Pen, 13-7/8 x 18-1/2, signed *Taber*. Inscribed *Sher-
man's march from Savannah / Destroying railroad
track*.
Engraved: *Century* 34:930, Oct., 1887; *Battles and
Leaders* IV-684.
PLATE 349

545.   APPOMATTOX STATION, VIRGINIA
After a photograph by Timothy H. O'Sullivan,
April, 1865.
Pen, 5 x 9-1/4 (sight size), signed *Taber*. Inscribed
title.
PLATE 360

546.   THE MCLEAN HOUSE
Appomattox Court House, Va., after a photograph
by Timothy H. O'Sullivan, April, 1865.
Water color, 6-1/4 x 9 (sight size); signed *Taber*.
Inscribed title.
Collection of Robert B. Mayo.
PLATE 362

547.   THE ESCAPE OF CONFEDERATE SECRETARY OF
        WAR BRECKINRIDGE
After a sketch by John Taylor Wood.
Pen, 2-3/4 x 2 (sight size). Inscribed *Initial / Es-
cape of Gen. Breckinridge*.
Engraved: *Century* 47:110, Nov., 1893.

548.   AFTER THE WAR
Original illustration.
Pen 4 x 4-3/4 (sight size). Inscribed *Rifle Pit cov-
ered with trees*.
Engraved: *Century* 30:294, June, 1885; *Battles and
Leaders* II-347.
PLATE 364

549.   BLOODY HILL, WILSON'S CREEK
After a photograph, c. 1885.
Pen, 3-3/4 x 10-1/2 (sight size), signed *Taber*. In-
scribed *Bloody Hill from the East*. On verso: unat-
tributed description of battlefield site.
Engraved: *Battles and Leaders* I-298.
PLATE 366

550.   BLOODY LANE, ANTIETAM
After a photograph, 1886.
Pen, 3-5/8 x 3-1/8 (sight size), signed *Taber / After
Photo*. Inscribed *Bloody Lane looking towards
Hagerstown Pike / Antietam*.
Engraved: *Century* 32:302, June, 1886; *Battles and
Leaders* II-668.
PLATE 371

551.   BLOODY LANE, ANTIETAM
After a photograph, 1886.
Pen, 10-11/16 x 9-1/2, signed *Taber / After Photo*.
Inscribed title.
Engraved: *Century* 32:303, June, 1886; *Battles and
Leaders* II-668.

552.   ANDERSONVILLE AFTER THE WAR
After photographs, 1868.
Pen, 3-3/8 x 10-1/4 (sight size), signed *Taber*.
Three drawings. Inscribed *Andersonville Prison /
views taken 1868*.
Engraved: *Century* 41:100, Nov., 1890.
PLATE 373

553.   GETTYSBURG MONUMENT
After a photograph, 1886.
Pen, 9 x 14-1/4 (sight size). Inscribed *Monument /
Ninth Mass. Battery / Gettysburg 2nd Day*.
Engraved: *Century* 33:283, Dec., 1886; *Battles and
Leaders* III-307.
PLATE 374

554.   THE NEW HENRY HOUSE, BULL RUN
After a photograph, 1884.
Pen, 4-1/2 x 8-1/2 (sight size), signed *Taber*. In-
scribed title.
Engraved: *Century* 31:466, Jan., 1886; *Battles and
Leaders* I-229.
PLATE 375

555.   ROWLETT'S MILL
Fort Donelson, Tenn., battlefield: after a photo-
graph, 1884.
Pen and wash, 10-3/4 x 9-3/4 on mount, signed
Taber / 84.
Engraved: *Century* 29:303, Dec., 1884; *Battles and
Leaders* I-425.

JAMES E. TAYLOR

Newspaper artist and painter. Born Cincinnati,
Dec. 12, 1839; died New York, June 22, 1901. A
graduate of Notre Dame, Taylor enlisted in the
10th New York in 1861. Sketches he submitted to
Leslie's led that newspaper to hire him as a special
artist in 1863. After the war he traveled widely in
the West, focusing on Indian subjects. He left
Leslie's in 1883 to become a free-lance illustrator.

556.   SHERMAN'S 17TH CORPS CROSSING THE SALUDA
Columbia, S.C., Feb. 17, 1865; after an eyewitness
sketch by the artist.
Water color, 9-1/8 x 16, signed *J. E. Taylor*. In-
scribed *Advance of Sherman's Right-wing—17th
Army Corps crossing Saluda River S.C. 17th Feby /
Drawn by Jas. E. Taylor after his original sketch
published in Frank Leslie's Illustrated Newspaper
Apr. 8 1865*.
Engraved: *Century* 34:931, Oct., 1887; *Battles and
Leaders* IV-686.
PLATE 351

THURE DE THULSTRUP

Illustrator and painter. Born Stockholm, 1848; died
New York, 1930. After military schooling in Swe-
den, Thulstrup served in the French army in the
Franco-Prussian War. He left the military to study
art in Paris, and in 1873 emigrated to Canada. Moving to Boston, he worked for the Prang lithograph
firm and then settled in New York, becoming a
newspaper and magazine illustrator. His specialty
was military subjects.

538

543

547

551

555

561

562

563

564

567

568

557.   BUELL'S TROOPS ARRIVING AT PITTSBURG
        LANDING
Battle of Shiloh, April 6, 1862; original illustration.
Tempera, 14-1/16 x 12-5/16, signed *Thulstrup*. In-
scribed *Battle of Shiloh / Landing of reinforce-
ments on the night of April 6th*.
Engraved: *Century* 29:608, Feb., 1885; *Battles and
Leaders* I-518.
PLATE 66

558.   TAKING DOWN THE STATE FLAG, NEW ORLEANS
April 29, 1862; original illustration.
Pen, 12-1/2 x 15-3/4, signed *Thulstrup*.
Engraved: *Century* 32:457, July, 1886; *Battles and
Leaders* II-94.
PLATE 84

559.   THE BATTLE OF MALVERN HILL
July 1, 1862; original illustration.
Pen, 12 x 18-1/2, signed *Thulstrup*.
Engraved: *Century* 30:631, Aug., 1885; *Battles and
Leaders* II-417.
PLATE 117

560.   FIELD HOSPITAL AT SAVAGE'S STATION
Federal wounded; after a photograph by James F.
Gibson, June, 1862.
Pen, 9-3/4 x 10-1/4 on mount, signed *Thulstrup*.
Engraved: *Century* 30:459, July, 1885; *Battles and
Leaders* II-387.
PLATE 168

UNKNOWN ARTISTS

561.   THE STONE HOUSE
Bull Run battlefield; probably after a postwar pho-
tograph.
Pen, 10-1/2 x 10-3/8. Inscribed title.

562.   THE WOUNDING OF LIEUTENANT WORDEN
Aboard *Monitor* in the battle with *Merrimack*,
March 9, 1862; original illustration.
Pen, 20 x 12-1/2. Inscribed *The blinding of the
commander Worden in the wheel house*.
Engraved: *St. Nicholas* April, 1887.

563.   GUN MONUMENT, NATIONAL CEMETERY,
        CORINTH, MISSISSIPPI
After a postwar photograph.
Pen, 13-3/4 x 11-3/8.

CHARLES A. VANDERHOOF

Illustrator and etcher. Died Locust Point, N.J.,
1918. Vanderhoof was active as an illustrator in
the 1880's, particularly for *Century*, and he contributed
to perfecting the technique of soft-ground etching.
He was an instructor at Cooper Union and active in
the formation of the Art Students' League.

564.   FORTIFIED HOUSE, FAIR OAKS
Peninsula campaign; after a sketch by Robert K.
Sneden, c. June, 1862.
Pen, 10-11/16 x 9-5/8, signed *V*. Inscribed title.
Engraved: *Battles and Leaders* II-257.

565.   FIELD HOSPITALS, FAIR OAKS
Peninsula campaign; after sketches by Robert K.
Sneden, c. June, 1862.
Pen, 9-5/16 x 12-1/2. Two drawings. Inscribed
*Farm House—Fair Oaks Va. / Hyer's House /
Union Hospitals*.
Engraved: *Battles and Leaders* II-254.
PLATE 108

566.   THE BATTLE OF GLENDALE
June 30, 1862; after a sketch by Robert K. Sneden,
June, 1862.
Pen, 7-1/16 x 12-1/8 (sight size). Inscribed *Head-
quarters of Maj Genl Heintzelman, Glendale, Va.
June 30, 1862*.
Engraved: *Battles and Leaders* II-405.
PLATE 114

567.   GENERAL HEINTZELMAN'S HEADQUARTERS,
        MALVERN HILL
Peninsula campaign; after a sketch by Robert K.
Sneden, July, 1862.
Pen, 6-1/4 x 11-1/8. Inscribed title.
Engraved: *Battles and Leaders* II-424.

568.   TURKEY CREEK BRIDGE
Peninsula campaign; after a sketch by Robert K.
Sneden, July, 1862.
Pen, 6-1/4 x 12-1/2. Inscribed title.
Engraved: *Battles and Leaders* II-424.

569.   UNION ENTRENCHMENTS, WESTOVER CHURCH
Peninsula campaign; after a sketch by Robert K.
Sneden, July, 1862.
Pen, 13-1/4 x 18-3/16. Inscribed title.

570.   WHITTAKER'S MILL
Peninsula campaign; after a sketch by Robert K.
Sneden, 1862.
Pen, 8-3/4 x 10-5/8.

571.   GENERAL HEINTZELMAN'S HEADQUARTERS,
        ALEXANDRIA, VIRGINIA
After a sketch by Robert K. Sneden, Sept. 3, 1862.
Pen, 7-1/4 x 12. Inscribed *Head-Quarters of Maj.
Gen. Heintzelman & Slave pen. Alexandria Va.*
Engraved: *Battles and Leaders* II-541.

572.   VIEWS OF DAMAGE TO FORT PULASKI
Savannah River, Ga.; after photographs by Tim-
othy H. O'Sullivan, April, 1862.
Pen, 15-1/4 x 12-1/4, signed *V*. Three drawings.
Inscribed *Fort Pulaski / 1. Interior view of breach.
2. Interior view of front parapet. 3. Close view of
breach*.
Engraved: *Battles and Leaders* II-11.

573.   CASTLE PINCKNEY, CHARLESTON HARBOR
After a wartime sketch by Robert K. Sneden.
Pen, 13 x 16-1/4, signed *V*. Inscribed title. On
verso: commentary on drawing by consultant John
Johnson, former Confederate major of engineers.
Engraved: *Battles and Leaders* IV-6.

574.   FORT MORGAN AND LIGHTHOUSE, MOBILE BAY
After photographs credited to McPherson and
Oliver, Aug., 1864.
Pen, 18-1/4 x 14-3/16, signed *C. A. Vanderhoof*.
Three drawings. Inscribed *Light House Mobile
Point / Fort Morgan S. E. Bastion / Citadel from
North Side*.
Engraved: *Battles and Leaders* IV-382.
PLATE 224

575.   THE CHANCELLOR HOUSE, HOOKER'S
        HEADQUARTERS
Chancellorsville battlefield; after a photograph
taken before the battle.
Pen, 7-5/8 x 10-1/2, signed *C.A.V.*
Engraved: *Battles and Leaders* III-190.

576. THE CHANCELLOR HOUSE
Chancellorsville battlefield; after sketches by Robert K. Sneden, May, 1863.
Pen, 9-3/4 x 9-5/8 (sight size). Two drawings. Inscribed *Headquarters of Maj. Gen. Hooker / The Chancellorsville House / Ruins of Chancellorsville House.*
PLATE 232

577. ROSECRANS' HEADQUARTERS AND OVERALL'S CREEK
Murfreesboro battlefield; after photographs, 1884.
Pen, 9-1/4 x 10, signed *C. A. Vanderhoof.* Two drawings. Inscribed title.
Engraved: *Battles and Leaders* III-620.
PLATE 268

578. MCFADDEN FORD, STONE'S RIVER
Murfreesboro battlefield; after a photograph, 1884.
Pen, 14-9/16 x 18-3/16, signed *C. A. Vanderhoof.* Inscribed title.
Engraved: *Battles and Leaders* III-631.

579. HULK OF THE "STAR OF THE WEST"
Tallahatchie River, Miss.; after a photograph, 1887.
Pen, 12-3/8 x 15-1/4. Inscribed title.
Engraved: *Battles and Leaders* III-550.

580. THE VICKSBURG COURTHOUSE
Vicksburg, Miss.; after a photograph, 1880.
Pen, 14-5/8 x 18-1/8, signed *V.* Inscribed title and commentary on dating of source photograph.
Engraved: *Battles and Leaders* III-480.

581. FORT SANDERS, KNOXVILLE
After a photograph by George N. Barnard, 1864.
Pen, 11-7/8 x 15-1/4. Inscribed title.
Engraved: *Battles and Leaders* III-747.

582. ALDIE GAP, VIRGINIA
After a sketch by Robert K. Sneden, 1863.
Pen, 14-5/8 x 18-3/16. Inscribed title.
Engraved: *Battles and Leaders* IV-83.

583. BEALTON STATION AND BRANDY STATION, VIRGINIA
After sketches by Robert K. Sneden, c. 1863.
Pen, 14-9/16 x 18-1/4. Two drawings. Inscribed *Bealton Station Va. / Brandy Station (Both on the Orange and Alexandria RR) Va.*
Engraved: *Battles and Leaders* IV-98.

584. FORT RAMSAY, UPTON'S HILL, VIRGINIA
Federal fortification; after a sketch by Robert K. Sneden, 1863.
Pen, 5-11/16 x 9-13/16 (sight size), signed *V.* Inscribed title.
Engraved: *Battles and Leaders* IV-82.
PLATE 287

585. WARRENTON JUNCTION, VIRGINIA
After a sketch by Robert K. Sneden, 1863.
Pen, 6-11/16 x 10-7/8 (sight size). Inscribed title.
Engraved: *Battles and Leaders* IV-86.
PLATE 288

586. FORT DE RUSSY, RED RIVER
Red River campaign; after a sketch by James M. Alden, c. March, 1864.
Pen, 6-1/4 x 13 (sight size). Inscribed title.
Engraved: *Battles and Leaders* IV-371.
PLATE 314

569

578

570

579

571

580

572

581

573

582

573

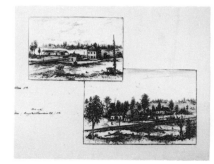

583

587

588

589

590

591

592

587. FAYETTEVILLE, ARKANSAS
After a postwar photograph by Hansard & Osborn.
Pen, 12-3/8 x 14-7/8.
Engraved: *Battles and Leaders* III-448.

588. HELENA, ARKANSAS
After a photograph, 1888.
Pen, 12-1/2 x 15-1/4, signed *C. A. Vanderhoof.*
Engraved: *Battles and Leaders* III-455.

589. CONFEDERATE ENTRENCHMENTS AT RESACA
Resaca, Ga.; after a photograph by George N. Barnard, 1864.
Pen, 16-1/2 x 20-3/4, signed *C. A. Vanderhoof.*
Engraved: *Battles and Leaders* IV-280.

590. UNION LINES AT ALLATOONA PASS
Allatoona Pass, Ga.; after a photograph by George N. Barnard, 1864.
Pen, 16-1/2 x 20-3/4, signed *C. A. Vanderhoof.*
Inscribed title.
Engraved: *Battles and Leaders* IV-344.

591. UNION LINES IN FRONT OF KENNESAW MOUNTAIN
Marietta, Ga.; after a photograph by George N. Barnard, 1864.
Pen, 16-1/2 x 20-3/4.
Engraved: *Battles and Leaders* IV-308.

592. CONFEDERATE WORKS, CHATTAHOOCHIE RIVER
Atlanta, Ga.; after a photograph by George N. Barnard, 1864.
Pen, 16-1/2 x 20-3/4, signed *C. A. Vanderhoof.*
Inscribed title.
Engraved: *Battles and Leaders* IV-310.

593. THE VALLEY PIKE, CEDAR CREEK, VIRGINIA
After a photograph, 1885.
Pen, 16-1/2 x 20-13/16, signed *C. A. Vanderhoof.*
Engraved: *Battles and Leaders* IV-522.

ALFRED R. WAUD

Newspaper artist and illustrator. Born London, Oct. 2, 1828; died Marietta, Ga., April 6, 1891. Before emigrating to the United States in 1850, Waud studied art at the School of Design of the Royal Academy. In the fifties he was a newspaper artist in Boston and New York, and when the Civil War began he was working for the *New York Illustrated News.* He spent nearly the entire war traveling with the Army of the Potomac (in February, 1862, he left the *News* for *Harper's*). After a postwar tour of the South for *Harper's*, Waud turned free lance in 1869 and continued his travels, reporting on the West as well as the South for various magazines and such publishing projects as *Picturesque America.* His *Battles and Leaders* illustrations were among the last of his career.

594. CONFEDERATE RETREAT THROUGH MECHANICSVILLE
Peninsula campaign, May 24, 1862; after a sketch by the artist, May, 1862, and a photograph by John Reekie, April, 1865.
Pen, 13-1/8 x 14-3/4, signed *A.R.W.* Inscribed title.
Engraved: *Century* 30:313, June, 1885; *Battles and Leaders* II-322.
PLATE 103

595. WHITE HOUSE, PAMUNKEY RIVER
Peninsula campaign; after sketches by the artist, June, 1862.
Pen, 13-1/4 x 15-3/8, signed *A. R. Waud.* Two drawings. Inscribed *The White House—before & after the fire.*
Engraved: *Century* 30:131, May, 1885; *Battles and Leaders* II-179.
PLATE 105

596. SUMNER'S CORPS CROSSING THE CHICKAHOMINY
Battle of Fair Oaks, May 31, 1862; after an eyewitness sketch by the artist.
Water color, 10-1/8 x 15-3/4, signed *ARW.*
Engraved: *Century* 30:133, May, 1885; *Battles and Leaders* II-246.
PLATE 110

597. DESTRUCTION OF AN AMMUNITION TRAIN
Peninsula campaign; after a sketch by the artist, June, 1862.
Water color, 4-9/16 x 5-9/16 on mount, signed *ARW.*
Engraved: *Battles and Leaders* II-371.
Collection of Robert B. Mayo.
PLATE 115

598. ENGAGEMENT AT WHITE OAK BRIDGE
June 30, 1862; after an eyewitness sketch by the artist.
Pen, 12-15/16 x 17-1/4, signed *ARW.*
Engraved: *Century* 30:462, July, 1885; *Battles and Leaders* II-389.
PLATE 116

599. BERKELEY, HARRISON'S LANDING
Peninsula campaign; after a sketch by the artist, July, 1862.
Pen, 10-3/8 x 13-1/2, signed *ARW.* Inscribed *Birthplace of Wm. Hy. Harrison. Road front of Harrison house. Occupied as a hospital and [as] a signal station. Scaffolds [for] that purpose built about the chim[neys].*
Engraved: *Century* 30:639, Aug., 1885; *Battles and Leaders* II-427.
PLATE 118

600. WESTOVER, HARRISON'S LANDING
Peninsula campaign; after a sketch by the artist, July, 1862.
Pen, 10-3/4 x 14, signed *A.R.W.* Inscribed *Headquarters of Genl Fitz John Porter July 1862. Westover Mansion. Road foreground headquarters in background.*
Engraved: *Century* 30:638, Aug., 1885; *Battles and Leaders* II-425.

601. THE FATE OF THE RAIL FENCE
After a sketch by the artist, 1862.
Pen, 9-1/4 x 8, signed *A. R. Waud.* Inscribed discussion and anecdotes about troops using split-rail fences for firewood.
Engraved: *Century* 34:918, Oct., 1887; *Battles and Leaders* IV-668.
PLATE 167

602. SAILOR ON PICKET DUTY
Federal sailor; probably after a wartime sketch by Horatio L. Wait.
Pen, 6-1/2 x 5 (sight size), signed *ARW.* Inscribed title.
PLATE 184

603. FISHING TORPEDOES OUT OF THE POTOMAC
After a sketch by the artist, 1861, and a wartime photograph by James F. Gibson.
Pen, 12-1/2 x 9, signed *A.R.W.* Inscribed title and *near Shipping point by the crew of the Freeborn Capt. Ward.* On verso: description of the mine and of minesweeping operations.
PLATE 185

604. BLOCKADE RUNNERS
After wartime sketches by Horatio L. Wait.
Pen, 10-3/4 x 15-1/8, signed *ARW.* Inscribed *1. Conf. Blockade Runner "Neptune" captured off Mobile 1863 by U.S.S. Lackawanna / 2. Conf. Blockade Runner Vesta / 3. Conf. Blockade Runner Alliance.*
Engraved: *Century* 56:920, Oct., 1898.
PLATE 199

605. SINKING OF THE MONITOR "WEEHAWKEN"
Charleston Harbor, Dec. 6, 1863; after a sketch by Horatio L. Wait, 1863.
Pen, 11-3/16 x 14-1/8, signed *ARW.* Inscribed title.
Engraved: *Century* 56:828, Oct., 1898.

606. ON PICKET DUTY OFF MOBILE
Federal blockade; after a sketch by Horatio L. Wait, 1863.
Pen, 11-1/8 x 14-1/16, signed *ARW.* Inscribed title.
Engraved: *Century* 56:914, Oct., 1898.

607. RECEIVING THE MAIL OFF MOBILE
Federal blockade; after a sketch by Horatio L. Wait, 1863.
Pen, 11-1/8 x 14-3/16, signed *ARW.* Inscribed *Receiving the mail off Mobile from Quartermaster's Tug "Sykes."*
Engraved: *Century* 56:922, Oct., 1898.

608. "SACHEM" AND "MISSISSIPPI" AT PORT HUDSON
Port Hudson, La., March 14, 1863; after an unattributed wartime sketch.
Pen, 12-1/2 x 15-1/8, signed *ARW.* Inscribed *The Sachem falling back. The Mississippi floating after in flames. Pt. Hudson. April 14, 1863.*

609. THE DEVIL'S DEN, GETTYSBURG
July 2, 1863; after an eyewitness sketch by the artist.
Pen, 6-5/8 x 9-1/4 (sight size), signed *ARW.* Inscribed *Vincents brigade falling back from the Devils Den July 2nd 1863.*
Engraved: *Century* 33:299, Dec., 1886; *Battles and Leaders* III-323.
PLATE 240

610. THE ATTACK OF SMITH'S CORPS, COLD HARBOR
Battle of Cold Harbor, June 1, 1864; after an eyewitness sketch by the artist.
Pen, 7 x 12-3/4, signed *A.R.W.* Inscribed on verso *Fight on June 1st 1864 (Smith's Corps) near Cold Harbor. Prisoners and wounded coming in from the front. The lines face the Chickahominy which is beyond the distant crest, held by the rebels.*
PLATE 298

611. ENTRENCHING AT COLD HARBOR
Battle of Cold Harbor, June 3, 1864; after an eyewitness sketch by the artist.
Pen, 6-1/4 x 9-1/2 (sight size), signed *A.R.W.* Inscribed *June 3d 1864 Cold Harbor. Hancock's front. There were no picks and shovels. The men threw up breastworks by their hands with the assistance of bayonets, tin plates and old canteens.*
Engraved: *Battles and Leaders* IV-156.
PLATE·299

612. IN THE FEDERAL LINES AT PETERSBURG
Siege of Petersburg; after sketches by the artist, July, 1864.
Pen, 12 x 15, signed *A.R.W.* Two drawings. Inscribed (left) *Sharpshooters, 18th Corps front. Siege of Petersburg;* (right) *Bivouac of the 5th Corps in the rifle pits.*
Engraved: *Battles and Leaders* IV-560.
PLATE 302

613. A SAP ROLLER
Siege of Petersburg; after a sketch by the artist, 1864.
Water color, 9-15/16 x 14-3/8, signed *A.R.W.* Inscribed title.
PLATE 304

614. EXPLOSION OF THE PETERSBURG MINE
Siege of Petersburg, July 30, 1864; after an eyewitness sketch by the artist.
Pen, 16 x 20-1/2, signed *A.R.W.* Inscribed title.
Engraved: *Battles and Leaders* IV-561.
PLATE 305

615. THE BATTLE OF THE CRATER
Siege of Petersburg, July 30, 1864; after an eyewitness sketch by the artist.
Pen, 12 x 15, signed *A.R.W.* Inscribed *The advance upon the Crater after the explosion of the mine. Petersburg July 30, 1864.*
Engraved: *Battles and Leaders* IV-552.
PLATE 306

616. ON PICKET DUTY
Siege of Petersburg; after a sketch by the artist, 1864.
Pen, 12-1/2 x 15-1/4, signed *A.R.W.* Inscribed *One of the Pickets in front of Ft. Hell* and on verso description of pickets' activities during siege of Petersburg.
PLATE 328

617. FORTIFIED BATTERY, PETERSBURG
Siege of Petersburg; after a sketch by the artist, Dec., 1864.
Pen, 9-3/8 x 11-1/2 on mount, signed *A. R. Waud.* Inscribed *Casemated field work in the siege lines. Petersburg, Va. Dec. 1864.*
PLATE 330

618. GENERAL WARREN'S HEADQUARTERS, GLOBE TAVERN
Siege of Petersburg, after a sketch by the artist, 1864.
Pen, 12 x 15 Inscribed *Genl Warrens head-qtr's Yellow Tavern* [sic].
Engraved: *Battles and Leaders* IV-571.
PLATE 331

619. THE BATTLE OF CEDAR CREEK
Oct. 19, 1864; after an eyewitness sketch by the artist.
Pen, 12-1/2 x 15-1/4, signed *ARW.* Inscribed *Battle of Cedar Creek. Recovery of guns lost in the morning and troops pursuing the enemy. Scene on the turnpike. In the middle distance are remains of a camp burning (crossed out: 12th Maine and others of the 19th Corps), about 1-1/2 miles from Strasburg.*
PLATE 340

620. THE THUNDERBOLT BATTERY, SAVANNAH
Confederate fortification, Savannah, Ga.; after a sketch by William Waud, Dec., 1864.
Pen, 6-3/8 x 15-1/4, signed *A.R.W.* Inscribed title. Inscribed on verso *This fort was built in 1861. It was of immense strength and was designed to protect Wilmington* [sic] *from attacks by the river.*
PLATE 348

593

600

605

606

607

608

621. FORCING A CROSSING OF THE LITTLE
SALKEHATCHIE
Near Bamberg, S.C., Feb. 6, 1865; after an eyewitness sketch by William Waud.
Pen, 8-1/2 x 12 (sight size), signed *A. R. Waud.* Inscribed title and *Wever's brigade 2nd brigade 3rd Div. 15th Corps charging the enemies defenses across the river.*
Engraved: *Century* 34:925, Oct., 1885; *Battles and Leaders* IV-678.
PLATE 350

622

622. FEDERAL SKIRMISHERS CROSSING THE NORTH
EDISTO
Near Orangeburg, S.C., Feb., 1865; after an eyewitness sketch by William Waud.
Pen, 8 x 12. Inscribed *Col. Wells Jones brigade crossing the North Edisto at Shillings bridge. The men passed over on a floating foot bridge to charge the works before the pontoons were laid.*
Engraved: *Century* 34:929, Oct., 1887; *Battles and Leaders* IV-685.

625

623. RAISING THE COLORS, COLUMBIA, SOUTH
CAROLINA
Feb. 17, 1865; after an eyewitness sketch by William Waud.
Pen, 12-1/2 x 15-1/4. Inscribed *Hoisting the Union flag upon the old State House, Columbia, S.C.*
Engraved: *Century* 34:933, Oct., 1887; *Battles and Leaders* IV-687.
PLATE 352

628

WILLIAM WAUD

Newspaper artist and illustrator. Born England; died Jersey City, N.J., Nov. 10, 1878. In the 1850's, after serving as an assistant to Sir Joseph Paxton in the construction of the Crystal Palace, which housed Britain's Great Exhibition in 1851, William joined brother Alfred in the United States. At the beginning of the war he was on the staff of *Leslie's*, but in 1864 he switched to his brother's paper, *Harper's*.

624. SHERMAN'S 14TH CORPS CROSSING JUNIPER
CREEK
Near Chesterfield, S.C., March 9, 1865; an eyewitness sketch.
Water color, 9 x 12. Inscribed *Gen. Slocum, Baird &c / Houses up to the right full of rosin.* Inscribed on verso *Juniper Creek March 9th / 3rd Div 14th A.C. (Gen. Bairds) Houses & Barrels filled with rosin on fire running down the banks into the creek & floating on the surface of the water. Troops running across, fire catching the bridge.*
Engraved: *Harper's Weekly*, April 29, 1865, p. 269; *Century* 34:934, Oct., 1887.
PLATE 354

631

JACOB WELLS

625. CASEMATE, FORT HINDMAN
Capture of Confederate Fort Hindman, Arkansas Post, Ark., Jan. 11, 1863; after a photograph.
Pen, 5-7/8 x 7-7/8. Inscribed title.
Engraved: *Battles and Leaders* III-454.

632

JOHN D. WOODWARD

Illustrator and landscape painter. Born Middlesex County, Va., July 12, 1846; died New Rochelle, N.Y., June 5, 1924. Woodward's first illustrations were for *Picturesque America* (1872-74), after which he traveled widely in Europe and the Middle East, working with Harry Fenn to prepare illustrations for *Picturesque Europe* and *Picturesque Palestine, Sinai and Egypt*. After 1905, when he settled in New Rochelle, Woodward devoted himself to landscape painting.

626. THE ROBINSON HOUSE
Bull Run battlefield; after a photograph, Aug., 1862.
Pen, 4-3/8 x 5-3/4 (sight size), signed *JDW.* Inscribed title.
Engraved: *Battles and Leaders* I-213.
PLATE 19

627. SUDLEY CHURCH
Bull Run battlefield; after a photograph by Alexander Gardner, March, 1862.
Pen, 3-7/8 x 5-1/2 (sight size), signed *JDW.* Inscribed title.
Engraved: *Century* 31:469, Jan., 1886; *Battles and Leaders* II-510.
PLATE 20

628. CONFEDERATE FORTIFICATIONS, COLUMBUS,
KENTUCKY
After a sketch by Henri Lovie published in *Frank Leslie's Illustrated Newspaper*, March 22, 1862.
Pen, 12 x 14-5/8 signed *JDW.* Inscribed title.
Engraved: *Battles and Leaders* I-354.

629. THE SHEBANG AND POST OFFICE, BRANDY
STATION, VIRGINIA
U.S. Sanitary Commission (top); after a photograph by James Gardner, Dec., 1863. Federal Post Office headquarters (bottom); after a photograph by Timothy H. O'Sullivan, Nov., 1863.
Pen, 13-1/4 x 15-3/8, signed *JDW.* Two drawings. Inscribed title.
Engraved: *Battles and Leaders* IV-90.
PLATE 43

630. CHICKAHOMINY SWAMP
Virginia peninsula; after a photograph by Mathew B. Brady, 1862.
Pen, 7-1/2 x 6-1/2 (sight size), signed *JDW.*
Engraved: *Century* 30:455, July, 1885; *Battles and Leaders* II-385.
PLATE 107

631. FORTIFIED CAMP, HARRISON'S LANDING
Peninsula campaign; after a sketch by Alfred R. Waud, July, 1862.
Pen, 8-1/4 x 12-1/2, signed *JDW.* Inscribed *Camp of the 1st Mass Artly Harrisons Landing.*
Engraved: *Century* 30:637, Aug., 1885; *Battles and Leaders* II-429.

632. FOX'S GAP LOOKING EAST
South Mountain, Md.; after a photograph, 1885.
Pen, 5 x 9-5/8 (sight size), signed *JDW.* Inscribed *Renos field—looking east.*
Engraved: *Century* 32:146, May, 1886; *Battles and Leaders* II-572.

633.   FOX'S GAP LOOKING SOUTH
South Mountain, Md.; after a photograph, 1885.
Pen, 5 x 9-5/8 (sight size), signed *JDW*. Inscribed
Renos Field—looking south.
Engraved: *Century* 32:147, May, 1886; *Battles and
Leaders* II-573.

634.   THE PRY HOUSE, MCCLELLAN'S HEADQUARTERS
Antietam battlefield; after a photograph, 1886.
Pen, 13-1/2 x 11-3/4, signed *JDW*. Inscribed title.
Engraved: *Century* 32:128, May, 1886; *Battles and
Leaders* II-638.
PLATE 132

635.   BOTELER'S FORD ON THE POTOMAC
Shepherdstown, Md.; after a photograph, 1885.
Water color, 9-7/8 x 13-3/8, signed *JDW*.
Engraved: *Century* 32:441, July, 1886; *Battles and
Leaders* II-673.

636.   ROSTRUM, NATIONAL CEMETERY, SHARPSBURG,
         MARYLAND
After a photograph, 1885.
Pen, 11-1/4 x 12, signed *JDW*. Inscribed title.
Engraved: *Century* 32:121, March, 1886; *Battles
and Leaders* II-555.

637.   FREDERICKSBURG, VIRGINIA
After a wartime photograph by Mathew B. Brady.
Pen, 12-1/2 x 16-1/2, signed *JDW*. Inscribed title.
Engraved: *Century* 32:632, Aug., 1886; *Battles and
Leaders* III-118.

638.   WELFORD'S MILL ON HAZEL RUN,
         FREDERICKSBURG
After a wartime photograph.
Pen, 8-1/4 x 12. Inscribed title.
Engraved: *Century* 32:611, Aug., 1886; *Battles and
Leaders* III-84.

639.   RUINS OF MANSFIELD, FREDERICKSBURG
After a wartime photograph by Alexander Gardner.
Pen, 5-1/4 x 8-5/8 (sight size), signed *JDW*. In-
scribed *"Mansfield" or Bernard House below Fred-
ericksburg Va.*
Engraved: *Century* 32:637, Aug., 1886; *Battles and
Leaders* III-134.

640.   TODD'S TAVERN
Virginia Wilderness; after a wartime photograph.
Pen, 4-3/8 x 8-1/2 (sight size). Inscribed *Todd's
Tavern as it was*.
Engraved: *Century* 34:302, June, 1887; *Battles and
Leaders* IV-146.

641.   CONFEDERATE ENTRENCHMENTS AT SPOTSYLVANIA
Spotsylvania Court House, Va.; after photographs,
1864.
Pen, 15-1/4 x 12-1/2, signed *JDW*. Four drawings.
Inscribed title.
Engraved: *Century* 34:289, June, 1887; *Battles and
Leaders* IV-133.
PLATE 293

642.   EXTREME RIGHT OF THE CONFEDERATE LINES,
         COLD HARBOR
Cold Harbor, Va.; after a photograph by John
Reekie, April, 1865.
Pen, 6-1/2 x 9-1/4 (sight size), signed *JDW*. In-
scribed title.
Engraved: *Century* 34:298, June, 1887; *Battles and
Leaders* IV-142.

633

639

640

635

642

636

637

638

644

645

647

648

643. THE PETERSBURG BATTLEFIELD
An 1886 field study.
Pencil, 6-7/8 x 17-1/2. Inscribed *Gracies and Colquits Salients from Union picket line—S by W from Fort Haskell* and identifications.
Engraved: *Century* 34:784, Sept., 1887; *Battles and Leaders* IV-542.
PLATE 300

644. RESERVOIR HILL, PETERSBURG
Siege of Petersburg; after a photograph, 1886.
Pen, 10-5/8 x 16-3/4. Inscribed *Reservoir & Ravine of Lieutenants Creek / Petersburg* and identifications in margin.
Engraved: *Century* 34:764, Sept., 1887; *Battles and Leaders* IV-537.

645. PROFILE OF THE CRATER
Siege of Petersburg; an 1886 field study.
Pen, 8-1/2 x 21-1/8. Inscribed identifications in margin.
Engraved: *Century* 34:766-67, Sept., 1887; *Battles and Leaders* IV-546-47.

646. RELICS OF THE CRATER
Petersburg battlefield; after museum exhibits, 1887.
Pen, 13 x 10-1/2. Inscribed title and identifications.
Engraved: *Century* 34:775, Sept., 1887; *Battles and leaders* IV-559.
PLATE 308

647. PHOTOGRAPHER'S STUDIO, CORINTH, MISSISSIPPI
After a wartime photograph by George Armstead.
Pen, 8-5/16 x 12-1/2. Inscribed *The Artists Studio Corinth Miss.*

648. FORT WILLIAMS, CORINTH, MISSISSIPPI
After a photograph, 1884.
Water color, 7-3/16 x 11, signed *JDW*. Inscribed *M & C R.R. Cut Ft. Williams. Earth works on the right.*
Engraved: *Century* 32:913, Oct., 1886; *Battles and Leaders* II-747.

649. THE GRAVE OF COLONEL RODGERS
Corinth, Miss.; after a photograph, 1884.
Water color, 6 x 10-5/8 (sight size), signed *JDW*. Inscribed title.
Engraved: *Century* 32:913, Oct., 1886; *Battles and Leaders* II-752.
PLATE 376

RUFUS F. ZOGBAUM

Illustrator and painter. Born Charleston, 1849; died New York, Oct. 22, 1925. Trained at the Art Students' League and in Paris, Zogbaum dealt almost exclusively with military and naval subjects in his illustrations, murals, and paintings.

650. HEADQUARTERS IN THE FIELD
Federal officers; original illustration.
Pen, 9-1/2 x 15-1/4 on mount.
Engraved: *Century* 32:121, May, 1886; *Battles and Leaders* I-298.
PLATE 58

MAPS

651. MISSOURI
By Jacob Wells.
Pen, 12-1/2 x 10-3/8, signed *J. Wells.*
Engraved: *Battles and Leaders* I-263.

652. BATTLEFIELD OF WILSON'S CREEK, MISSOURI
Aug. 10, 1861; by Jacob Wells.
Pen, 11-7/8 x 8.
Engraved: *Battles and Leaders* I-290.

653. BATTLEFIELD OF WILSON'S CREEK, MISSOURI
Aug. 10, 1862; by Jacob Wells.
Pen, 11-1/4 x 8, signed *J. Wells.*

654. BATTLEFIELD OF BALL'S BLUFF, VIRGINIA
Oct. 21, 1861; by Jacob Wells.
Pen, 7-1/4 x 7-1/8, signed *J. Wells.*
Engraved: *Battles and Leaders* II-126.

655. BATTLEFIELD OF SHILOH
April 6-7, 1862.
Photo or proof copy, 8-3/8 x 5-5/8 on mount.

656. BATTLEFIELD OF SOUTH MILLS, NORTH CAROLINA
April 19, 1862; by Fred E. Sitts, after a map in Confederate General Huger's report.
Pen, 5-1/8 x 4 on mount.
Engraved: *Battles and Leaders* I-656.

657. BATTLEFIELD OF FAIR OAKS
Peninsula campaign, May 31, 1862.
Pen, 8-1/8 x 11-1/8.
Engraved: *Century* 30:118, May, 1885.

658. BATTLEFIELD OF BEAVER DAM CREEK
Peninsula campaign, June 26, 1862; by Jacob Wells.
Pen, 8 x 10, signed *J. Wells.*
Engraved: *Century* 30:300, June, 1885; *Battles and Leaders* II-328.

659. SECOND BULL RUN CAMPAIGN
Aug. 27, 1862; by Jacob Wells.
Pen, 7-1/2 x 8-1/4.
Engraved: *Century* 31:447, Jan., 1886; *Battles and Leaders* II-467.

660. BATTLEFIELD OF SECOND BULL RUN
Noon, Aug. 29, 1862; reproduction of a drawing "lent by General John Pope."
Photo or proof copy; 7 x 5 on mount, signed *Winstanley, Topogr.*
Engraved: *Battles and Leaders* II-472.

661. BRAGG'S INVASION OF KENTUCKY
By Jacob Wells.
Pen, 9-1/4 x 12-1/4, signed *Wells.*
Engraved: *Battles and Leaders* III-6.

662. Gettysburg Campaign
June 3-15, 1863; by Jacob Wells, compiled by General Abner Doubleday.
Pen, 12-7/8 x 10-7/8. Five maps.
Engraved: *Century* 33:119, Nov., 1886; *Battles and Leaders* III-262.

663. Gettysburg Area, Looking South
Relief map by A. E. Lehman, 1886.
Photo reproduction, 11 x 13-3/4.
Engraved: *Century* 33:627, Feb., 1887; *Battles and Leaders* III-292.

664. Battlefield of Gettysburg
July 1, 1863; by Jacob Wells, compiled by General Abner Doubleday.
Pen, 10-7/8 x 10-3/4, signed *J. Wells.*
Engraved: *Century* 33:131, Nov., 1886; *Battles and Leaders* III-282.

665. Battlefield of Gettysburg
Afternoon, July 3, 1863; by Jacob Wells, compiled by General Abner Doubleday.
Pen, 11-1/8 x 8-1/2, signed *J. Wells.*
Engraved: *Century* 33:454, Jan., 1887; *Battles and Leaders* III-344.

666. Farnsworth's Cavalry Charge at Gettysburg
July 3, 1863; by Jacob Wells, after a sketch map by Capt. H. C. Parsons.
Pen, 7-3/4 x 11-15/16, signed *J. Wells.*
Engraved: *Battles and Leaders* III-394.

667. Lee's Retreat from Gettysburg
By Jacob Wells, compiled by General Abner Doubleday.
Pen, 9-3/4 x 7-1/2. Two maps.
Engraved: *Battles and Leaders* III-382.

668. Red River Falls and Dam
Alexandria, La.; by Gregor Noetzel.
Pen, 6-5/8 x 12-3/4, signed *Gregor Noetzel Draughtsman.*
Engraved: *Battles and Leaders* IV-358.

669. Battlefield of the Wilderness
May 4, 1864.
Pen, 11-1/2 x 12-3/4.
Engraved: *Battles and Leaders* IV-153.

670. Area of Petersburg and Appomattox Campaigns
1864-65; by Jacob Wells.
Pen, 8 x 11-5/8.
Engraved: *Battles and Leaders* IV-569.

671. Atlanta and Vicinity
From *Memoirs of General William T. Sherman* (1875).
Tearsheet, 11-1/2 x 8.

672. Tennessee and Alabama
By Jacob Wells.
Pen, 8-1/4 x 12-1/8, signed *J. Wells.*
Engraved: *Battles and Leaders* IV-414.

652

658

654

659

656

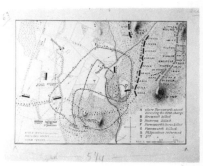
666

657

668

673

677

674

679

673.   BATTLEFIELD OF FRANKLIN, TENNESSEE
Nov. 3, 1864; by J. Cowen.
Pen, 11-3/8 x 7-3/4, signed *J. Cowen.*
Engraved: *Century* 34:602, Aug., 1887.

674.   BATTLEFIELD OF NASHVILLE, TENNESSEE
Dec. 15-16, 1864; by J. Cowen.
Pen, 9-1/2 x 11-5/8.
Engraved: *Century* 34:611, Aug., 1887.

675.   SHERMAN'S OPERATIONS IN NORTH CAROLINA
From *Memoirs of General William T. Sherman*
(1875).
Tearsheet, 8 x 11-1/2.
Engraved: *Battles and Leaders* IV-694.

676.   SHERMAN'S MARCH FROM RALEIGH TO
        WASHINGTON
From *Memoirs of General William T. Sherman*
(1875).
Tearsheet, 11-1/2 x 8.

677.   FORT FISHER AND VICINITY
Wilmington, N.C.; by Jacob Wells.
Pen, 9-3/4 x 5-1/4, signed *J. Wells.*

678.   PLAN OF FORT FISHER
Wilmington, N.C.; by E. E. Court.
Pen, 11-3/4 x 8-1/2.
Engraved: *Battles and Leaders* IV-645.

679.   POSITION OF UNION ATTACKING FORCES, FORT
        FISHER
Wilmington, N.C., Jan. 15, 1865; by E. E. Court.
Pen, 13-7/8 x 10-1/2. Inscribed *Topography taken
from Coast Chart of 1866—details from Comstock
Map of 1865.*
Engraved: *Battles and Leaders* IV-644.

Library of Congress Cataloging in Publication Data
Main entry under title:

The American Heritage Century Collection of Civil War
Art.

    Illustrations originally appeared in Battles and Leaders of
the Civil War, published 1887-88.
    1. United States—History—Civil War, 1861-1865—Pic-
torial works. I. Sears, Stephen W., ed. II. Battles and Leaders
of the Civil War.
E468.7.A58   973.7'022'2   74-11398
ISBN 0-07-010267-8